Past and Future Lives

Wisdom Journeys through Time

Heather Bray

Heather Bray

BUTTERFLY PRESS

Butterfly Press
PO Box 257
Marazion
TR18 9AD

www.keystowisdom.co.uk

British Library Cataloguing-in-Publication Data
A catalogue record for this book is available from the British Library

Disclaimer
The contents of this book do not constitute medical advice. Neither is it intended
to be used in any way as a teaching manual. The services of a qualified therapist
should always be sought.

Cover design by Heather Bray.
Front cover painting, "The Garden of the Heart" by Heather Bray.

First published in Great Britain in 2007 by
BUTTERFLY PRESS

ISBN 978-0-9550954-1-2

Printed and bound in Great Britain by R Booth Ltd, Penryn Cornwall

Thanks

Special thanks are due to my loving family, who always support and encourage me in everything I try to do, and also to Melody, author of a series of crystal books, full of amazing and truly wonderful insights, called Love is in the Earth, without whose wisdom my work would be much depleted.

A special thank you to her also for her personal support and encouragement along the way in the writing of both Keys to Wisdom and Wisdom Journeys through Time, for her unshakeable belief in me, and the work that we do here.

DEDICATION

This book is dedicated to my husband Barrie, our two lovely daughters Lucie and Vania, all the many special people whom I have met through Healing over the years, and last but not least, all the many Helpers, Guides and Angels it has been my privilege to work with from the World of Spirit.

In 1989, two years after her death, I asked my daughter, Vania, for a maxim for Life. A maxim is a piece of wisdom, expressed in a sentence. This is what my pendulum spelt out. "By adjustment do we learn our lessons".

OPENING QUOTE

"Amit Goswami, the Indian Physicist, believes that by means of reincarnation identities are passing through the information field, exchanging data with new identities, which feel like a new "Me," but are actually transmutations of indestructible zeros and ones strung into long chains of ideas and experiences. Right now you are a bundle of information in mind and body. You have unique memories. Your souls have undergone chemical changes shared by no one else in the world. When you die none of this information will vanish, because it can't. There is nowhere for plus and minus, positive and negative to go, since the field contains nothing but information. Therefore the only alternative is to recombine. How do they do that? The answer lies in the root word of information, which is FORM. We *inhabit* an *informed* universe, according to scientist Ervin Laszlo, which strings atoms along the double helix of DNA, and bits of information in physical form, just as it strings the same information, in non physical form as ideas. This brings us one step closer to the breathtaking notion that the whole universe is God's Mind.

Samskaras★ can be dismantled or changed only by affecting the right level of the mind. A change at the subtlest level is the most powerful. J Krishnamurti put it beautifully when he said that the highest form of human intelligence is to observe yourself without judgement, that is, if you can stand aside from how your beliefs are behaving, how various energies of desire and repulsion are pulling at you, how the stored consciousness of memory makes you see the world, you can witness the field itself. This is true enlightenment. In many spiritual traditions, such as Buddhism, the key seems to be stillness, detaching oneself from the internal dialogue, whose stream of ideas and impulses comes from the past. Witnessing allows us to see and understand with an intelligence which is contextual, nurturing, wholistic, without a win or lose orientation. This gives us a chance to experience the mind field, or what we popularly call, "Having an open mind."

Ultimately dying will carry each of us into the mind field. ... The issue of an open mind bears directly upon how much baggage we'll have to carry."

Quote from Deepak Chopra in his book, Life after Death; The Burden of Proof

★Samskaras are impressions derived from past experiences (in previous incarnations or in this life) that influence future responses and behaviour.

CONTENTS

INTRODUCTION

"The only real valuable thing is intuition." Albert Einstein.

When we pick up a book for the first time we are curious: something has drawn us towards it. Maybe a catchy title or a bright and interesting cover first caught your eye. Is it a good read? Has it new and meaningful things to say on a subject which interests you? Is it worth adding to your collection? If you are interested in the wisdom and healing potential of regressions, progressions and soul journeys I believe it is, because it contains a wealth of experience from different contributors, whose amazing, fascinating stories will reward your time and attention, so may I, the facilitator and co-ordinator, introduce myself?

I am a healer of some twenty years experience working in my own busy, successful clinic. My story is an unusual one, because I have never been to any other person or place to learn the skills at my disposal and yet there are many 'tools in the tool bag.' I have, undoubtedly, been guided along the path by intuition: I have been taught by unseen guides, "from within." How can that be?

I have been a dowser for more than thirty years. My 'celestial telephone' is a pendulum which is constantly moving, its chain held very short, (2 centimetres or so) between the thumb and forefinger of my right hand. It is passing me information which I believe is coming both from within me and from the realm of Universal Consciousness.

My first book, "Keys to Wisdom," published in 2005, describes my personal journey into healing and my unique working practices as a healer using crystals, flower essences and 'Hands on' healing. The keys, the many and varied movements made by a pendulum, (which is any small symmetrical object attached to a piece of chain or string,) are truly the keys to wisdom. Ced Jackson of The British Society of Dowsers acknowledged the book to be, "One of the most important and thought provoking books on dowsing to be published in recent years."

I am essentially a practical person, and this second book is a record of a just a few of the extraordinary journeys I have facilitated over the years with the purpose of healing at the very deep mind level possible only in a 'Lucid dream' state. The so-called seed points are sought out in order to release the traumas of such patterns from our psyche. Once again I facilitate healing using a pendulum, the movements of which are here interpreted by a further extended language. And so it is we journey together from scene to scene, through space and time, past and future.

Two different aspects of the work are studied in depth here and for clarity I have set out the book in four parts. The second part contains the account of regressions which happened as a result of people coming to me with specific questions around matters of health or perceived psychological problems.

The third part is somewhat different, but, in a sense, comes out of Part Two. The journeys here started because Hannah came to me with a physical problem of psoriasis which was first treated by my normal healing methods. The psoriasis was greatly improved by those means, but did not completely go away, and so a regression was suggested. This regression is recorded in Part Two as Chapter 11. This is an extraordinary journey anyway, but what makes it even more extraordinary is what happened right at the end. Hannah's voice changed and she was taken over by what we now know to be a Light Being, who issued us with an invitation, and a wish to, "Entertain your presence at a future date." Having thought about this invitation very carefully, we eventually took up the offer, and, in fact, to date, ten journeys have taken place, eight of which are fully recorded here. Each journey contains deep wisdom for ourselves and the planet, while more journeys may well follow. Incidentally yes, the psoriasis did get healed!

Scientists are very much aware these days that space and time are indivisibly linked, in what is known as the space/time continuum. Soul journeys, triggered by a question, in order that specific lives are re-experienced, have been undertaken and vividly described by the clients themselves. We work with the character of the immortal soul, put through the filters of temperament of a particular human personality and the capacity of their current human brain. Important insights are gained and amazing messages from Beings of Light are received.

Progression is the ability to go forward in time in a search for vital wisdom and understanding, while Regression is about the ability to re-member, put back together again, that which has been forgotten, and in so doing, to heal at a very deep level of the soul. Clients and readers alike become more aware of the Divine Order of things and gain a greater understanding of their present purpose here on earth.

Most people take the everyday primary level of consciousness very seriously, not realising or acknowledging that there are other levels. It is always a spiritual awakening of some kind that allows the realisation that other levels of consciousness are possible. This awakening can happen in many ways, for example meditation, near death experience, the death of a loved one and deja vu as well as through regression. As Eckhart Tolle said, "The flower of consciousness grows out of the mud of experience, just as the beautiful lotus blossom grows out of the mud of the river."

These transcriptions are a record of exactly what happened on the day and are as impeccably truthful as I can make them. If they seem amazing, it is because they are amazing, even to me, even after all these years! There is little in the way of procedure that I follow prior to the regression, other than a very quick last minute check through the client's major chakras, just to ensure that we don't have one that might need a crystal placed either on or beside it in order to hold the energy on. It's a bit like the cabin crew cross checking that the doors of the aircraft are closed (or in this case, open!) before take off. Then I simply take a reading from the pendulum that everything is ready and off we go.

The names of clients may be changed to protect their identity. Other than that, the accounts in this book are recorded exactly as they happened.

Chapter One

Where science and mysticism meet

"Ultimately, I suppose, we all believe what we want to believe. I guess that's what reality is. One thing though. The line between science and mysticism... is just a line." Victor Bergman, from "Journey through the Black Sun."

Primordial humans possessed an instinctive knowledge of the profound interconnectedness and sacred unity of all things. In our modern, sophisticated world, this sense of interconnectedness is, thankfully, once again beginning to be recognised and, this time around, the knowledge is backed up scientifically.

The modern scientific concept is of a Holographic Universe. The idea behind the Holographic Universe hypothesis is that all information, concerning our universe, is stored two dimensionally around its periphery, and that this two dimensional information then reappears, three-dimensionally, inside the universe itself. This links the macrocosm and the microcosm together in a unique way, as we can, in fact, liken a single living cell to the whole universe. Discoveries have now been made concerning the importance of the membrane or brane surrounding a single cell. It was previously believed that if the nucleus was taken out of a cell, that cell would die. However it has now been shown that in fact this does not happen, that a cell can continue to sustain life for several months, following the extraction of its nucleus. The membrane surrounding the cell is acting like a lens through which the relevant in-formation can pass and is the reason for the continuation of life. We could liken this membrane, or brane, as it is known, to the All Seeing Eye of Horus of Ancient Egyptian mystic tradition, the permeable layer through which the order and watchful awareness of an all-powerful God Figure becomes instated with the human psyche of the pharaoh, so that the pharaoh is not merely seen as God's representative on Earth, but actually is God. As above, so below. A possible implication from this is that the universe could be re-in-formed, as and when necessary, from the hologram surrounding it, thus extending or even reinitiating its life span.

Ervin Lazlo, in his book, "Science and the Akashic Field," recognises that the genetic makeup of even the simplest living organism is so complex, and the way in which it fits in with every other living thing in its environment is so perfectly balanced, that if it were not for perfect attunement, no species could mutate into a viable form before being destroyed by the process of natural selection. It is here, in the space of a single cell, that we see the timeless battle of destiny versus free will re-enacted. If a dead beetle is put into a Petri dish, it has been shown that mycelial mats on the far side of the dish will very quickly grow towards the food source. The distance involved is huge in their terms and yet they are still able to target it. It has also been reported, by scientists in Japan, that a slime mould can repeatedly negotiate a maze in which a food source has been deposited, in the most efficient manner and with the least possible cell production. This suggests that the existence of some form of cellular intelligence is at work

It is accepted, by some, that conscious awareness is fundamental to all sentient beings, including plant life, and yet an individual's consciousness, it has *also* been shown, is not uniquely their own. There is potential for a group consciousness. We see this demonstrated, for instance, in the studied reciprocal behaviour of twins or those who are emotionally very close. For example, one twin is suffering with appendicitis. The other twin, living at a considerable distance and having had no news of the illness of her sister, suffers the pains with her, at the same time and in exactly the same way. The mind of one person (or indeed animal,) appears to be able to act on the mind and body of another, even at a distance, and, most recently, it has been shown to be possible, even when one is in a so-called vegetative or unconscious state. Note the use of the word 'mind' here. The brain is finite, its function being curtailed by death, while the mind is infinite. This causes such confusion in the scientific world. The brain has been shown to be dead. so how can a person continue to know things? Documentary evidence from Near Death Experiences shows that, even though the body is classified as clinically 'dead' the mind continues to function normally. The implication of this is that the mind of a 'dead' person could act on the mind and body of a 'living' person, which is one explanation for the so-called Demons of Trauma. These we shall discuss later. Traditional cultures did not regard transpersonal communications as an illusion, but many of us living in modern societies do.

All the great spiritual disciplines describe the evolutionary stages through which the soul of Man must pass, in order to attain enlightenment, heaven, nirvana and so on. These evolutionary stages are traditionally simple but all encompassing. Christianity asks that we become, "as a little child," Buddhism preaches non-attachment, Don Miguel Ruiz, a descendant of Aztec stock, preaches the beautiful four agreements, through which we can identify the error in our lives, while humanists say we should treat others as we would wish to be treated ourselves. We are given many beautiful, simple codes of behaviour to follow, stemming from the different spiritual backgrounds.

According to the Mayans, we are now in a time of transition, moving from the fifth sun towards the sixth sun of consciousness, an important time of evolution for the earth and all her inhabitants. It is said that this sixth sun will usher in a new level of awareness, and that this new level of awareness may well be embodied within the increased development of humanity's so-called sixth sense. My experience right now is such that a trained person, with the aid of a pendulum and a fully comprehensive language with which to work, has the potential, **at will**, for reaching a functioning super consciousness, or *seventh* sense, which is a very subtle level of intuition, induced when the soul and the spirit blend and harmonise within the transfigured consciousness of man. A simple pendulum held in the hand, and an extended pendulum language have proved once again to be the **Keys to Wisdom** for me and they could be for you also. They compare with the sling and the five smooth pebbles with which a David of Wisdom slew the Goliath of Ignorance.

David Bohm, Ervin Lazlo and Jude Currivan are among a number of cutting edge scientists who believe that interactions between Nature and Mind are mediated and informed by a fundamental information field, or memory bank. Information on the state of the whole has the potential to travel almost instantaneously from anywhere to anywhere in the known and unknown universes.

What is the implication of our ability to take up this information? An enlightened society, hallmarked by transpersonal consciousness, is not likely to be materialistic and self centred. Realisation amongst the nations of the truths expressed here would change our world for ever. This has certainly been my experience with each individual, in the life changing work undertaken for this book and Keys to Wisdom, the one that preceded it. Education changes lives. (Latin: e, from. Ducere, to lead.)

"Those who walked in darkness have seen a great light." (Isaiah 9:2) Our desire for light stems from our experience of darkness. The prophet Isaiah speaks to a despondent and bewildered people and promises that God is not done with them. The context for this oracle or poem is the apparent failure of Ahaz, King of Judah, to provide stability and peace for the nation. The dire threat of Assyrian occupation is staring them in the face and hope is all but extinguished. There is but one place to turn, one possibility that joy may break into their hopelessness, one source of light that might shine in their darkness: God who hears the cries of the people and intervenes to bring about a new thing. In this intrusive act, by which the Divine Will is made manifest through a human agent, everything becomes possible.

Now let us spend a few minutes looking at the four aspects of the 'ocean of consciousness.' First let us liken our normal waking level of consciousness, working with the gross world and our conscious minds, to a walk along the shoreline, (Vaishvanara in Sanskrit.) Where the shoreline meets the ocean, Vaishvanara meets Taijasa, waking meets dreaming, conscious meets unconscious and the gross world meets the subtle world. It is possible to go further into the ocean from the shore, without actually going deeper. This is the dreaming state. (Taijasa) It is concerned with the active unconscious and the subtle realm proper. Very few people will venture into the *depths* of the ocean of consciousness, (Prajna,) which we can liken to the floor of the ocean. The vast majority seek only to know about the shoreline and the surface of the ocean, exploring the Waking state and the Gross world, along with the Dreaming state and its Subtle plane. For many of us, the paradigm of reality is so fixed in our minds that anything which doesn't fit in we won't even admit exists! There are only those rare few who seek to know Prajna, (pra, supreme, and jna, knowing,) the latent, formless Causal plane of pure potential, and the fourth state, Turiya, the Absolute, which permeates and is the support of the other three. But it is in this direction, the direction of the Garden of the Heart, that the journeys in this book take us. It was Decartes who first linked the causal mind to the pineal gland, and it was Leonardo da Vinci who linked the pineal gland to the soul.

The quantum vacuum, the zero point energy field that fills all cosmic space, appears to transport light, energy, pressure and sound. The question scientists are asking is, could it also be a sea of information, with a means of both conservation and conveyance? The quantum vacuum is considered by science to be a frictionless medium. In the absence of contrary forces, objects move without resistance, and could, at least in theory, continue to move for ever. This is exactly what my practical experience of the pendulum has been. It will continue to swing for literally hours at a time, when necessary, such as in a healing or regression situation, while it is in use as a vehicle for retrieving information from the Akashic Record, or what the scientists call the Akashic Field. I have often wondered why this apparent disregard of the laws of physics, with regard to friction, comes about when dowsing with a pendulum. In fact I constantly have a callous on the outside of the index finger of my right hand, caused by friction, which fails to prevent the action of the swinging pendulum against it

In a holographic recording, created by the interference pattern of two light beams, information is held in a distributed form, so that all the information that makes up a hologram is present in every part of it. This makes all information available almost instantaneously everywhere, provided of course that you have the means to unlock it.

And so Lazlo makes the all important point - The quantum vacuum, which existed before the first universe was born and will continue to exist if all matter in the universe vanishes, "generates the holographic field that is the memory of the universe."

These are words that express our personal feelings and ideas about energy, but we could just as well be using the words, God/Goddess and the Mind of God/ Matrix, instead of the scientific words of quantum vacuum and holographic field. It is the, "rose by any other name," *eternal* quality of the *energy* that is important, and not the words used to record and express it. Andrew Harvey, in his book, "Radiant Heart - The radical teachings of Jesus and the Christian mystics" writes

This path of love in action and the transformation that it necessitates has a unique urgency for our time, threatened as it is by world wide disaster. In Christianity, and throughout the mystical experience of Christian mystics, has been a thread of awareness that knows that the Cosmic Christ is the child of both the Father and the Mother aspects of the Godhead, of both the formless and the absolute law and order of the Father and the embodied love, the embodied Godhead, that is the Mother. It has been the disastrous loss of this dimension of the Sacred Feminine, through the increasing Patriarchalisation, both of the Church and of the message of the Church, that has resulted in the ethereal Christ being celebrated and not the full Divine, Human Christ, that is at once transcendent and imminent, in link with the transcendent Father and passionately in love and embodying the imminent Mother, that is the source of all real transformation on this path.

However, this still does not take things far enough to match up with my experience. Lazlo follows up with, "We must admit there must have been an original creative act, an act of 'Metaversal design.' (Metaversal Universe meaning " Mother Universe which then went on to inform all other universes.") If the Metaverse was in existence before all other universes, the burning question is: **"By what creative, intelligent energy force were the initial conditions and directions for the Metaverse laid down?"**

The ancient Egyptian name for the Creator was Amn, from which the amen' of Christian prayers is derived. Amn is also linked to the cosmic sound or word, Aum or Om, as in the Biblical phrase, "In the beginning was the Word, and the Word was God and the Word was with God." And so the word or sound represents the primal sound of the Cosmos, and is equivalent to the Big Bang of science. What then is the one thing, from which we are all descended and to which we will return? In Chapter Fifteen I ask a parallel question to the one posed above.

Heather: What started the Creative Energy, God? What brought the Creative Energy of God into existence?

Hannah: (Immediately) Dust, (pause) Dust.

Heather: Where did the dust come from?

Hannah: Dust Was, Is, Was, Dust always was.

A quote now from Eva's story, Chapter Nine:

Heather: ... your Guardian Angel, or angels or guides are moving in closer now. If you get a sense of their presence, maybe you could let me know.

Eva: Yes, there are *two* things. One, I don't know *what* it is. It's not a person or an animal, it's something very, very primal, like .. the stuff that everything is made of. I don't know what that would be, .. some sort of basic stuff.

Heather: DNA, or something like that?

Eva: Even before that. Something not even really living in the sense that we know it. It's *really* the stuff that the cosmos is made of. That's *one* thing. And the deer is there as well.

Many months later, when transcribing the tapes of those journeys, I decided to do some research on the internet about dust, and what did I find? I found that the American Astronomical Society have published an article in 2003, which begins, and

I quote, "Dust grains play a crucial role in the formation and evolution history of stars and galaxies in the early universe."

I am a believer, but I believe in the Unknowable and Ineffable, and can no longer believe in the God of my childhood. The image of an Old man with a beard, sitting on a golden chair in the sky, no longer holds for me, although I must admit, there's something about personification which is significantly good for approachability. I believe in a Creative Consciousness that knows each and every living thing intimately and cares about its well-being, because this has been my experience, but there will always be the need for the final leap of faith that each of us must make for ourselves, as expressed in the quotation, "Lord I believe, help thou my unbelief." Truth can be expressed in many different ways, and still remain truth. Our ways of expressing truth track the path of our personal path towards enlightenment. Many of us have a portion of the truth, but *none* of us can, or ever will, while we live, have it all. Let us remember this. It will enable us to remain more open to the opinions of others.

We are all on the journey back to the Light. This is what enlightenment stands for, to merge with the LIGHT, the Divine Creative Spark. We must all perform the "Labours of Hercules," and face many amazing and difficult challenges before enlightenment is realised, whatever the spiritual path to which we nail our banner. Our bodies are but vehicles which take us through the various experiences of life, but the purpose of those journeys is to experience the things of the Spirit, and so grow in wisdom and understanding. I so often hear of people having difficulty in discovering their life's purpose. I believe our experiences, every single one of them, good, bad and indifferent, are grist to that mill. And remember to always ask yourself the question, "What is the lesson for me in this?" I guarantee there will always *be* one.

The Akashic Field, the hologram within which all information is stored, does not in fact react with any of the five senses of sight, hearing, touch, taste, or smell. It requires investigation only from the so-called aforementioned sixth and seventh senses, the senses that exist beyond the ego. We need to be advanced enough, as beings, to be able to move the "**I**" of personal power and identity out of the way in order that the in-formation be given us. At that point there are no longer "only five slits in the tower," as Lazlo puts it, but instead you can, "Open the roof to the sky."

So, if all the information of everything is potentially available to us in a regression situation, how do we manage to make the right connection and go through the right door? This is due to two energy qualities, **space** and **time.** I have long known that the times given in regression, for example, three weeks forward, or ten years backwards in time, may or may not be intended to be taken literally in terms of linear time. They are devices for finding our way, identifying a certain location. I take care to explain this principle to my client before a regression takes place.

If you imagine a map of the world with a grid of latitude and longitude placed over it, the vertical line of longitude and the horizontal line of latitude and their point of intersection give you an exact location. These intersecting lines of latitude and longitude are known as co-ordinates. Similarly the backward or forward movement (**Space**) together with the movement in terms of duration, (**Time**) identify an exact location in the holographic record, known as the Akashic, or Zero point Field, which is really ironical because it is a hologram, the terms of which mean that everything exists everywhere and there is only the now! We cannot understand it, we simply have to accept it, but the spiritual guides are kind enough to use what we **do** know, in order lead us to what we **need** to know.

Further, as we are guided through the regression session, we sometimes feel the need to invoke **keys** from a previously selected collection, should any of the portals or doorways not be already open and available to us. The search for these keys is undertaken by us during a separate session prior to the regression session itself. It is conducted in an attitude of humility and diligence, in order that, during the regression, the correct key having been selected, we be granted right of passage to certain more esoteric information.

Why is all this permitted to happen? Because I and my assistant have a genuine deep love for our fellows who are struggling and, because, through work previously undertaken, we have sufficient standing in the World of Spirit to make it possible. We are all on a journey travelling back to the light from whence we came. For most of us the journey is long and slow, but we are given many chances to achieve it. We are known, loved and understood in every small detail and are, each and every one of us, of the utmost importance to the Divine Creative Energy. We are its Self Expression. We are made from the dust of the stars themselves, while the stars themselves are made of light. Our bodies arise from dust and to dust they return, from no thing to no thing, dust to dust, ashes to ashes, as it says in the Holy Books. We as individuals have no purpose and every purpose. It is not enough to **know** the truth, we must start to **live** the truth. We encompass the beginning and the end, which is the beginning, and even then, maybe, the journey starts over again.

Chapter Two

Telling the story

"Tell me a fact and I'll learn. Tell me a truth
and I'll believe, but tell me a story, and it will
live in my heart for ever."

Old Indian proverb.

How do we know what is a reality and what is an illusion? The difference between subjective and objective experience is the ability of that experience to bring about transformation within the psyche. Some would say subjective is not real, that only objective experiences are real, but experience does not, and indeed should not, depend on other people supporting it. It is connected with the ability of the experience itself to touch and activate the deepest patterns of transformation within us.

Spiritual disciplines also inform us that the dedicated seeker after truth, as a result of prayerful attunement to the Divine Source, is capable of achieving many different altered states of consciousness. Transformation of consciousness is also happening right here and now, on a planetary scale. At last there is scientific discourse on hologram energy, akashic fields, and the importance of intuition, these areas of discussion formerly being the exclusive territory of mystics.

Incarnation is the carnation of consciousness into form, (Latin, caro, carnis, flesh, the coming into flesh.) "The word was made flesh and dwelt among us." John chapter 1 verse 14. The formless becomes form. We incarnate many times, sometimes several times in the same lifetime, reinventing ourselves/being reinvented until we know we are beyond form. At that stage we only come into physical form again in order to help others with this realisation. So what does the knowledge of being beyond form really consist of and how is it achieved?

The realisation of being beyond form is about breaking out of Me and my personal story. I remember a French teacher asking the class, many years ago, when I was just beginning to learn to conjugate a French verb, "Who is the most important person in the world?" We struggled, as a class of twelve year olds, to answer to this question, and in the end, the answer emerged. "I am." Therefore the first case of any verb is "I." The world revolves around Me. The things that happened to me from my past, over the years, form images in my head. There is also a story of course. That is an intrinsic part of my image of Me, so everybody lives in a personal work of fiction created by the mind, and the Me, who is the main protagonist, the most important and central actor in this work. My story, which needs to be continually revived mentally, is backed up both by Me, and those around Me, by mutual agreement. Others largely accept what I put forward, so that My story does not get challenged, but is tacitly authenticated by others, who are fundamentally and primarily interested in their own story, where *they* are the central character. I will support Your story if you will support My story. This central character, to be found in all our stories, lives in resistance to what **is**, because the artificial, fictitious needs of Me cannot be sustained, except in a state of resistance to Now, or to put it another way, except in denial of the present moment. Therefore every life story, the Little Me story, both past and present, is ultimately unsatisfactory. This is because, finding the present unpalatable, we have relied too heavily on the future, or maybe, indeed the past. If the present is unpalatable there is always hope for the future and a happy ending. This in itself is not necessarily wrong. We need our dream. but what *is* wrong is an inability to also adjust to and accept what is, here and now, for this moment is all we have to work with in order to achieve our dream, the dream of getting well, having a home of our own, getting a good job, or finding love. These concerns, of course, are of much importance to us, particularly to those of us who are still very attached to living in the world of form. For those of us who are managing to move **out** of the world of form, towards the formless, these problems are of much less concern and worry, because these people are recognising that the growth of the soul, and successes on a soul level are of paramount importance. This has not been so much acknowledged in the West.

Take an extreme example of a Holy Man who sits on a pole in India for many years. Some will say, "How lazy and useless he is, letting people bring everything to him while he just sits there. It's disgusting. He should get a job!" Others will make extremely long and arduous pilgrimages to him, believing him to be God's representative on earth and the possessor of great gifts of Healing. And it has to be said that the power of that belief is contributory to the success of the healing. Healing energy may be blocked if the recipient thinks, "What a load of mumbo jumbo and old rubbish this is!"

For those still very attached to the world of form, the future is fundamentally important because this is where the happy ending of the story of Me could possibly be found. The problem lies when there is no escape to the future because there is little or no future left, and we have to face the inevitability of our personal form translating itself into the formless. Never having remembered facing this before, the prospect may be terrifying. We identify ourselves only by the physical things we possess, including our body. Our identity, however, has been constantly changing throughout our lives, as we move from baby to teenager, to young adult, to middle age, to old age and finally, if we manage to avoid all the world's many hazards, to the seeming degradation of extreme old age, ending up as Shakespeare put it, "sans teeth, sans hair, sans everything." How sad this would seem if that was all there was to life. No, we are here to be in school, to try many things, to experience much, without judgement as to whether it be good or bad. As Emmanuel, the discarnate Being, with whom Pat Rodegast has long been in contact, said to the well known spiritual teacher Ram Dass, we are in school and we may as well study the curriculum. What we do not learn this time around, we shall surely be asked to study again, in another time and place.

Human beings are like icebergs. There is so much of the human memory stored in a place deep below the surface, unseen and irretrievable, unless certain specific trigger circumstances prevail. We none of us know the other's true story. Even the most enlightened of us have difficulty in discovering our own true story and finding out more clearly who we are. For some the challenge of self discovery proves too much, and alcohol, drugs or abusive behaviour may be resorted to, dulling the sense of personal pain.

As well as dream experiences, an even more powerful tool for personal transformation can be regression, particularly, I have found, the accuracy of regression as directed through the space/time language possible with a pendulum. More particularly, this is the retelling of a personal story by the individual themselves, and, as such, perfectly fills the gap in the long term memory. Here, we are exposing the story of Me, and even just by recognising it's nature, by looking at it, we are beginning to step outside of the story, because it can only sustain itself if it remains unconscious. When you choose to look at it, you are witnessing. You are standing in the Place of Witness, watching the mind and the structure of the mind, both your own little mind and its link with universal consciousness. You have your eye on it, you are aware. The recognition of this is already the beginning of the end of the unconsciousness that sustains that particular story. The story of Me is what has been running humanity in general and Me in particular for many thousands of years. The simple change required is to step outside and take a look at the mechanical unconscious nature of mind structures. The experiences that follow arise from a memory bank of experiences and feelings concerning current and past lives, healing the very soul.

The story of Me is the personal battlefield of the battle of the Self, the battle of Archetypal Light and Darkness fought out within ourselves, which is repeated in the mind of every person on the planet. This is humanity's ultimate challenge, the fighting of the **personal** battle for enlightenment. The ego, (the Me) will resist this to the last, because enlightenment is the ego's ultimate deterrent, bringing about its demise. It is by such means that the personality become reformed, (re-formed). What we carry forward into the next world, from this world of form, into the formless, are our gifts and our personality. This is why it is so important to work on these two areas of ourselves while we are still in form. As the German proverb says, "A shroud has no pockets." We can carry forward only that which is intangible, leaving the tangible

(Latin, tangere - to touch,) behind.

So how do we initiate this deeply healing process? The client goes into a gently altered state of consciousness, which deepens as the regression gathers momentum. This is achieved largely by the tone of my voice, an air of quiet confidence, and the trust that has built up between us. The previously composed question is then stated by the client, which helps direct the guides as to what information to bring forward, and from which lives. Once the state of relaxation has been achieved, the task of the facilitator will be to help the client establish contact with the subjective reality of the space in which they find themselves.

A client who is new to regression may find it a little difficult to release themselves from the objective reality of the surrounding room. This depends on how relaxed and comfortable they are, both psychologically and physically, and so this technique is very unlikely to be attempted with someone who is not known to me, someone, that is, who had not experienced more general healing sessions, as described in detail in my first book, "Keys to Wisdom." These sessions build up a situation of familiarity and trust between us, as well as pointing out the need for healing at such a deep Soul Mind level as regression.

To help ensure the success of the therapy, I need to ascertain the right day and time of day (the auspicious time/space) for both the putting together of the so called 'keys', and for facilitating the actual regression itself. I always take advice from my guides on this. I need, further, to check that the 'far memory mind' is attainable and is in fact on the energy vibration of the Love/Truth/Gift/Healing Line, representing connection with the Divine Source. As these Journeyings are very demanding in terms of concentration, I have never carried out more than one a week alongside my other healing work, and often they are facilitated much less frequently than that, because of the deep healing of both mind and body made available through my more usual healing methods.

As far as the keys are concerned, there is a two hour appointment, arranged a few days previous to the regression itself. I always like to allow plenty of time for this. It is very important that these discussions and decisions are not hurried. Keys are artefacts which have a particular significance to the person themselves, for example, a crystal, an angel's name, possibly their guardian angel, a totem or power animal. We could also be led to the name of a particular goddess or ascended master that we may call on, or the name of a close friend or member, (deceased) of the person's family. Those who hold a strong affection for us can sometimes be even more able to help us from their vantage point on the other side of life than they were while on earth. Also, both my colleague and I may be led to place certain artefacts and name-links that are particularly relevant to ourselves, within the group of keys, so, as you see, they can be many and varied in nature, but their purpose is always the same. They are there to aid the progress of the regression once it gets started; to open the doors, or portals to the Spirit World, as we call them, and indeed to keep them open, granting us rite of passage to information which previously lay out of reach. You will realise that the information we are trying to retrieve for our client is secret, and if we did not have sufficient 'rites of passage,' it might not be possible to complete the task well.

The knowledge of certain keys, specific to a person, is very important and comes from the power vested in us through the use of our divinely given gifts, because we are going to use it towards the ultimate healing, not only for our client, but also, potentially, for our client's forebears, or for those in the "cast of characters" appearing in the unfolding story. We believe there can be release of trauma and deep healing for some of the other characters who appear in the stories also. For example there may be an opportunity for the client to grant someone forgiveness for past actions, the guilt from which could be impeding their progress on the next level of existence.

One of the things that can concern a person after the experience of regression is that they can start to recoil or spring back, feeling that they may simply have been imagining things. This may be the effect of the so called Demons of Trauma, who have long fed on the fears inflicted on the individual, through the gap in their personal story. They, not wishing at all to be ousted, not feeling themselves ready to face the curative power of transformation, not wishing to let go of the sense of control and individuality of the age old situation they have long enjoyed, try to restate their claim.

This is one of the ways in which a shaman builds his/her standing in the Spirit world, because those transmuted and transformed personalities, once tamed, make the switch from the energies of Fear, Pain and Ignorance, to the energies of Love, Truth and Healing, as shown in the third cross of the pendulum language,★ and then are able to help the shaman, as reformed characters. This is to personify forces which are basically energy, but personification aids explanation.

So what of the extended pendulum language needed for accurate navigation of the regressional voyage, moving from scene to scene, as in a play? I hold the pendulum in my right hand throughout, and its movements are constantly changing, charting our course and passing very explicit information to me. These many movements are set out in the appendix, where you may discover them at will, but next I would like you to take a look at a regression session.

★ See my first book, "Keys to Wisdom," ISBN 0 955 0954 0 9

Chapter Three

A regression session

"The light of the body is the eye. If therefore thine eye
be single, thy whole body shall be full of light."
Matthew 6, verse 22, King James version.

The single eye, or Third Eye as it is more usually called in the West, is the eye of inner seeing, of intuition, of being taught from within. "As above, so below" is also a saying which helps to express the inner and outer nature of cognition, (Latin, (g)noscere, to know.) The in-formation which we seek, and indeed the power to do so, is both within us and without, but, should we not acknowledge the wisdom which is *not* inherently within us, we would be insufficiently open and too tied up with the story of Me, to be truly successful, in *whatever* it is we choose to do.

My first task in a regression session is to check whether the major chakras in the physical body of my client are in balance. This is done quickly and simply, by means of the pendulum. I place my hand on or over the major chakra points, as directed by my guides, and simply read off the energy. If the energy is registering as being on any other line than the Love/Truth/Gift/Healing line, or Balance line, then we have an imbalance.

If I discover a minor energy imbalance the correction is made by means of an appropriate crystal, intuitively chosen and verified by the pendulum, being laid either on or beside the body, to hold the correct energy in place. I would not expect to find more than one chakra out of syncronicity at this stage, or else a special Energy Clearing session would be required as a first stage procedure. This is because working at this level of intensity and not the "ordinary" level of healing, there could be a serious risk of an attachment to the client being present.

An attachment can be likened to a suitcase or attaché case as it is sometimes called. This can contain considerably more than 'dirty washing,' and may well contain, at the very least, a mischievous entity or energy spirit. Until the situation is 'opened up,' as happens in regression, there is often little cause for alarm. It is, to extend the metaphor, locked away, but a regression session is one of those things which opens the persona up, (overindulgence in drink and drugs, for example, being others,) and

Positions of Chakras and Colours

gold	4th chakra above crown	
silver	3rd chakra above crown	
white	2nd chakra above crown	
magenta	1st chakra above crown	
violet	crown	SAHASRARA
indigo	third eye	AJNA
blue	throat	VISHUDDI
turquoise	thymus	THYMUS
green/pink	heart	ANAHATA
yellow	solar plexus	MANIPURA
orange	sacral	SVADISHISTHANA
red	root	MULADHARA

The colour red protects from the top of the legs to the soles of the feet.

it is then, if careful preparation has not been meticulously followed, the trouble can start. This clearing session would either be facilitated by myself and my colleague, or by someone else well qualified in the field, before a regression session could be allowed to proceed.

Our aim is always to give the client as good a quality of help as possible, and that may mean going just that little bit slower and putting in that extra healing session. This amount of attention to detail is very important to the success and safety of the venture. As always, it is a question of Ease and not Dis-ease. For good results, an impeccable working practice is imperative.

It has been my custom, over a period of years now, to work the regression sessions with a colleague, picking up on the particular gifts that this colleague can bring. As the Kashmiri proverb goes:
"One plus one make eleven.
In unity there is strength. Two heads are better than one."

Hannah's technique is a little different from Yvonne's who used to work with me, as she has a background of Medicine Wheel work and understands the placing of the keys, as if on a Medicine Table, and so they are moved around the table, like chess men on a chess board, in order that optimum energy is achieved.

My job is to facilitate the regression, while my assistant's job is to introduce the keys at the appropriate time, to keep the energy optimum and the information flowing. However, I also have access to a card on which all the keys are named and clearly set out, so that either one of us could call one in at any point. In addition, the assistant's ability to "hold the energy" and to "bear witness" is very important. As I indicated previously, we have occasionally found, following a hunch, that, on checking chakra energies at an additional and specially arranged initial Discussion session, our client has a major block in one of the chakras, making regression unsuitable, even dangerous, at such a time. There may even be a force emanating there which doesn't wish to respond to either myself or my colleague. Our sense of this is to do with our awareness and precognition of such things. Bear in mind that the most gentle and pleasant of persons may be carrying a very dark force with them, (I have several times experienced this,) rather in the manner, as I said before, of a traveller with a suitcase. It is rather like a virus being contained within an attachment on a computer document. However the person with the attachment may well feel themselves, "Held back," in life, by something indeterminate, not knowing by what, or whom, or what to do about it.

The other requirement is for me to be assured, by the guides, that the person's Soul Memory or Far Memory Mind is on the receiving wavelength, in other words, is on the Love/Truth/ Gift / Healing line. This assures me that the information, no matter how 'old,' and it may be thousands of years old in linear time, can be brought close enough to be retrieved, and that the guides of all three, that is to say, the facilitator, the helper and the regressee, are willing and able to bring the relevant material forward, by which means the question formatted by the client is answered. This is strictly their question, formulated and spoken by them, and takes them into the **telling of their own story.** This helps make what happens both real and acceptable to them.

So, the question is stated clearly, in a short sentence or two, the chakra energies of the regressee are checked for Balance, and the sound system, with its three microphones, (one for the regressee, one for my assistant, and one for me) following a previous sound check, is switched on. Now the client is assured that their spirit is resting in a bubble of consciousness at the top of their head, and the pendulum will give me a signal, (Truth Line,) when we are ready for departure. The regression takes place on a couch, in a quiet, darkened, but not dark room, lit by a single candle. I have my list of the keys to hand, written clearly on card, and a small torch with which to read them if necessary. Although I have an assistant who is very reliable, sitting at her table with the actual keys set out in front of her, it is important that we are both in possession of all possible information, because the passage of a regression can be tough and demanding, and we may need to confer, and/or take avoiding action quickly.

I always put a 90 minute tape in the recording machine, and have a second one open beside, although have never, so far, used the second tape. I *do* have to take a moment out, at some very carefully chosen moment, for turning over the tape, but I *am* able to speak to my client about the necessity to do this, and they are quite happy to "hold" for me, provided the moment is sensitively chosen.

The client has been told that they are perfectly safe, which is what I truly believe, and that they can get up and walk around, at any time if necessary, for example, in order to go to the bathroom. This is very reassuring because people are naturally uncomfortable with the feeling that they might lose control over their thoughts and actions. This is in fact not true. Nobody can be coerced into doing or saying things that are not natural to them or into acting out of character. They will be aware that they are here in the Healing Room, with us, but they will be even **more aware** of being in another place and time.

Firstly their consciousness is taken to a place where they are put in touch with their Guardian Angels and Guides. Next we go to a sacred place, which may, or may not be a place familiar to them in the current lifetime. It could, for instance, be a church they have visited, a place remembered from a holiday visit, a favourite place from childhood, or a favourite haunt in nature, ... or they may suddenly find themselves somewhere, like the client who found herself sitting in a water lilly on a pond, and who reached the far memory mind by sliding down its stalk! Some have found a little boat on a beach, or by a river, and they have got in and made a short journey into the first scene of their regression. One person was in his living room and got into regression by going up the chimney!

However a 'standard' way might be for the client to see a staircase or lift in front of them, and to use one of these to take them down deeper and deeper into the levels of the mind. On reaching the bottom, they usually see a door, which they are able to describe.

I ask them if they can see a handle on the door, and can they use it to open the door? Then, having been reassured that it is perfectly safe to do so, and that they can return to the comfort and safety of this room whenever they wish, they open the door and step through into the first 'scene' of the regression.

These are the notes issued to the client at the meeting previous to the regression itself, where the 'keys' are collected together and discussed.

★★★★★★★★★★★★★★★★★★★★★★★★★★★★★★

Helpful Information for a Regressee

Past Life regression therapists work with the physical and mental body imprints of former lives that may be disabling to their client's current body. Typically, these people come to us after traditional medicine has not given them relief, or they may simply feel that certain information that they need is missing. For example, a physical problem may be referred discomfort from a violent past life death. We are also able to effect relief from anxiety related problems in this life by giving back to the client the 'story' of where this anxiety originates. Once it is seen that these anxieties have their root in what has occurred in the past and are not related to what is about to happen in the future, great release is possible. Part of our job is to deprogramme these "carryovers" whenever they become debilitating to the client.

1 I will be asking you to find specific intervals of time. The times given (Time Slots, as we call them) may not be literal, but merely a device to enable you to find the next scene in the exposition of your "Story" accurately.

2 The information comes in as a thought or a visual image. Just let it come. Do not criticise it at this stage, because any thinking, left brain work tends to stop the flow. Time enough for analysis later. Even if you did think to yourself, "Could I be imagining this ?" it wouldn't render the information invalid in any way.

3 Do not get anxious about periods of silence. There are bound to be periods of silence while either you (or we,) are finding things, and encouraging the "Story" to unfold, so times when nobody speaks is fine.

4 Do say whatever you need to say: express whatever you need to express. This session is all about getting you back in touch with yourself. If you find yourself speaking 'out of character' or even in a foreign language, don't be surprised. All these many different experiences are what makes you who you are today.

5 The "Get Out" clause.

If there is a painful experience being revealed, we will let you be in touch with that, because it is important to recover it, but then we can either, "fast forward" as on a video tape, or you can get out of your body and view what is going on, either as if on television or from a safe distance, often from above, or maybe to one side.

6 The slightly altered state of consciousness you will be in is very much what you have experienced countless times before, on waking or dropping off to sleep. You will be fully aware that you are in this room with us, but be equally aware that you are somewhere else at another time and place. However it is quite safe, and you are safe, and you can return whenever you wish, merely by requesting it.

7 We set up lights, crystals, energies, artefacts, as you will know from the " Preliminary to Regression" session. We prepare as thoroughly as we are able. I check the balance of your chakras, (body energy vortexes) and maybe place a crystal on or beside you to hold that balance. Everything is done to help you to relax and put you at your ease so as to be able to "let go"

8 Your spirit then "sits" in a bubble of consciousness at the top of your head, ready for "Take off." Then at a signal from the pendulum, and knowing that your Soul Memory Mind is being made available to us, off we go.

9 First we go up. Up, up, higher and higher, to a place where you may experience contact with your Guardian Angel, who is always with you, right through your life, although you may not always be aware that this is so. There may also be other angels or guides present. They may be male, they may be female, or even androgynous. (A mixture of both male and female) They may be a child or even an animal. They are there to help, to guide and to protect you.

10 Next we go to a sacred place of your own choosing. This may be some place that already feels very special to you. It might be a garden, a church, a library, a cave, or, maybe, somewhere you have visited on holiday. You might just suddenly find yourself somewhere that, in a strange way, you both know and don't know. It may be somewhere where you have often imagined or remembered being. The reason that we visit this sacred space is to be given access to your pages of the Akashic Record, or Book of Lives.

11 Finally we take a staircase or a lift, to go deep down into the unconscious mind, which is linked to the One Consciousness, where everything is remembered, and

so you will be able to remember everything. When you reach the bottom, you will find yourself in a room or space with a door or some way through. On the door is a handle, and, knowing that you are completely safe, that no harm can come to you and that what happens next is for your healing benefit, open the door.

12 Do please bring along to the Regression session anything which you would like to have with you for help or support, anything that you feel would help you to relax and feel confident. Also please understand that anything that you will experience will be happening in Real Time and is unlikely to be forgotten by you. The whole procedure is about helping you re-member (put back together again) your own Story. That is where the Healing power of Regression Therapy lies. Do expect to feel a little unsettled for a few days after Regression. This is simply because the information you have received is still being reintegrated into your Soul Story where it belongs.

★★★★★★★★★★★★★★★★★★★★★★★★★★★

Having explained things this carefully, beforehand, clients are asked to 'go with the flow' of whatever happens and trust the truth of wherever they find themselves. They need to abandon the necessity for control over the situation, 'freewheel,' and trust the process. An open mind and an open heart are what is required. They are also encouraged to speak up, (this reminder is necessary because regression is a process of looking within the Self and so often this has a tendency to turn the volume of the voice down as well,) speak clearly and to tell us, in as much detail as they can, what is going on, without censure.

The sound system is an added responsibility for me, but I have found that it is well worth the trouble, as it provides confirmation of exactly what happened. In fact this book could not have been written without it, although that was the last thought on my mind at the time I decided to record each session! The recordings were carried out to give the client as much insight and information as possible, and they always leave the regression session with a copy, unless they specifically state that they do not require one.

The "door" in regression is, in fact known as a portal, a way through to the next dimension, and it has, in a sense, a one way valve on it for the 'characters' in the story. They may, in fact, be better able to go forward in the light themselves after a regression, because they have been willing to help, but they are not permitted, by the portal guardians, to come back.

Finally, when the regression or journey has come to a natural conclusion, the thanking of guides and helpers takes place, followed by a couple of minutes of silence. Then I quietly address the client, telling them that I am going to monitor the movement of their consciousness back down through the body again until it is firmly rooted in the physical body, taking it right down to the soles of the feet, in order to ground the psyche, just as I would after a healing.

Of course, bearing in mind that we probably have had many lives, and there may be various things to correct, there could be different 'levels' of healing necessary. This is why it is sometimes important to regress the same subject on more than one occasion.

Take, for example, the client bothered by a difficult pain in his abdomen. All kinds of treatments were tried, and eventually regression seemed to be the only solution possible. Under regression, he was found to have been a female of French nationality, working for the Resistance movement at the time of the second world war. After the war, she settled in a small French village, where, in the aftermath of a village fete, she fell foul of the appreciably older village schoolmaster, and so became pregnant by him. She was determined, however, to have nothing more to do with him. He, nevertheless, had other plans, and came to her cottage one day, in order to persuade her to marry him. A nasty argument ensued, as she was adamant that this was in no way going to happen. Then things turned **really** nasty. She caught the gleam of the blade of a large kitchen knife, which the schoolmaster had pulled from his pocket. For a few minutes, the two of them 'played cat and mouse' around the kitchen table. Then she seizes an opportunity for escape, and makes a dash for the back door. She is impeded, however, by being quite heavily pregnant, and the schoolmaster catches up with her in a quiet copse, at the bottom of the garden. His intention is that if he can't have her nobody shall, and so he comes at her from behind, wraps both arms around her, and, in a rage, plunges the knife deep into her abdomen, killing both her and her unborn child.

The point at which the knife entered the abdomen, is the exact point at which my client was experiencing all the pain in this current lifetime. He even said to me, "Do you think we could run that through again, with me standing in the place of a television cameraman? I want to be absolutely sure at what point the knife entered my body." This request was granted by Spirit, the scene was rerun, and he got the confirmation he needed!

The body was hastily buried in an unmarked grave, covered with leaves, and the woman, who mysteriously arrived at the village, and lived quietly, keeping herself to herself, mysteriously disappears once more. No serious enquiry as to her disappearance was ever made.

There were two consequences of this regression. One was that the pain in the abdomen of my client largely, although not completely, disappeared. The second was that the woman, because of the circumstances surrounding her death, was trying, but was not quite able, to move on fully to the light. She needed acknowledgement, both for herself and for her baby. Armed with this knowledge, my client was then able to write her a short letter of explanation, and recognition, facilitating both his own, the woman's and the baby's release. The resulting benefit from this regression to my client was an approximate 85% reduction of experienced pain.

However, about a year later my client was still experiencing some difficulty. A second regression, so I was being told, by Spirit, would be beneficial. I remember saying to him that, "Lightening very seldom strikes in the same place twice," but this, so I was being told by my guides, "was the case in this instance." And so, once more I took him into regression, because I was told that there was still a pattern of trauma, laid down by a past life experience, in this man's current life body template.

This time, he was a young man, living in the Port of Falmouth, Cornwall in the 18th Century. His father was the skipper of a cargo boat, which plied between the French and English coasts, carrying goods. They were a respected family, but, of course, not of the aristocracy. However the young man fell in love with a lady from a wealthy family living in the area. It was a love match but things, they knew from the start, would not be easy for them, because of their different background and upbringing. She was "Landed Gentry," and he was an ordinary fellow, working on his father's boat. And there was another problem! Her father appointed a new steward of the estate, when his old steward died. This man was ambitious and clever, in many ways, not least in his desire to marry his master's daughter, and achieve "Landed Gentry" status for himself.

The steward was a very crafty fellow, and the beautiful young girl was not in the least interested in him, in fact, she despised his crafty ways, and was very conscious of his designs on her. There was a poisoning incident on board boat where the young sailor became very ill, and his old father actually died. The suspicion, which was never proved, was that he had been poisoned by one of the crew, working on behalf of the steward for a fee. Although at the time he was extremely ill, the young man did, in fact, eventually recover. However, when he heard rumours of an agreement between the girl's father and the steward, for her hand in marriage, he managed a secret meeting with her. She told him that in no way did she wish to associate herself the steward, who had managed to charm and impress her father with his knowledge and education, until the father had agreed to their marriage. Also the steward, was, by this time, in possession of certain information to do with the estate, which could spell trouble for the old man, if it was made public. The steward was a character the old man knew it was best not to cross, hardworking, thorough and crafty!

The young sailor was incensed! He was a young man who was not able to control his fits of temper when they came on him, and in this mood he devised a plan. He knew the road that the steward took at the end of each day, on his way home on horseback, and so he decided to lie in wait for him. He devised a plan to attack from above, and so he hid in the branches of a tall tree, which grew out over the road. At last, in the twilight, he spotted the steward approaching, and just as he got right under the branch, the young sailor jumped down. A violent struggle ensued and it quickly turned into a "kill or be killed" situation. Finally the young sailor triumphed.

Now he was a fugitive on the run. In the narrow streets of old Falmouth town, he was being chased by some Red Coat soldiers, and, looking back over his shoulder, to check their progress, he inadvertently ran on to the pike of another Red Coat soldier stealthily searching, coming around the corner in **front** of him, and killed! The pike, you may not be surprised to learn, entered his body at **exactly** the point of current life pain! And this second story, remembered, finally released the demons of trauma and the body template pain problem.

When the same person is regressed on more than one occasion, it is very interesting to observe the similarities and differences in personality traits. The same character is, in a sense, there, but there does seem to be a honing, and lessons do appear to be learned, from lifetime to lifetime. In my experience, progress occurs. The more lessons learned, the more enlightened we become. All life is a process towards enlightenment.

The future can be even more significantly changed with the possibility of progressions into the future. Also the space between lives is another potential for healing of the soul, and both are opportunities of the spirit for direction and education to be given. These areas are naturally becoming part of my current work. There is a certain urgency, and indeed opportunity, for people to learn faster now, as the whole world of science and technology speeds up.

Olga Kharitidi, in her book, "The Master of Lucid dreams," writes that fighting the memory demons is the first stage of immortality. Its successful resolution is connected, celestially with going through the Sun's Gate. This is the stage at which most people have to face a second death, because they forget who they are. They become terrified by their memory demons and lose the connection with the loving power of the Sun, which is always connected with our own heart and has the face of the goddess, Anakhita, a female form of the divine creative energy. She grants us salvation from the second death when we know how to connect with her in the first transformational stage following physical death. After that is accomplished, Olga Kharitidi writes that the individual awareness goes through the next stage of passing through one of the gates. It becomes attracted to one of the seven star gates, depending on what type of future experience is needed. In other words the seven star gates each open the way to a different type of afterlife or next incarnational experience.

I believe that the seven stargates are linked to the seven major chakras, and are to do with our stage of spiritual development as we finally pass through the doorway commonly known as Death. Life is like a game of Snakes and Ladders and we slide down the snakes as well as climb the ladders. There is a long snake, and downfall waiting for a false move, even up to the last square on the board. We need to be constantly attentive to matters of the spirit. As Don Miguel Ruiz says, in his book, the four agreements: Be impeccable with your word, don't take anything personally, don't make assumptions and always do your best.

These are such important standards to live by, and if something is going wrong in one of life's many relationships and correspondences, a simple but careful check through this list will help you identify the error.

Whether you, the reader, are prepared to accept that the stories obtained under regression are true, is your choice, but what I need to make clear is that whatever information is released from the client's unconscious or subconscious mind, that information can only be significant, especially when the healing potential and self realisation from these releases are obviously so great. I do not put a client into the necessary altered state of consciousness, unless I am convinced that it is as safe as can be to do so. Anyone who is in any way considered insufficiently mentally stable would certainly not be a candidate. Anyone whose energies are not sufficiently well known to me would not be a candidate. Anyone whose energies could not easily be held in balance by means of a crystal would not be considered suitable, neither would anyone for whom a regression was not considered an important part of the healing process, in other words regressions are not carried out for curiosity. There are many other very effective ways of initiating the healing processes, besides regression. These are discussed at length in my book entitled 'Keys to Wisdom,' the details of which you will find listed at the back of this book. We do not go "poking around" in the world of Spirit for entertainment idle curiosity or amusement. Neither do we do it without a wealth of relevant information to hand. It is not a practice lightly undertaken. We are well aware of the potential for harm in regression situations ineptly handled. We do not wish to place either ourselves or our clients in situations of potential danger, either in the short or long term.

Having said all this, of course, as I always say, we cannot work with "gloves" on. There is always the Gap; there is always the leap of faith in which we trust, and if we do inadvertently uncover some unexpected negative entity, there is always the protection of The Lord's Prayer or the 23rd Psalm, or some other deeply spiritual text, such as, "Holy, Holy, Holy, Lord God of Hosts," in which to take refuge, and with which to hold the negative energy in abeyance. Some of the work revealed in this book is definitely in the "cutting edge," category, but we have long experience and certain means of protection, because of our personal standing in the Spirit world. **Do not attempt this at home**. Thorough training in these matters, working as a personal student with an accomplished, and fully trained practitioner is **essential**.

Chapter Four

Naomi's Story

Naomi had suffered the pain and immobility of a frozen shoulder for many months and no amount of conventional treatment and physiotherapy cured the problem. I felt that there was a deeper trauma responsible for the problem which could only be released by the wisdom and insights gained while in a regression state.

The question:

I would just like this afternoon to free me up. With what's left of my life, I want to make a difference to people who come in contact with me, however small. I know what it's like to be loved. I've been loved by my parents, I know what it's like to be loved by a partner, and I know what it's like to be loved and to give love to children. Sometimes I'm so full of love myself, but recently I've been blocked. I want to touch people's lives physically and emotionally in some way, to put them in touch with something that I've been in touch with, and I know how great it is. I just want to be freed up, to just let it flow. Free me up please.

Heather: I am just waiting for your spirit to be ready and waiting in a bubble of consciousness at the top of your head, ... which it is now, ... and we're going to go higher and higher, up to a level where you can be put in touch with your Guardian Angel, or angels or guides. They may be male, they may be female, they may be androgynous, there could be a child or even an animal. I'm just waiting to get the signal, from the pendulum, telling me that they are there with you. ... And I feel that they *are* there. Do you get the sense of anything?
Naomi: I experienced an incredibly rapid heartbeat, ... which has just calmed down, so I think that that was just like a rush of energy, and it feels as if it's slowly calming down to a regular sort of beat.
Heather: Right. Well, now we can move. We are going to go to a sacred place, of your own choosing, in which, or through which, you can be put in touch with your Book of Life, your page of the Akashic Record. Your special place could be out in the

country, … it could be a special room, … it could be in a church, … it could be by the sea, but if you find yourself there, please let me know.

Naomi: My special place is the old harbour at Marazion. I'm on the beach, and that's my special place, and it's full of sea glass in beautiful colours.

Heather: Is there something waiting for you, like, possibly a little boat, or something? (Pause) There may be steps, or you might see a hole in the rock, anything that will enable you to move, from your sacred place, through a portal, which will take you from this life into another lifetime. A portal is merely a doorway, so you are looking for some special little way through, that you may never have noticed before.

Naomi: I need to find a certain stone. I always collected them when I was little and I always held them in the palm of my hand. I need to find a smooth stone, with a hole in it.

Heather: I wonder if the stone we've got there with the hole in it, might be helpful Yvonne? The piece of ivory, with a hole in it?

This is, in fact, a very ancient artefact. It comes from Mesopotamia, modern day Iran, and is around 4,500 years old. I believe it to be made of ivory, and to be part of a very small and simple spindle for spinning silk. I call it the "Insight Stone' because it often gives special insights when placed on the third eye.

Yvonne: So I'm going to invoke the insight stone.

Heather: Now, there's information coming. (Pause) Just tell me anything that's happening to you now.

Naomi: I feel like I'm stuck.

Heather: What's going on around you? Just talk to me, in general terms, about what's going on around you. What can you see? What feelings are you experiencing?

Naomi: There's light, which I was hoping would turn bright, but it's just grey light. I've just got greyness.

Heather: Let's see if we can get some sun to shine for you.

Yvonne: The guides keep giving me a boat, Naomi. Is there a boat somewhere on that sea? It's not a big boat, it's a small boat.

Naomi: (Petulantly) Well, I want it to come!

Yvonne: I'm going to invoke the rudder.

This is a little wooden boat rudder that Naomi's husband, Guy, gave her to bring to the regression. Guy makes very special art pieces in the form of boats and this is a rudder he made for one of them.

So that it's directed towards you. I'm going to invoke the fluorite as well .. and the ruby record keeper is stepping forward.

Fluorite increases the ability to concentrate, balancing the positive and negative relationships of the mind. It helps one to see both reality and the truth behind illusion. Also the energy of fluorite can inspire the universal energies to activate the nourishing energies of the body, assisting one in the attainment of the ultimate state of physical perfection.

The energy of the ruby is intense, bringing lucidity to the dream state. This quality would be magnified by a record keeper, which stores ancient knowledge.

Heather: (Realising the energy has now shifted to the Truth line, the line where information and images can be received) Now, what can you feel now?

Naomi: (Sadly) Still haven't come for me. (Gets really upset and bursts into tears.)

Heather: Don't worry, you're probably trying too hard. If you can just relax .... it'll happen. You're on the right wavelength to receive information.

Yvonne: I'm going to bring the yin-yang energies in to help give a bit of balance Naomi.

Heather: We've got a working energy now.

Yvonne: Moonstone is stepping forward ... and the Buddha crystal.

Once called the 'traveller's stone', moonstone is used for protection against the perils of travel.

Buddha crystal has been used to contact and promote the transfer of information from the elders of the ancient civilisations of India, Tibet and China. It is a stone of Shukri la or Shambhala, a mystical city in Tibetan Buddhist tradition.

Naomi: (Excitedly) He's, he's going to come! I know I've dreamt about this.

Heather thinks to herself: *He's* very powerful whoever he is! She got two strong blasts of spiritual energy though her body at this point.

Naomi: It's a very small boat. He's a very tall man. He has a sort of turban on his head and he's basically brown, brown robes and a turban. He's a dark man, but he's not black, and he has red/orange dust on his face, but underneath it he's got olive skin.

Heather: More information coming.

Yvonne: I'm going to invoke the rhodocrosite at this stage.

Using rhodocrosite during the meditative state, one may melt into the sphere of golden ecstasy: an encounter with one's twin soul is highly likely.

Naomi: He's come from the Mount, across to the beach, but he doesn't live there. He's from the Nile.

Heather feels more blasts of energy.

He's come up the Nile for me. (Naomi breaks into sobs) He's come up the Nile, and he's got a pole! And he's come from the Mount, but really he's come from the Nile! This is so stupid 'cos it's Moses and the bulrushes! (still sobbing) There's a baby! It's the baby in the bulrushes! The baby's in the bulrushes! (Sobbing loudly) The baby's in the bulrushes! My baby! He's the baby in the bulrushes. It's Little Mo! I've hidden the baby in the bulrushes. I've had to hide the baby in the bulrushes, ... had to *hide* him.

Heather: There's a little bit more that wants to come through, and then I think we can move.

Yvonne: The little Egyptian cat is stepping forward, so I Invoke the energy of the cat.

This is the Egyptian goddess, Bast, represented in the form of a cat. Bastet is the usual female form of the name, however this one wishes to be known as Bast, the name in its male form. In addition to her major symbol, the sistrum, an ancient Egyptian percussion instrument, Bast was also allotted one of the Divine all seeing Eyes of Horus, in the form of the Uraeus, or Serpent of Wisdom.

Naomi: I wrapped him up tight .... He's secure. He's wrapped up in swaddling and he's secure. I've had to hide him and I've had to leave him ... and the man's still there, in the boat.

He's going to have to take me away. He's a *lovely* man, he's a really lovely man. He's, he's helping me with this. He's there to help me. ... And it's, it's my little Mo, mine, my little Mo. (Obviously still upset)

Heather: And now I think we can move, forward, minutes, hours, one hour forward, just about one hour forward, in time.

Yvonne: Mother of Pearl energy is stepping forward.

This carries the energy of the Universal Mother.

Heather: Information is coming. ..... Now, what can you feel now?

Naomi: (Sniffing back tears) It feels as if it's dealt with now.

Heather: Where are you? Can you tell me where you are?

Naomi: I'm not on the river. We're in between.

Yvonne: The Cross energy is stepping forward.

In the Sinai Desert, the mature Moses was introduced to the god of the Midianite tribes, a god of storms and war, whose symbol was the crucifix-like motif, worn on their foreheads. It later became known as the 'Yahweh mark'. This god, who lived in the mountains, and, in particular Mount Horab, or the Moses Mountain, as it is still known, became the God of the Jews, following Moses' conversations with Him, when he was leading the Israelites on Exodus through the Sinai. Interestingly, although dates are difficult to establish, Moses is believed to have lived around 1,200 BC, in the same time period as Akhenaten, the Pharaoh who also believed in One God.

Heather: When you say you're in between, can you define that a bit more? In fact "In between" turns out to be the space between lives. You've come out of that very painful incident. Are you on your own? Is there somebody with you? .... Information coming! Now!

Yvonne: Pegasus is stepping forward, so I invoke his energy.

Pegasus is the winged horse of mythology, who is introduced by the guides to help carry Naomi forward from a very difficult place.

Heather: Tell me a little bit about you. Are you an Egyptian? Are you an Israelite? Are you the mother of the child?

Naomi: Mm, I'm the mother. He's my baby.

Heather: Are you indoors, or outdoors?

Naomi: I think I'm hiding.

Heather: Where are you hiding?

Naomi: I'm on the riverbank.

Heather: What time of day is it? Is it bright sunshine , or is it evening?

Naomi: It's early evening.

Heather: If you look around you, what can you see?

Naomi: I can see an ancient hill, with ancient buildings, and it's very dusty.

Heather: There's a bit more information coming.

Yvonne: Madagascan sapphire stepping forward.

Madagascan sapphire allows one to approach the metaphysical realm with ease.

Heather: I think the guides want you to tell me a little bit more about where we are now, before we move. Tell me absolutely anything that you can experience, see, or feel, about where you are.

Naomi: (Simply sighs, but says nothing.)

Heather: Are you cold? Are you hungry?

Naomi: It feels .... detached. I've detached myself from .... um .. having to hide the baby. I've just had to .. detach myself.

This is a highly significant statement about Naomi's personality that the guides needed to be voiced.

Heather: And now I think we can move, forward, minutes, hours, days, weeks, one, two, three, between three and four weeks, forward. (Pause) Just tell us anything at all that you can.

Naomi: I've shut off. I've shut down. I've just had to .... shut off .... and I do that in this lifetime. I have to close down.

Heather: More information coming. ...... Now, what's come into your mind now?

Naomi: I want to .... I want to move on to another lifetime, but the little Mo thing is so strong

Heather: That you can't leave him behind?

Naomi: That I can't move on. I'm stuck.

Yvonne: I'm going to invoke the rainbow amethyst and I'm actually going to invoke the *energy of the baby.*

Amethyst, especially with rainbows inside, is to activate the energy to produce realignment of the energy bodies, while providing for stimulus to rectify disassociation between the aspects of cause and effect. It further allows for the integration of cause and effect, providing insight into which portion of the actualised self requires remodelling in order to facilitate change toward the ultimate state of perfection.

Heather: Now we've got a working pattern.

A working pattern is an indication to me that certain work is being carried out, by the guides, on our client's persona.

Naomi: It's OK now, because I can see he becomes a man, he lives to become a man. That's **good**.

Heather: So now you feel able to move?

Naomi: Yes, yes.

Heather: OK, well we'll go forward, minutes, hours, days, weeks, months, years, decades, centuries, one century forward, so you go forward one hundred years, into a completely different space and time. You could be a child, a man, a woman, you could even be an animal, … and there's information coming. Now, give me your first impression now.

Naomi: I think I might be an animal.

Heather: More information coming. Now!

Naomi: I think I've been a dove. (Then more confidently) I've been a dove in Egypt!

Heather: More information coming.

Naomi: And it's to do with love, because you mate for life, with one partner. (Starts to sob, as if heartbroken.)

Heather: There's more information coming.

Naomi: (Still upset and struggling to speak) We're in the olive trees, and there's lots of us. We're just filling the olive trees, and we're all doves, and I haven't got a male dove.

Heather: More information coming ..... now.

Naomi: The tree is full of doves, and I've lost my dove, (still sobbing) and I'm just on my own, and everybody else has got a partner.

Heather: (Gently) More information coming.

Naomi: My partner, I know, I found in the road. (Sobs as if her heart would break.) Someone had killed it in the road. I took Kit (Naomi's younger son) to school, and I came back and my dove was in the road, and it was still warm, and I had to stop the car and pick it up, and it was still warm, (between sobs) and I wrapped it in pink tissue paper. And I knew what that was, when I held it in this lifetime, I knew what that warmth was! I buried it in the garden. (Sobbing) That was my *dove. That was my soul mate dove!* And I've got an olive tree and it just had one olive on it. I've got an olive tree in this lifetime and there's just one olive on it. It came off and it's special, like I've kept it. And I love olive trees, and I love eating olives, and it's to do with my dove. (Sighs and begins to compose herself.)

Heather: And now we can move. We're going to go forward again, minutes, hours, days, weeks, months, years, decades, centuries, another hundred years, forward. Go forward another hundred years.

Naomi: It's to do with my arm. It is hurting. It's hurting, just at the top. And I'm a lady.

Heather: There's more information coming.

Naomi: I've got black hair and I'm very beautiful, and I'm wearing a turquoise robe and it's got gold around the edges, and I've got my eyes on, (fully made up in the Egyptian fashion) with my kohl around my eyes, and I've got a gold crown around my head.

Heather: A little bit more information coming ..... now. (Naomi is still very upset.) You're doing really well, *really* well.

Naomi: I've got a beautiful necklace on. It's gold and lapis lazuli. And I've got my ring on. I've got the ring. It's the turquoise and gold ring that I wear. I've got it, and it's about love conquering all. It's the only thing that's important. Nothing else is important, in *any* lifetime. You've got to *love*.

Gold, lapis Lazuli and turquoise is what ancient Egyptian jewellery was made of. Turquoise has long been mined in the area west of Sinai.

Heather: There's more information coming ... now.

Naomi: I think I'm in some sort of palace, and there's polished stone, and it's cool, the stone is cool.

Heather: Little bit more.

Naomi: Peacock feathers.

Heather: What is the significance of the peacock feathers?

Peacock feathers are a symbol of death.

Naomi: It's hot, and there's a fan. Someone's fanning me. And I've got both arms. I don't know why the top of my arm is hurting, but I think it's 'cos there's a bangle, and it's *digging in*. I've got bare arms.

Heather: Now I think we can move, forward. It's a *very short space of time.* It's like the next minute! Does something happen suddenly?

Naomi: Well I don't know ... I feel that I'm a queen, but I don't know where my king is.

Rulers of Egypt were known as Kings, not as Pharaohs, until the period of the New Kingdom 1550 to 1295 BC

I'm sitting on a throne, but, on the left hand side there should be the king, and he's not there.

Heather: And now I think we can move, forward, minutes, hours, days, one day, forward, so the next day.

Naomi: The man on the Nile in the boat, that collected me and waited for me while I was hiding the baby, this tall man is trying to 'be there' for me. I think he's already dead, but he's come back in the boat again and he's like ... he's ... he's waiting in the wings for me, the man in the boat, the tall man.

Heather: And now we can move, forward, it's just like, almost instantaneously, it's like the next minute, something very quick.

Naomi: The king thinks .. I've had lovers.

Heather: More information coming. ...What now?

Naomi: He's going to cut my arm off.

Heather: More information coming.

Naomi: He wants me to be maimed, and unattractive!

Heather: More information coming.

Naomi: (Pause) I think he *hates me!* .... *He's jealous,* ... because of all the young men in the court. I *don't have* lovers. I don't have lovers! I'm faithful to the king, and I like, I like the young men, because they're beautiful, very, very beautiful young men, and their beauty is just exquisite, but I'm not unfaithful to the king, and I think that one of these beautiful young men is Kit, who is my younger son in this life, (starts to get upset) and the other beautiful young man is Elliot! (Kit's very best friend in this life now) And they're together! They're both very very beautiful young men. And they have beautiful dark skin, and black hair, and they have lovely gold bands around their heads, ... And I think they might be brothers. Elliot is older than Kit, and they have bare chests, and they have gold bangles around their wrists, and they're physically beautiful young men, and I'm taken with their beauty. And the one that looks like Kit reminds me of Mo. (Mo is the little baby who was hidden in the bulrushes, the remembrance of whom makes Naomi start to cry again.) And I'm in this palace, and I'm sitting there and I want the king to be on the other side and he's not! There are all these beautiful young Egyptian men and there's Elliot and Kit, ... and he comes, the king comes, and, in front of these beautiful young men, he cuts my arm off .... in front of Kit, who carries the energy of Mo. ....

The young Egyptian men at court would certainly have been sophisticated and physically beautiful at this time. Egyptians today are a mixture of Arab, European and Negro racial types, creating a variety of skin tones and features. Many of these are strikingly beautiful, and some of these are identical to the images found in the ancient tombs within the pyramids. This beauty is not merely skin deep, as they have always been friendly, and by all normal standards, a tolerant nation. As believers in Ma'at, (Righteousness, Truth and Justice,) the Ancients would also have appeared psychologically beautiful, by contrast, to the Queen, because, in the Hyksos period of Egyptian history, (1782 - 1570 BC) falling between the Middle Kingdom and the New Kingdom, the Hyksos or Desert Kings ruled in Upper Egypt. They were a mixed group of Asiatic people, of desert background who were certainly not followers in the ways of Ma'at, and, in their search for power, they initially dealt cruelly and roughly with anyone they felt was an obstacle to their cause.

Heather: And now we can move, forward, minutes , hours, days, ... well, it's about 23 hours, it's almost a day, nearly a day.

Naomi: (In a flat voice) I die. I die .. and ... I don't know that Kit is Mo, but, certainly Kit and Elliot, the two beautiful young men at court, had to witness .... this, this abuse. And it stays with them both, Kit and Elliot. I think they're brothers, but Elliot is the eldest brother.

Heather: So now we're going to move, forward again, minutes, hours, days, weeks, months ... it looks like one month, but don't try and work that our mathematically. So move one month forward.

Naomi: The king gets them. The king gets Kit and Elliot, because they showed their emotions to the queen, and he thinks that that must mean that they had relations with the queen, but they just loved her. He's going to seek them out.

Heather: And now we move, forward again, it's minutes only, 5, 10, it's about 12 minutes forward.

Naomi: I don't know how, but Elliot saves Kit's life. I think he has to give his life for Kit. He protects him, to the end. (Sighs)

Heather: More information coming.

Naomi: And he gives his life, to save Kit.

Heather: And now we can move, forward again. Minutes, a matter of minutes. It's only about one minute. One minute forward. ..... don't think of it logically.

Naomi: The man in the boat has come again. He's come for Elliot.

Heather: More information coming.

Naomi: He's come to take Elliot away, in the little boat.

Heather: And now we can move, forward, minutes, hours, days, weeks, months, years, decades, centuries, millennia, one, we're going forward a thousand years, one thousand years or so, forward. .... I think you're in incarnation, I don't think you're between lives. You're in incarnation. I get that you might just have been born.

Naomi: Guy (Naomi's husband in this life) is my father.

Heather: Are you a baby?

Naomi: Yes, I'm a girl.

Heather: More information coming .... now.

Naomi: I think it's China, and ... I don't think I have a mother.

Heather: More information coming.

Naomi: So Guy brings me up...

Heather: More information.

Naomi: ..which is unusual for a man.

Heather: And now we can move, forward, minutes, hours, days, weeks, 1, 2, 3, three weeks or so forward. .... What are you feeling?

Naomi: Um, ... I don't know *why* it's just ... him and me.

Heather: Well, why would it not be?

Naomi: (Continuing to sound sad and flat) There's no mother, and no other children.

Heather: More information coming.

Naomi: And the wall. I think we're contained within this wall.

Heather: Do you mean you're *behind the wall*, or do you mean you're are actually *in the wall?*

Naomi: Just that the wall surrounds us; it's just a high wall. I think we live within the wall, within the space. It's surrounding where we live.

Heather: You don't sound very happy.

Naomi: I don't know where everyone else is.

Heather: And now we can move, forward, minutes, the next minute.

Naomi: I'm just stuck, I'm stuck in this space.

Yvonne: I'm going to invoke the gold leaf within this bottle, and the silver coin. These represent the twin energies of the sun and the moon. Gold, in this instance os for balancing the heart chakra, and for purification of the physical body. Silver is for drawing forth negativity from the physical body while transferring the positive forces of the other mineral.

Heather: Now, there's information coming. ... Now.

Naomi: Well, I think we're the only ones left. I don't know what's happened, but we're the only ones left. I think there's been a fire, in the village, and Guy's my father, and he was the teacher, and there's no one left.

Heather: More information.

Naomi: So he takes me away, safely, ... because it was very black there. We escape, and we go to somewhere very, very green, and very beautiful, beautiful landscape, like a beautiful garden. The whole of the landscape is a beautiful garden, and we've been in this black space behind a wall together, and now we've escaped to the green, and it's very, very beautiful, and there's water, and we both know the beauty of this place, and very few people get to this place, and we got there together, and he got me there, and it's so green, and healing. It's so green and healing and the water is so clear, and it's a beautiful garden to be in, and we're so lucky to be there. I want Kit in there, and Elliot, and Mo, I want everybody I know in this garden. It's *so beautiful.* And the river is running and it's rose quartz. It's *pink. The water is pink* and it's *clear. And it's **pink water. And it's pink against the green. And it's fresh, and it's clear. And the air is clear and icy when you breath it in, and it's so good for you. And it's what everybody needs. Everybody I know in this lifetime needs to be placed in this garden, and experience this garden, because everybody deserves to experience this BEAUTIFUL PLACE. And I must try and hold on to this feeling, and when I meet people and I touch people and I help people, I must visualise that I can take them to this garden. and Guy HAS SHOWN ME THIS GARDEN. Nobody else can show me this garden but Guy. And the doves are coming BACK.* I've got to put this garden in a bottle, and shake the green and the pink together, and try and sprinkle everybody that I love, or I don't love. When we meet, I have to sprinkle them, with this love. It's like magic, but magic has *no depth to it. The word magic is, is too shallow a word, it's just .....* I must bring this forward, I must **hold on to this and bring it forward**. (Breaths repeatedly, very deeply.) And, now this is the end of my regression, but I just want anybody, who's listening to this, to know that there is this place, and it's *very, very beautiful, and the doves always come back.*

Naomi's comments

The paragraph, where I say I've got my ring on, I actually wear the ring in this lifetime, so I'm recognising, in the regression, a ring that I wear every day. It came about through a very powerful dream I had. I was shown a ring, and after I'd been shown the ring, there was a message. The message that went with the dream was a very powerful, "Love Conquers All," message that has remained with me. And so I knew I'd got to go and find someone to make this ring up.

I found a jeweller who would follow my design. The ring is made out of 18 carat gold and a piece of Cornish turquoise, which is not very plentiful, found in the Cornish clay pits. If anyone was to look at it in this present day, it looks as if it's been dug up out of the ground, the sort of thing you would see in a museum. It's noticed a lot; many people remark on it. I always think they're connecting with something when they do that.

When I first had the ring, I had trouble wearing it. It burned my finger. I can remember picking it up from the jeweller and putting it on, and it was just exactly as I wanted. But one day I realised that, before I could actually wear it every day, I had to go across on the ferry to Saint Michael's Mount, wearing the ring. (Small motor boats, carrying the pilgrims, ply the 500 metres or so, to and fro to the Mount regularly.) As I was going across in the ferryboat, I trailed my hand wearing the ring in the sea water, while making the journey. Having reached the island, I briefly got out of the boat on to the island itself, and then returned to the mainland, doing the same thing with the ring on my return journey. After that it didn't hurt. It was as if I had to carry out the cleansing ritual, before I, in this lifetime, could be comfortable with wearing the ring. It happened that suddenly. In my lunch hour I thought, "I know what I've got to do! I didn't know why I had to do it at the time, but I knew it had to be done!"

This was because Naomi was last wearing the ring when her arm was chopped off.

Heather: There may be some quality, about the turquoise, which is now in the ring, and which wasn't in there before.

It can hereafter be used for attunement between those of the physical plain, as well as between one and the spirit world. It is valuable to provide strength and protection during vision quests and astral travel. It is of high spirituality and can bring both valour and protection on the spiritual level, and from the etheric plane. It is also a stone of Earth-grounding : hence, one can remain grounded during spiritual work. It acts to improve meditation and to further peace of mind.

Naomi: So this is why it is remarkable in the regression. It's a piece which I have had for many years now. I had it way, way before the regression. I would never do any "hands on" healing without wearing it. In fact I don't even leave the house. I would go back again if I'd forgotten to put it on.

I would like also, in some way, to explain a little bit about Elliot and Kit, who appear in the Egyptian lifetime. Kit is my son in this lifetime, and I *know* that, when he was born, he was sent to heal me. It was apparent, every time I touched him. He just made me feel better. I *knew* we'd been together before. And his very first friend, that he met as a baby, was the character who appears in the regression, called Elliot. These two, as little boys, maybe two and a half to three years old, loved nothing better than sitting down together watching National Geographic videos on Ancient Egypt. Kit was *obsessed* about Egypt when he was very young,, and so was Elliot. Kit used to collect anything to do with Egypt and lots of people knew that, so they were always giving me things, and he was thrilled. He even wanted his bedroom painted like a sarcophagus!

Heather: So what of your frozen shoulder Naomi? Did it recover?

Naomi: Yes. I'd gone for 6 months of treatment, after three months of it slowly coming on.

And so I'd been to see an osteopath. I'd had a lot of fantastic physiotherapy, from a very good source, which helped, but I was at a point when I decided to have the regression, when you said to me, " I really think you need to go for a regression Naomi. Nothing else is going to shift this." Before the regression I was taking really strong pain killers every four hours during the day and every four hours at night.

After the regression, the first night, when I got home, I didn't know what to do with my arm with the pain. I remember thinking, "Well, I've taken the pain killers," and the pain was so intense, I didn't know where to put myself. At one point I thought that I was just going to have to go to hospital because I was pacing around rocking this arm, thinking, "Oh my God! I'm just going to have to see somebody about this!" This pain was so *intense*. And then I got to the right painkillers, and I spoke to you next morning, and you said calmly, "Just give it 48 hours, and it will be fine." By the next morning that excruciating pain had gone and then it disappeared completely. There was no pain whatsoever, no trace at all!

Chapter Five

Richard's story

The question
Why do I still find difficulty in forming
meaningful relationships with women and what
needs to be cleared before that becomes possible?

Heather: We are ready to begin. Your spirit is resting in a bubble of consciousness at the top of your head Richard, and I'm waiting for permission to go forward further.... Off we go. We go higher and higher, higher and higher to a place where you can be put in touch with your Guardian Angel, or guide or guides. They may be male, they may be female, they could be androgynous, there could be a child or even an animal. I get the sense that whoever or whatever they are, they are actually with you. Can you get any sense of that for yourself?

Richard: I feel kind of confused. I feel that I'm down in a hole and they're looking down at me. They're grinning at me and there's a sense that they're wanting me to get on with it, wanting me to commit, .. come to their level maybe.

Heather: More information is trying to get through.

Richard: I feel that I'm coming up, that the ground is acting as a lift and I'm being lifted up. (Big sigh) I think I'm there. There's someone there. I think I had the sense of it being a Chinaman but I kind of dismissed it! (Laughs) but I don't know why.

Heather: More information is coming.

Richard: It's almost like someone with a painted face, or someone in a robe, maybe Japanese.

Heather: Could it be a mask?

Richard: It *could* be a mask. Yes. And I've got this image of a lion, but again not a real lion, a lion that's a Chinese ornament.

Heather: You're doing well.

Richard: Yes. I feel like I needed that reassurance. Actually I feel I need to clarify and focus my attention. I feel that I'm stood up now, and that I'm walking, .. I'm walking to some woods or some trees, and there's a building there, and again it's a sort of Chinese or Japanese style building, and it feels like there's someone there, waiting for me, and maybe that's the person who was there before. It's almost like he was doing magic, creating all these images of the masked person and the lion, almost to tease me, playing games. And I'm there and I'm going up the steps and he's there sitting. And there's tea, ... a tea ceremony. I'm invited to sit, and I feel quite in awe, because I've seen the sort of magic, the powers that he's able to bring about. And I'm sat there. But I feel at ease. I feel put at ease in his company. His presence feels very soothing. There's a sense of peace, a sense of harmony about him, that I feel bathed in and blessed by.

Heather: And now we can move. One hour forward.

Richard: I feel like I'm sat on the steps that lead up to his house, facing down, looking at the view. There are open plains and there are horses, but there's one horse in particular, a black horse is there and is coming towards me. I'm not sure whether it's a wild horse. It's not got any saddle or anything, but it's there and it's allowing me to stroke it and yes, even to mount it, and it feels like I just want to walk and go slowly, (Laughing) and it wants to gallop, and I feel kind of carried along, but exhilarated. It feels like I'm not going to fall off, whatever, even though there's no saddle and I've just got the mane to hold on to and it's almost as if it's a magic horse as well, that won't throw me. It's almost as if its feet don't quite touch the ground, so it doesn't jolt along.

Heather: And now I think we can move, forward, four days forward.

Richard: Mmm....

Heather: Maybe we're not quite far enough forward. Four and a half days?

Richard: It feels somewhat like a fortified house. It has big thick walls and a big gateway. I'm there and I think the horse is still there also. I'm knocking on the door, banging on this door. It opens, opens into a kind of courtyard with animals, cows and chickens and goats, and some people. It feels like I've come to meet someone, see someone, and I feels I can already see her, but ...

Heather: I think we move now. I think you *could* just catch a glimpse of her, but that it's time to move really. We're going to move forward, minutes, Two minutes.

Richard: Well, I'm there. I've gone up some steps and we're standing together on the balcony which looks out over the courtyard. And this woman, I can't quite see her face. I can see her hair, which is long and golden, and my feeling is that she's very beautiful, and I feel very attracted to her.

Heather: And now we move. We move forward, but there seems to be more to it than that somehow. Minutes, ten, twenty, thirty, thirty five minutes. No, somewhere between thirty and thirty five minutes.

Richard: (Says nothing,)

Heather: I think it's thirty minutes. The timing is crucial here, try thirty minutes.

Richard: I think I feel confused in my mind. It's almost as if I have one image and I'm not sure whether it's my (Laughs) my fantasy(Peals of laughter)

Heather: (Enjoying the fun of the situation) Is there a problem about putting it into words?

Richard: I don't *think* so. It feels like we're making love, but I was just caught in the sense of the thirty minutes! It was pretty quick work! (Laughs again) So I kind of hesitated!

Heather: *I* just asked you to find the thirty minute mark, and it all started from there! (Joins in the laughter)

Richard: Yes and it left me feeling a bit, I don't know, *exposed* maybe.

Heather: Well you've got the benefit of the visual images you see!

Richard: Anyhow it feels like there's a joy and a pleasure and a relaxed ease in our being together, so I guess we maybe knew each other before. It feel's like the scene is that of ..

Heather: Familiarity?

Richard: Yes, familiarity and sexual pleasure and just the goodness of being together. It feels very unifying and as if we belong.

Heather: And now we move forward, a very short space of time. It's almost down to seconds. Five, ten, fifteen seconds.

Richard: I don't know whether someone else is there. It feels like it's a big man, darkly dressed. I don't know whether it's armour, leather bound maybe, and I don't know whether it's her husband or her father or ... I feel some explosive kind of entrance and ....

Heather: Now we can move, minutes, hours, days, it looks like next day.

Richard: I don't quite know what's happened. I *think* he's dead. I think the man who came in .. was stabbed. I thought for a moment it was the woman who died, but I don't *think* so. I think it was the man. And it feels like now we're outlaws on the run, dazed and not quite sure where we are going ... in the woods I *think*. We still have the horse, and it looks like we're both riding on it, bareback, slowly winding our way, but subdued.

Heather: And now we can move. I think we go back in time. Minutes, hours, fifteen hours back.

Richard: I think that was the point at which the man had just come into the room, and he was angry, yes, .. but I think he was willing to talk. I think maybe he was the woman's husband but maybe he was impotent or... and in, in lots of ways a good man and just wanted to keep things hushed up, wouldn't make a fuss, but the sense of wanting life to carry on as it was, as if nothing had happened, and I don't know quite how it was that he died. There's some feeling that I was sat talking to him and that the woman came from behind with the dagger and stabbed him. And the feeling of it not being what I wanted and feeling that sense of his betrayal, and somehow it feeling that the love that I was feeling for the woman is now, somehow, irrevocably sullied by her action and deceit and it's almost like, yes, there's a feeling of disgust, or revulsion, but also a certain complicity in it, of feeling kind of trapped. It's as if she's saying, "Well, we're in this together."

Heather: There's a bit more that wants to come through.

Richard: Yes, now we're in this together and now we *can be together for ever*. And my feeling of just, "Yes, but not like that!" And feeling the sense of the void opening between us of mistrust and deceit and betrayal. It's almost as if there's a feeling I have of her having planned it, of her having known that he was around, was going to come in, and that that scene would happen, whereas I had been under the impression that the other man wasn't about, so I feel also kind of lied to and betrayed somehow, caught up in that tangled web.

Heather: I picked up an Anxiety pattern there, but it's gone on to the Truth line again, so there may be further communication around this particular scene Richard. .. More information trying to get through now.

Richard: It's almost like she was already packed, ready to go. She's got her things that she's wanted to take, so there's the feeling of, I don't know, just playing my part in a prearranged trap, a prearranged encounter that she has orchestrated from the start, .. that, suddenly, I don't know who this person is whom I thought was sweet and whose love I felt I enjoyed.

Heather: And now we're going to move, forward, minutes, hours, days, weeks, one week forward.

Richard: There's a sense of sitting, I'm not sure whether it's in a cave or just by some rocks, and there's a fire. Sitting there, hunched over, still very caught up in the events of the week before and the feelings of guilt and betrayal and dishonour and the woman there trying to cajole me and jog me out of that space. All she's expressing is about being free, and free for us to be together and what's wrong with that? You know it's what we said we wanted, and as if the end is justified by the means.

Heather: More information coming.

Richard: And for me I just feel the sense of a stranger, a part of her that I've had no experience of before, and I'm kind of confused and appalled and disgusted and angry and also I feel helpless. I feel in some way responsible and it's like I don't know what to do. My mind is just working hard at trying to resolve a course of action that feels true to me, honourable and right and, and I don't know what that is.

Heather: And now we can move, forward again, it looks like ten years forward.

Richard: And it feels like we're still together but, ... and I'm not sure if she's pregnant, but there's certainly at least one child, and there's a, I don't know, a *bitterness* between us, a feeling of lack of fulfilment, of things not said, truths not told, the living somehow of a deception, of a lie that built on one lie and then on to another and then another, so there's the feeling of being weighed down with that burden of not knowing now where the truth lies, within all that mire of of dishonour and dishonesty, so there's the feeling of, .. my feeling is of a heavy hearted burdened existence, of the past deeds, misdeeds weighing heavily on my mind, always there, not wanting to sully the lives of the children, not wanting to inflict it on them, but somehow it permeating every part of the life we're leading.

Heather: I'm going to invoke the little black and white spirit doll. That's bringing more information in.

Richard: (Pause) I feel myself pacing around. It's like a tiger trapped in the zoo. It's like an animal contained, confined, in a life that feels ignoble and petty, and it's almost as if as time goes on the burden doesn't diminish, it increases. It's the sense of just moving all the time further and further away from the truth and that each step further from the truth involves more weight, more burden.

Heather: A little bit more.

Richard: My heart feels like it's stretched on a rack. It's tortured and never at peace. (Pause) And I don't know how the thoughts are there to make amends, and so to offer recompense. What do I need to do to heal this? I think the horse is still there, I'm not sure whether tethered or in an enclosure. It's kind of always there and somehow always reminds me of the time before, the time of freedom, of truth, of when I lived, *when I lived*.

Heather: More information coming.

Richard: It's what I do. I go down to the horse and confess my sins. It's what I do. It's the only ease I have, the only contact that feels true and it's, it's almost like in the leaving, and the leaving of my children, there's the feeling of, (Huge sigh) I don't know. Can I do that? Can I take them? The punishment that would be to me in the leaving of them, the pain to them in my leaving. I toss the idea back and forth. What do I need to do?

Heather: And now we can move, forward, minutes, hours, days, one, two, three, between three and four days, forward, nearly into the fourth day really.

Richard: It feels like it's night.

Heather: Yes. I knew it was night. I could feel it was night.

Richard: We're in bed. I'm in bed with the woman. I'm not sure whether she's my wife now. And I'm not sure whether I'm unburdening my heart, but I'm telling her that I can't go on like this. And she's angry. I think she's also scared, scared that I will betray her and...

Heather: There's more information trying to get through.

Richard: And my feeling is that I need to go, though I don't know what I will do. I don't have it in my mind to betray her. I feel her deeds, her conscience is for her, but for me, a feeling that something is being torn irrevocably between us. But I must go. And, I don't know, I have a sense again that I find it hard to know, to see clearly, how many children. My sense is that maybe there are two, and that the boy will come with me, and (Pause) yes, there's a girl also, a little girl, who is the joy of my life, the kernel of that which has survived, and I feel I must leave her. Mmmm.... (Long pause) And it feels like she's there like this doll

holding on to me,

The black and white Spirit Doll which Richard brought with him as a key

begging me not to go, not understanding, feeling inconsolable and frightened and like her whole world is being torn apart, and it *is*.

Yvonne: I invoke forgiveness.

Heather: We have got confused energy here haven't we? Can you accept the forgiveness? Only part way I think.

Richard: I feel like I don't know where the forgiveness is coming from and, (Really struggling) I don't know, I don't know how to be with this. It's, it's....

Heather: It seems to me that the forgiveness would come from the self, in other words, can you forgive yourself?

Richard: (Long pause, obviously struggling.)

Heather: There's information that's coming through here, that's sort of being sent back again. It's like the ball over the net, in tennis. It comes over the net to you and you lob it back again. It comes over the net *again*, and you lob it back *again!*

Yvonne: I'm going to invoke Mother Meera now.

Mother Meera is the Indian Avatar, believed by some to be an incarnation of the Divine Energy, whom Richard has visited and received Darshan from on a couple of occasions. Darshan is given in silence and is the bestowal of love light and grace.

Heather: Can you take it a bit further Yvonne? The energy is not *quite* up to the angle of Healing on the pendulum. Can you invoke Mother Meera and *something else?*

Yvonne: Unconditional Love.

Heather to Richard: So can you accept forgiveness which comes from Unconditional Love? Of the One for Another?

Richard: It feels like I *can*, but then something is still holding on, resisting, kind of it's ..

Yvonne: I invoke the candle quartz at this moment in time.

The word "Candle" is used to convey the image of the dribbling wax after a candle has burned sufficiently to cause the same effect. Candle Quartz is a very tranquillising stone which can be used to dissipate the tedious and oppressive from ones character or environment. The presence of the stone in an environment acts as a clarifying agent 'to dispel the shadowy' and to acclaim the interior illumination.

Heather: Well that's holding the energy on the Healing Line now. The ball has stopped going over the net. It's actually on the right line now. You are held in time and space, and we are waiting for you to be able to accept forgiveness, to which we will be your witnesses.

Richard: It feels like there's, a , I don't know, there's a sense of, in my memory a sullying of something that, at the time, was of purer intent and intention, so it's like that sexual act, that love making, now has become distorted into a kind of shadowy lecherous memory, and so it's almost like, the need is to return to the source, the need is to return to that act, which was loving and joyful and not dark and deceitful.

Yvonne: I invoke the flame, in the Temple of Love.

Richard: And I'm still with the thought, the idea of forgiveness. Can that permeate through, can I be permeable to receive it? What's stopping me still? (Getting a bit annoyed with himself) It's almost like there's an arrogance of self righteousness, of some purity and perfection, some expectation of myself as superhuman, and is it possible for myself to allow myself just to be human, just to be me, that "warts and all" struggling being who makes mistakes and falls down .. rather than keep demanding, tightening, forcing myself into this *form, in which I don't belong*, which is that perfect, that perfect being that doesn't need to be forgiven, because it never gets it wrong! Like it feels, it feels hard to voice the words for myself, "Forgive me." They feel so unfamiliar, like they don't fit. "Forgive me." "Forgive me." It feels like I'm down on my knees. It felt like I was imagining Archangel Michael being there .... "Forgive me." I feel like I don't know how to be in my body. My shoulders, my chest, it feels like I've been carrying this weight like the cross piece of a crucifix, and my body has grown to that shape, to accommodate that. (long pause) I'm there on my knees in the dust, and the woman's there and the children are there looking at me, (SOBBING)

Heather: (Softly) You're doing well.

Richard: And I ... (sobbing as though his heart were breaking)

Heather: (As he calms down) Just say it.

Richard: And I feel so *ashamed*.

Heather: Well done.

Richard (Whispers) I feel so ashamed. I feel ... ashamed for my persecuting them with my high ideals, and I see them and I see the woman there in her softness and beauty. I see that she *has* suffered her own punishment through enduring *me*. (Deep breath in and breath out) And it feels like I want to shout out!

Heather: Go on! Go for it!

Richard: (Laughs) Almost it's jubilant. (Laughs)

Heather: Go on! Let's hear it!

Richard: It was going to be, "Forgive me" but it feels like that's not quite right. It's " I AM FORGIVEN! I AM FORGIVEN! I AM FORGIVEN!"

Heather: Amen.

Richard: And I feel now the possibility of joy and fun and lightness. Of just wanting to play and skip and dance and there's the four of us there, just dancing around in a circle, .. a sense of some natural balance, of equanimity and harmony being restored.

Richard's comments

Reading through the transcript of this regression two years on, it still has the power to move me and remind me of the stubbornness and rigidity of ideals and expectations that I can sometimes get caught up in. That habit of bearing the cross, of needing to be perfect, is softening gradually, with an increasing capacity for compassion.

The theme of forgiveness has permeated through all the regressions thus far with

Heather, and has been a central theme in my spiritual and emotional life. A definition of forgiveness, offered by Mark Bryan in his book, "The Prodigal Father," and which I recently read, had a profound impact on me. It stated simply that forgiveness meant, "letting go of the need for a different or better past." This regression feels like another piece of the jigsaw.

In the end, if we look widely and deeply and softly enough, even forgiveness becomes redundant as we recognise the place of Oneness and Unity, of the reconciliation of what, at an ego level feels irreconcilable. It felt that, for a time, both during and after the regression, this was a place I touched.

Chapter Six

Barbara's Story

The question:
I'd like to know why I feel fear in extremes of speed, enclosure or heights.

Heather: We are here this afternoon to help Barbara find her way forward in life and to have an answer to the question that she has formulated. Barbara, I have checked that your chakras are in balance, and your spirit is resting in a bubble of consciousness at the top of your head. I'm just about to get a signal for departure from the pendulum now, so it's a question of the ambient energies settling down ... and off we go. First of all we're going to go higher and higher, and the reason we go higher is to put you in touch with your guardian angel or angels or guides. There may well be more than one waiting for you. They are those special Beings who are there for you, not just for this afternoon, but always, right through your earthly life. I'm just getting a feeling of them gathering now, waiting to come fully in. .. I feel that that has now in fact happened, but you may or may not be conscious of it at this early stage. Do you feel different in any way?

Barbara: Mm, don't think so.

Heather: Sometimes the guides are male, sometimes female, sometimes androgynous, that is to say a mixture of both.

Barbara: (Amused) I feel someone's got hold of my foot!

Heather: I think that's just one way of saying,"Hey, I *am* here!" (Chuckles)

Barbara: They're touching the ball of my foot!

Heather: Mm, it feels to me like an androgynous energy, which would be very appropriate for an Angelic Being. So they've let you know that they are there, and now we're going to go to a sacred place. This may be a sacred place of your own choosing, or it may be more that some image will come into your mind, will choose you. It could be out in the countryside. It could be a special place in a church, or a library .....

Barbara: I keep thinking of my granny's back garden. She had two big wooden doors that opened up into what I remember as something like a blackberry bush. Tomatoes plants sometimes remind me of it. It was really overgrown.

Heather: And the doors are facing you?

Barbara: To the side. I *loved* those doors.

Heather: Can you open them and go through?

Barbara: Yes.

Heather: And having gone through, can you see anything?

Barbara: I can see my pinafore. I'm wearing a white pinafore.

Heather: Can you go *down*, from the hem of the pinafore, towards your feet, for a moment?

Barbara: I look like someone from "The little house on the prairie!" (Amused)

Heather: Can you describe how you are dressed?

Barbara: I've got boots on. I don't think they *are* shiny, but they're *meant* to be, ... some wooly socks, and then some sort of flowery dress, with a pinafore over the top, a white pinafore.

Heather: Have you any idea how old you are?

Barbara: Young, ten.

Heather: Is there anybody with you?

Barbara: No.

Heather: How you are feeling?

Barbara: I feel happy and .. just like a little girl! (Starts to giggle, as a ten year old might)

Heather: What sort of place are you in? Can you see any of your surroundings? Can you describe anything of your surroundings for me?

Barbara: No, I can't really see anything.

Yvonne: I'm going to bring in the Mother-of-Pearl energy.

This carries the loving energy of the universal Mother.

Heather: Now, that's actually brought things on line, (Truth/Healing Line on pendulum,) so can you see anything around you now?

Barbara: It's just dark. I want to go back out into the garden. The door is ajar. It was open when I came in and then it closed. Now it's really dark and cold. I want to go back out because it's sunny out there.

Heather: Fine, do that then.

Barbara: Mm, it's lovely. It's really warm and fresh. The sky is blue and the grass is long.

Heather: Wonderful. And now we're going to move, backwards in time, one year back in time, so the scene will change.

Yvonne: I've got some animal keys stepping forward. I've got the seagull, the horse, and the cat.

Seagull supports the emotional side of our nature and a carefree attitude.

Horse supports friendship, freedom and power.

Cat supports agility and clear perceptions, strength and fearlessness.

Heather: Now we've got a working energy, which suggests to me that some work is being done to your psyche Barbara. .. Now, what's happening now?

Barbara: I'm in a tunnel! Or it could be a forest. I'm not really sure. It looks really *dark*.

Heather: What about moving forward in the tunnel? Could you do that?

Jill: OK

Yvonne: I'm going to invoke the snowflake obsidian at this point as well.

Snowflake obsidian assists one in actualising the serenity of the isolated state.

Heather: The tunnel is often a connection to another level of awareness.

Barbara: Can I run in it?

Heather: Yes, that's fine.

Barbara: Mm, it *is* a forest. It's really overgrown and there's nettles and everything everywhere, bracken, and brambles.

Heather: There's more information trying to get through .. now. What's happening?

Barbara: I've stopped running and I'm in a meadow. Ohh! My leg hurts. I think I might have done something to my leg.

Heather: More information coming,

Barbara: It feels as if the leg, and I'm not sure which one it is, isn't *real*, .. that it's wood or something!

Heather: More information coming.

Barbara: Ohh! I don't even know if my leg is there! Am I a different person now?

Heather: Well, I get "No," to that. I don't *think* so.

This is later seen as a transition stage between one person and the next with the tunnel acting as the bridge between – same soul, different bodies.

There's more information trying to get through.

Barbara: I feel there's a soldier there. I feel like *I'm* the soldier, even though I haven't got a leg! That's how I feel. And I'm terrified. I've got battle dress on, and I'm in a meadow, but it's not nice. It's not a nice meadow. And I think my leg's been blown off. It's just the weight, it just feels dead from the hip down.

Heather: And now it feels to me as if we can move to another time/space.

Yvonne: Yes. I have to invoke the Madagascan sapphires at this point, both of them. *These are superior sapphire crystals and exhibit additional properties which include an approach of ease to the metaphysical realms. With the sapphire crystal, one may assess ancient scripts covering the esoteric principles of physical movements in the universal realm and during the life of our civilisation upon this earth. Two crystals were invoked because both Yvonne and I had placed our personal crystals on the table as keys.*

Heather: Right, so we're going to move, forward in time, to next day.

Barbara: I'm lying there in the meadow, still lying there where I was.

Heather: More information coming.

Barbara: I can't see anyone. I don't know if the grass is longer or if I just don't want to look, but my leg's *really* heavy.

Yvonne: I'm going to invoke the dolphin and the whale energy at this point.

Whale energy asks us to go deep within our past and listen to its stories so that we can creatively heal old wounds.

Dolphin energy allows us to enter the waters of life and call forth the wisdom that we need.

Barbara: And I don't know if I should have my kit, not my clothes, but stuff that I should have as a soldier. I feel desperate, and no-one knows I'm here. They've all gone, and my kit's gone too!

Heather: More information trying to get through.

Yvonne: Clear quartz is being invoked.

Heather: Now!

Barbara: It's going really dark.

Heather: Now we can move, forward, one hour forward.

Barbara: Everything is really dark. I don't really know where I am. I feel like I'm in Scotland.

Heather: I could move you, but I'm told to wait. I don't want to move you until we've finished with the information available at this location.

Barbara: I'm on Culloden Battle field. (16th April 1746) It's near Inverness. We went there in the summer ... I'm *lying* there. The grass is soft and long and and it's really comfortable.

Heather: This is to do with Cordor Castle isn't it?

Barbara: Yes.

Heather: Ohh! ... Oh my goodness, ... I felt that *energy!!* (Heather had an experience a few years ago when visiting Cordor Castle, of becoming very aware of the spirit of Lady Cordor, who sat looking out through a window on a high landing, facing toward the Battlefield of Culloden, awaiting the return of her dead husband. She had been waiting a long time in this world's terms. As she realised help was at hand, and wished to go forward, she made her presence known to Heather and some release work was undertaken, at a distance, through the following night, to that end. Therefore the spirit of Lady Cordor made itself felt at this point in the regression, prompted by the reference to her castle home and the battlefield, thus demonstrating the awareness of which those on the next level are capable. Even as I'm writing she's making it known by huge swings of the pendulum on the Truth Line, that she wishes this to be spoken about.

Barbara: The grass is hiding me but I can see rocks and it's not comfortable, but it is comfortable in another sort of way.

Heather: And now we can move, forward. It's just like the next minute really.

Barbara: I think it might be night time, and that's why it's so dark. My back hurts though, and I think I'm really *hurt*. I'm not in *pain*. My leg's dead and my back's dead.

(Very deep breath in and out.)

Heather: There's more information trying to get through.

Barbara: I'm covered in blood. My uniform is really tatty.

Yvonne: Pegasus is stepping forward.

Pegasus is come in preparation, as the 'take away figure' for Barbara's impending death, of which we, at that time knew nothing. He is the flying horse – the thundering horse of Jove or Jupiter, who carried lightning bolts for Zeus, supreme ruler of Mount Olympus and the pantheon of gods who resided there.

Barbara: Ohh, I've got a pain in my head. OOOhh I've got a pain in my head. I think something is in my head, or my head's on something which hurts it maybe. I can't move.

Heather: And now we're going to move in time, forward, forty-five minutes forward.

Barbara: All the pain's gone. ... Everything I felt .. is gone! And lying here, I feel as light as a feather.

Heather: Do you think it possible that you might have died?

Barbara: Yes, I think I have. I think I've died.

Yvonne: I invoke the ruby.

The ruby encourages one to follow bliss. It is said that ruby will light the darkness of one's life, giving birth to a spark of light which progresses throughout the body and spirit, conquering darkness on all levels.

Barbara: That's really weird. (referring to her death as the soldier)

Heather: I think we are to stay in this space between lives for a moment.

Yvonne: That feels right.

Barbara: I feel I'm floating on clouds.

Yvonne: I invoke the two crosses at this point as well.

The twin crosses, one of which Heather bought as a souvenir from the Holy Island of Iona, and the other, which Yvonne's daughter bought locally in a "Collectables" shop in Cornwall, have a unique quality, in that they are identical in every aspect and appear to be made by the same hand! They represent the twin energies of Love and Knowledge, gained through willing sacrifice of the Self.

Heather: I've got an energy coming in now, which looks, from the shape the pendulum is giving me, like an angelic energy, so an angelic presence is with you.

Barbara: (Deep breath in and out) I just feel as if I'm floating.

Heather: That angelic energy pattern is opening out now, so that certain work can be done (on the client.) There's a working pattern going on at the moment, and that means to me that work is being done on your spirit. .... Now I have to pull out some negativity. The pendulum has gone on to the Healing Line. .... And we've got the angelic presence back again. ... Now the energy's gone forward, but I still need to pull out a little bit, and it's gone on to the Healing Line again. To let you know what is going on, this is a mending process. This is a form of what's known as psychic surgery, and there's a mending process going on, on your spirit. It is the angel who is using this space/time opportunity for the mending to take place.

Barbara: Ahh. (A little sigh is heard.)

Heather: That seems to come to an end and I'm just waiting to pick up the story. ... Now, can you tell me anything, that you *feel*, or *see?*

Barbara: I feel really calm and quiet and relaxed. I can't really see anything though. It's all really dark.

Heather: Information trying to get through.

Yvonne: Can you invoke Apollo at this stage?

Apollo: Greek God of the Sun, son of Zeus. One of Apollo's famous children is Asklepios, God of Healing.

Heather: Yes, Now.

Barbara: ... I can see something really big, and white. It's kind of like the white cliffs of Dover.

Heather: More information coming.

Yvonne: I invoke the smoky quartz.

Quartz is said to bring the energy of the stars into the soul. Traditionally, the natural quartz crystal was said to both harmonise and align human energies - thoughts, consciousness, emotions - with the energies of the universe and make these greater energies available to humanity. Smokey quartz however does not astound one with its speed; it is prolonged, yet intense and gentle in its action.

Barbara: It's like desert, desert rock, that's what it is. And it's cold, I'm cold.

Heather: More information coming,

Barbara: And there's nothing around me.

Yvonne: The Icelandic quartz record keeper crystal energy is stepping forward.

A record keeper crystal is a crystal within which wisdom is stored. It is recognised by a raised, {or several raised} perfect equilateral triangles located on one or more of its faces. Record keepers exist only in ruby or quartz crystals. The "three" of the triangle(s) located upon the face(s) of the crystal represents perfect balance achieved when the physical, mental and emotional aspects of one's being is aligned with love and purity of the highest spirituality. The triangular shape of the "doors" which lead to the records also symbolises the third eye, the creation and preservation of the state of perfection which serves as a pathway toward the enlightened state.

Barbara: I think I've got a, whew, an Araby thing on,

Heather: Just look down at your feet a minute. Can you see your feet.

Barbara: Bare! They're just .. a mess! They look all rough .. all rough. They just look like the feet of someone who doesn't wear shoes, and they're huge from that. I've got long hair. I don't know if it *is* long hair, or if it's a beard! I've got on a white head cloth, with a knitted band around the top.

Yvonne: The two bears are stepping forward.

The two bears represent the twin energies linked to Gemini, of love and wisdom.

61

The difference between knowledge and wisdom is that knowledge is researched and wisdom is intuited.

Barbara: I think it's a beard. Ugh, I think I'm really mean! I think I'm a mean man. (Sighs)

Heather: I *think,* we can move! (Chuckles, and everybody joins in, which breaks the tension in the room.) I think we can move forward, one year forward.

Yvonne: I invoke the rose quartz wand.

Rose quartz can be used for the spiritual attunement to the energy of Love, Truth, Gift, Healing. The wand itself provides for the directional focus required to provide the maximum penetration of the energy.

Barbara: Ohh, I can *feel* something .. a pain, like a wound! I think I'm quite old, for the times I think I'm old, or weather-beaten. It might be weather-beaten.

Heather: Right. More information coming.

Barbara: I can see the desert, and whatever you call a small expanse of water, or that sort of thing in a desert.

Heather: An oasis.

Barbara: And there's all sorts of people sat there. And I've got stuff to sort out. I don't know what it is I've got to sort out.

Heather: Are they not pleased with you?

Barbara: No, it's not *that.* There's not many of them, eight maybe, and they're all sat down. I can see water canisters and .. I've got to look after them. That's what I've go to do! I just keep seeing my face. I've got teeth missing. There's a tooth there, (points to her mouth) and the rest are all rotten. Mm, brown, dark brown eyes. Hot sun, *so hot!!*. But we've got lots of clothes on, lots of desert kind of clothes. It's hot for us, but we're used to it. Abdel, that's who I am.

Heather: Bit more.

Barbara: I'm a leader. There are more people there behind. Oh, there's lots of them! I can see the big, not pavilion, but like a tea tent! Ha! And behind that there's *loads of people, loads of them.* It's not a city, but it's where we all live. I don't know why we're all sat around here. It might be all my family, where we sit to eat. There's lots of noise and bells and clanking of tins and animals. Ahmed, .. ohh! I don't know who *that* is. I don't know who *he* is, *that* name.

Heather: There's more information coming.

Barbara: I think I'm the leader of all these people, I *think* they *chose me.* I'm not a *prince or anything.* (Whispers, referring to the pain from the wound) That pain's gone. I think they *chose* me as their leader, and I think they're *happy* with me. I don't think I am *really* mean, I think I'm just mean at war. (Sighs) There's children, but I don't know if any of them are mine. A pretty girl keeps coming into my mind, but I don't know if she's mine. Mm, I think I've got to run. *Everyone's* running. There's chaos, but I don't really know what's happening. Maybe more confusion than chaos. I don't think there's any trouble. I think it's just something going on. I don't feel that everyone's got to run away and hide, or there's trouble brewing. It's just something that's happening that I can't work out. I think I'm going to go into the .. it's like a bazaar. Ohh, there's some cold water in a big metal cup, and ugh, I thought it was going to be cold and it's not, ugh *horrible*, ugh, (spits it out.) It stinks, stinks of urine! Ugh, I'm getting out of here.

Heather: Do you feel ready to move?

Barbara: (Lazily) Yeh...

Heather: OK, so we'll move. We'll move forward again, about three and a half days, forward.

Barbara: I'm in a room where I've been living. It's just a cave really. I'm doing a deal. I don't know what the deal's for, but I'm doing a deal. And I've been successful! Hm! I got the better deal! And I think this other person's an idiot. I *don't really* think he's an idiot, I just think that he didn't know how to work out a cunning plan. (chuckles craftily)

There are men all around the place. I don't know where the women are. Mm, the deal's done and I'm going. Ha, ha!

Heather: So, now we can move?

Barbara: Yes.

Heather: Ok, so we go forward again, about eight years forward.

Barbara: I can't see anything.

Yvonne: I'm going to invoke the amethyst.

It assists in the assimilation of new ideas. By carrying, wearing or using amethyst, one can remember and apply the myriad ways which can be used to overcome any crystallised or stationary areas within one's physical form, intellectual activities, emotional attitudes, and states of consciousness.

Barbara: I don't think I'm still there, I just don't see anything.

Heather: The information is a bit far out yet. I may not have got the time quite right. Try eight years, three months. (Long pause.)

Barbara: I'm in a bed. I'm in a hospital bed.

Heather: Right, more information is coming,

Barbara: It's my arm.

Yvonne: I'm going to invoke the Buddha quartz.

It has been used to contact and promote the transfer of information from the elders of the ancient civilisations of India, Tibet and China. It is a stone of Shangri-La, and is said to have been used to bring the harmony and accord of this civilisation to those who share the energy.

Barbara: I'm in a hospital bed, but nobody is really looking after me. I don't think they think I'm going to, you know, die immediately .. but there's nothing they can do for me and I'm lying there in the bed. I know they think that, but it's OK. I'm still in the body of the Arab.

Yvonne: I'm going to invoke the Three in One.

Barbara: ... I want to say "little old arab" now, but... I'm just lying there still, and I don't think I can even see properly. It's a building, not a cave like we were in before. The beds are made of iron, and the sheets, .. I think there's just a blanket thing and then a piece of material over me.

Heather: We don't move. We stay with it at the moment, because there's more information coming in.

Barbara: (Sighs) I can't really see anything, and when I can, things are blurred. Oh, someone's coming over to me. They've got a cross. They're holding a cross up to me. I don't think it's a vicar. Someone's holding a cross to me, but it's not my religion, and I want to laugh at them. I'm kind of thinking, "Silly fool," but I know they mean well, and I don't care.

Yvonne: I'm going to invoke the energy from the little goddess figure.

Heather: Now, what now?

Yvonne: I'm going to invoke the Sami shamanic piece,

Sami piece: A shamanic reindeer-tracking bone that came from way inside the arctic circle at North Cape, Norway.

And the butterfly.

The butterfly stands for transformation and release of the spirit.

Heather: It sounds as if the spirit is waiting to release.

Barbara: I think I'm waiting to die. I think I'm just dying of old age.

Yvonne: I'm going to invoke the praying hands.

The painting by Albrecht Durer, the study of praying hands

Barbara: It's busy, but it's not busy for me. The nurses have got those tall hats on, like nuns. .... I've just seen the numbers 1811. Oh, there's a clock and a calendar, September, 1811! Let's see if I can tell what the time is. Five to eleven I think! (chuckles)

Heather: Now I'm getting a working pattern from the pendulum, which suggests that some work is being done on you again.

Barbara: The 3rd of September, 1811.

Heather: Just pulling out some negativity. Now this is work being done on a fairly subtle level of your psyche. The pendulum is showing me a very small circle. Pulling out again. On the Healing line. (Stays on this line for about 30/40 seconds.) (Jill sighs deeply.) Do you feel at ease?

Barbara: Yes.

Heather: Do you think you might have slipped quietly away?

Barbara: I think I *have*. My body's still there though. I can see me lying in the bed. No-one's noticed, but they're busy. (Pause) But I *am* dead. Mmm ....

Heather: The energy is starting to go forward again now, quite strongly, as if there's more information coming. You may find you're in another life, or you may find you're in the space between lives.

Barbara: .. I can't see anything.

Heather: There's information trying to get through.

64

Yvonne: I'm going to invoke azurite at this point.

In the Native American Indian history, azurite has been used as a sacred stone. The nodule and crystal forms have been used to facilitate contact with ones spiritual Indian guide, to allow one to both feel the presence and to understand the message.

Barbara: I feel cold, I don't know *why.*

Heather: More information coming.

Yvonne: I'm going to invoke black velvet.

Velvet Black stands for a State of Grace.

Barbara: I can see a big black shiny horse, like Black Beauty.

Heather: More information coming.

Barbara: I think I'm that little girl in the pinafore again. And there's this big black horse. *It's beautiful, and* it's galloping in a meadow full of flowers. It's really *lovely.*

Heather: More information coming.

Barbara: (Starts to breath noisily.) I think the horse has just kicked me. I think it's trodden me. Yes! (experiences difficulty with breathing)

Heather: And now?

Barbara: (Talking with difficulty) I don't know if I'm the little girl, or if I've seen this happen, but the hoof's here. (Points to a place on her body.)

Yvonne: I am going to invoke the ruby. (In ancient cultures it was used in the practice of "casting lots", to assist in the determination of resolutions and decisions.)

Barbara: (Experiencing continuing difficulty with breathing,) There are trees and the wind's blowing and it's a meadow, but I can't see any buildings, and the horse has put the hoof down on the little girl. Whew! I don't know what to do. I don't know who I am.

Heather: There is more information that wants to come in, otherwise I would move you, but there's more information trying to get through here.

Barbara: I don't know what I am - if I've watched this happen, if I'm the little girl, or if I'm the black horse! My head is pounding with the fear of what's happened.

Yvonne: I'm going to invoke the energy of the rose quartz wand.

The rose quartz wand is to focus and bring about the power of Healing.

Heather: So you obviously feel involved in *some* way.

Barbara: Yes. I feel as if I'm looking at a clip of film over and over again, and nothing, nothing's happening. ... *I can't move.* **I can't move.** Can I be in a wheelchair? (Sounds really panicky) I can't move from where I am! Like physically *move!*

Heather: I'm going to move you forward in time again, to the next day.

Barbara: Everyone's crying.

Heather: Information trying to get through.

Barbara: There's a big room, with a big fireplace and it's cold in there, except near the fire, and there's lots of people who've got shawls on. Everyone's sad, but I'm not sure *why* they're sad.

Heather: Do you not feel part of it?

Barbara: It's to do with yesterday. Ohh, .. I've got a bad pain in my leg. I think I really *am* in a wheelchair. It's a really old type of chair, a wooden chair! I think I've broken my leg. There's certainly something wrong with it. I don't know! I've got a couple of images in my head. One is of an old woman with grey and white hair, wearing glasses, with shawls and in a wheelchair, and the other is of a leg supported out on a wooden chair with wheels on it, as if the leg is broken.

Heather: It feels to me as if those two images are connected somehow, as if they both belong to the same person.

Barbara: There is the old woman, the little girl, and the broken leg, and I don't know which is which. It's all muddled, as if there are three existences and they're all one, all at the same time, but the black horse isn't around.

Heather: Could you possibly be clicking into different levels of awareness? If we imagine time to be as a tower, could it be that you are clicking into different "floor levels" in a tower of memory?

Barbara: What, like it's the same person? Well yes, that's the only image I can see. That's the only way I can *see* it.

Heather: Right, so we need to be able to find a way forward here. I think the best thing to do would be to move you. ... I'm going to move you *back*. Perhaps we've got to rerun something here, so we're going backwards in time, decades, one, so ten years back.

Barbara: I'm the little girl trodden by the horse. That's me, ten years before. I don't know whether I'm five or ten, but I'm *little*, and I've been trodden on by a horse and I think I've **really** been hurt!

Heather: Any more information?

Barbara: No, but it's quite clear. I'm in the field. I've been trodden on and no-one knew I was out there.

Heather: So obviously the accident was even worse than it might have been.

Barbara: Yes!

Heather: Right. So now we go forward again.

Barbara: Yes, I'm ..

Heather: Do you want to say anything else?

Barbara: I'm in a wheelchair now.

Heather: Right, so obviously you've gone forward.

Barbara: Time's past and I'm older. I'm still a young girl in a wheelchair though and everyone feels sorry for me but ... you see no one knew I was out in the field.

Heather: Now we can move again, (Deep sigh from Barbara,) forward, oh my goodness! It looks like eight decades forward, so either you're a very, very old woman or....

Barbara: I am. I *am*. I'm a very old lady, and I can see now that that is me, with the shawl and the glasses, and even though I've spent all my life in a wheelchair, I outlived everyone.

Heather: Can you give me a bit more information?

Barbara: We're in the same *house, that same house with the fire.* Everyone's sad again. I don't know why they're sad. It's not about me, because I'm sat in the kitchen. I'm sat in the kitchen, and everybody's kind of doing their thing. *Someone's* died, but, I don't think it's *very* sad .., it's not a tragedy! I think maybe it's a man.

Heather: More information coming.

Yvonne: I'm going to invoke the clear quartz at this time.

The clear quartz crystal can be used to facilitate both speaking with, and receiving information from, the spiritual and otherworldly masters, teachers and healers.

Barbara: It's my son that's died but he was quite old as well. I think I might be ninety three!

Heather: I would say you would be in your nineties.

Barbara: Yes I think I'm ninety three, and I think my son was seventy.

Heather: A bit more information trying to get through.

Yvonne: I'm going to invoke Apollo.

Apollo is invoked for his ability as Sun God to throw light and clarity on the situation.

Barbara: It's not my son. (whispers) It's my daughter's husband, Wilfred, Wilfred Williams. That's who it is, definitely, and he's seventy something, I think he's seventy eight. Yes, he's seventy eight, that's why I didn't think he was my son, because I thought I might be too young. It's my daughter's husband, and, like I said, I'm outliving everybody ... and grandchildren, there's just like *generations galore!* I don't know how I had children, when I spent my life in a wheelchair.

Heather: Through great determination I expect! Information coming.

Barbara: I've got three daughters.

Heather: And now I think we can move.

Barbara: Mmm, I can smell baking bread.

Heather: Does that mean you want to go into the kitchen.

Barbara: (assuming I would know) I'm in it!

Heather: Oh! Right! So we move, and we move forward, six days forward, or thereabouts, just under a week.

Barbara: Ah, what can I see? I just see the kitchen and the coldness of the granite and the fire roaring and .. I think there's a broth on. Ugh! There's a dead goose or a duck or something hanging up. That's disgusting! .. I think my daughter's skinning a rabbit. But she's old. We really live off the land and I'm sat at the table chopping vegetables, that's what I'm doing. It's a real working kitchen. We're farmers.

Heather: Now we can move again, forward, next day.

Barbara: I think I'm fine, but I'm sat in bed in the morning. Maybe I don't get up in the morning, but there's nothing wrong with me, well, apart from being ninety odd, but I'm well and happy. Do you know, I think it might be my birthday, and that's why I'm in bed. Everybody said stay in bed, but I don't want to, I want to get up. Yes, it is, it's my birthday!

Heather: And now we can move, forward, about twenty hours, just under the full day, twenty to twenty one hours forward.

Barbara: (Wearily) I think I'm going back to bed. Is this the night I die?

Heather: More information coming.

Barbara: I hope not, 'cos I'm happy. I *like* this life! Now they've got a fire lit in the room, and it's just low, and crackling away. The room's quite cold, but, it's not Winter, it's just cold stone houses, and I'm going off to sleep. I've got my shawl around me. I always have that. Everyone calls it Granny's shawl. (Whisper's) I'm going to sleep. ..... I'm sleeping in bed. It doesn't look very comfortable, the bed. I think we might have *made* the bed ourselves.

Heather: More information.

Barbara: I think, I'm not sure about this but, I think it's a feather bed. I hate feather beds. I've never heard of a feather farm, but I think it might be a feather farm. There's something going on about animals being plucked and feathers being used *somewhere*. (Long pause) It's nearly morning I think.

Heather: More information.

Barbara: I'm lying in bed. I can see the sun rising. I like getting up early. It's a *beautiful* morning.

Heather: Keep telling me about it.

Barbara: The sky looks orange. The window has got no curtains, and I'm not sure that it has glass in it, but there might be shutters on the *outside. The window is really deep.* Someone's lit the fire for me! Oh, they got up so *early,* just to do the fire for Granny. It's crackling. Oh I can really smell it! (Sniffs the air.) It's lovely! ...

Heather: More information coming.

Barbara: I can't see anything through the bedroom window from the bed. Oh! Where my chair's gone!

Heather: And now we can move, forward, minutes, five or six minutes.

Barbara: I think I've just got in my chair, because I'm exhausted!

Heather: More information coming.

Barbara: I'm so old that I can't really do anything, but my head isn't. My head's fine! My head's switched on and it's just my body can't *do* it. I've got a book I'm reading. I'll have a look at the cover and just see what it says. It's got a red cover. It's an old book, and it's tatty. The pages are like parchment. Oh, let's see what it says. There's a picture on the cover. Oh it's the Bible! I think it's some kind of local bible, I'm not really sure, but I love this book. The picture seems to be of a yew tree, with two little deer underneath, like Bambi. It's only a little picture. One deer is standing up and one is lying down. Ahh, (Chuckles) yes, that's what it is. The pages have got gold edging on them. Oh gosh, can I read something in it? Oh, I want to try and do that! I really want to open it at a page and see a page number. It's a psalm. Now I don't know anything about psalms, I don't even know what a psalm is,

A psalm is a devotional song or hymn in a Bible.

but that's what it is and I know what the page number is, but I can't read any of it, because my eyesight's gone. 102, 122, 1022, that's what it is, page 1022. It's beautiful. The pages are like parchment.

Heather: There may be a way that we can actually get the psalm for you. Would you like me to try?

Barbara: Yes, yes I would.

Heather: Well, is it in the first 10, second 10, third 10, fourth 10, fifth 10, sixth 10, seventh 10, so, 70,1,2,3,4,5, .. 75.

Barbara: Do you know I think it's just happened! I think I've just passed away! With this book on my lap!

Heather: Well, I'll finish the number because I think it's alright to do that, but I think it was Psalm 75. It might be worth looking later to see what's in psalm 75.

The pendulum later picked out verse 9 from the King James Version:

But I will declare for ever; I will sing praises to the God of Jacob.

Barbara: Do you know, I don't know if I *have died*, or if I'm asleep. I keep thinking that people are downstairs, but I don't think there is an upstairs .. I'm not in my own room. I've got a corner of the living room. They don't know that I've, that I'm asleep in the chair. .. I want to say the name Carol, but it's not Carol. Oh, I can't think who it is! I can see her. She's got her hair tied in a bun. She's about 50 odd and she's got *really grey hair!* She's the one who's doing all the cooking. She's my granddaughter. I feel that fashions should have changed, and yet they haven't. We're all wearing prairie clothes. The name is not Carol. It's a name that Carol would have been derived from. Maybe I don't know her name because I'm so *old*. I can see my hands, all wrinkly. Coral! That's what it is! It was a name we liked. We all thought it was a lovely name, and I've never been able to *say* it. Huh! That's a typical granny! There's a church nearby. I can't see it and it's only small. It's our church though. It's got a bell outside that rings in a little steeple .. Saint Stephens.

Heather: There's a bit more information coming.

Barbara: When I was talking about Coral, she had a newspaper in her hand. She finished the cooking and sat down to read the paper. It's an old style newspaper, like when they came out first, and I'm sitting watching all this, from where I am, whatever's happened to me. I can see the church and I think I'm going to be buried at the church. I can see a road name, but there aren't any roads. The road might be St Stephens, St Stephen's Road.

Heather: (Having tested against the pendulum,) I think you are right.

We're going to move one last time, probably, forward in time, nearly four weeks.

Barbara: I have this really clear picture of two images. One is, I'm in a grave under a Yew tree, and the other is, I'm still in the house. They're the same, there's nothing *different* about them. It's the same time!

Heather: Well, maybe you were so fond of that house that you ..

Barbara: I'm still in it!

Heather: Yes. Your spirit, in a sense, stayed in it.

Barbara: I can see a big black shining gravestone, and yet it's like a hundred year old piece of granite slab.

Heather: So it's very worn is it?

Barbara: It's both new and old. Let's see if I can see what's on it. Let's look at the shiny one. I think they called me Ma. I can see 'Beloved,' and those typical words, and then it's got Ma.

Heather: *I* think they called you Ma as well!

Barbara: I want to see my name.

Heather: Maybe they didn't call you by another name. Maybe they felt that was who you truly were, that Ma was sufficient.

Barbara: Maybe my name was Williams, but all I can see is Will. I think I was over a hundred. I'm still sat in the chair *anyway,* so I don't care about the writing on the gravestone *or* how old I was! (Laughs contentedly)

Heather: Now we're going to thank the guides and helpers very much for this afternoon. I'm sure there's been a lot of ground covered and a lot of difficult areas which we have gone into and come out of again, with great adeptness and safety, and I personally thank my guides and yours for their wonderful help. I'm sure Yvonne also wishes to thank her own guides for their kind assistance this afternoon.

Yvonne: Many thanks to all our guides and helpers. Thank you.

AFTERWARDS

Heather: You moved forward in time in each of those three lifetimes didn't you? You started with the soldier who died at the battle of Culloden in 1746 and then moved to the life as an Arab male. In that life you saw 1811 on the calendar when you were admitted to hospital remember, and then lastly you moved to the life as the little girl living on the American Prairies, who was badly crushed by a horse, but who then went on to become Matriarch of a large family. We don't know much about the soldier, except that he was mortally wounded in the leg.

Barbara: I think he was just a young boy when he died.

Heather: Yes. We don't know much about his character, but there was quite a contrast in character between the Arab, Abdel, and the lady in her wheelchair. Shrewd, obviously a shrewd personality, in both the Arabic life and the life of the old lady, and indeed this life I think! And quite a lot of .. I want to say "wisdom," but I'm not sure that that's quite the right word. Experience, I suppose, may be a better word.

Barbara: That's the old lady?

Heather: Yes, but the Arab as well. He had a canniness and experience of life about him. He also showed strong qualities of leadership.

Barbara: Yes, the thing that struck me most about him was that he had been chosen as a leader by the people. He wasn't born into it, but had been elected to it.

Heather: And so Ma was a leader in her own way wasn't she? What about the original question, "I'd like to know why I feel fear in extremes of speed, enclosure or heights." Do you feel that it was answered?

Barbara: I don't know. (This conversation took place immediately after the regression, which is good, because everything is fresh in the mind at that stage, but also not so good, because the client can be quite 'spaced out' still.)

Heather: You were in quite a few positions where you couldn't move weren't you?

Barbara: Yes, trapped.

Yvonne: And then again in that last life with granny in the wheelchair.

Barbara: Ohh, that's scary!

Heather: The injured soldier couldn't move on the battle field either, and obviously took many hours to die alone. However his experience of that was not nearly as anguished as we, as onlookers, might imagine.

Barbara: And then I had that pain when I was the Arab .. but that went. I think I'd been injured in some way, but I'd recovered.

Heather: Also, the story of the old lady doesn't make the situation clear, but I wonder if you were not in fact riding the huge black horse, or at least trying to. Just maybe, you were somehow on his back and he sprang into a gallop. If that was what happened, that would explain the fear of speed, and height. Also being trampled and very badly injured would be yet another reason to fear tight spaces. Of course all this takes time to absorb and to integrate. This is the advantage of the tape because you can go over it and you can see what actually went on. This is why I'm so keen on getting a tape, if I possibly can. It's not always helpful to play it again, but in the majority of cases it is.

There were those three lives going on and there was also, actually, at least two sessions of psychic surgery that were going on as well, the purpose of which is to clear away negativity from your psyche. That is never planned by me, although sometimes I'm told to expect it. The guide introduces it when the time is right, and I'm shown, by means of the pendulum, that we are going into it.

Barbara: Yes. ...

I feel that the old lady was very wise, but she was more than that.

Heather: She was very experienced wasn't she?

Barbara: Mm, .. for someone who had been in a wheelchair, since being a little girl. I think perhaps that gave her the opportunity to watch and read, and analyse her thoughts ..

Heather: Well she was very very interested, in life, right up to the very end. She was very inquisitive. Do you recognise any of your own characteristics today in those people?

Barbara: I think I do, but I don't know if I can think of that just yet.

Heather: No. I understand and respect that. It's too early for that question because your persona is still too much with those other personalities, for you to be able to stand back and look objectively at Barbara Those events you have just re-experienced, which are now in your consciousness, will become integrated over the next few days and weeks.

Barbara: Yes, I don't know where they came from. I mean I was aware of what I was saying and if I started to add my own thought to it, then I knew, very clearly that that was not what I should be doing, nor what I was actually seeing. But sometimes, like with the old lady at the end, it isn't always easy to know what reality you are in. Was I in the grave or was I in the chair, and did I, in a sense, have a choice?

Chapter Seven

Clare's Story

Opening questions: What do I need to be shown to help me integrate the feminine more fully within my psyche and continue to fulfil my life purpose? Sometimes my right foot feels as if it simply isn't there. What happened to it and can I have it back?

Heather: Clare, I'm just waiting for the energy of the pendulum to go around to the Truth Line showing me that the Akashic Record energy is available, so I know I can begin. .. That looks fine now. Your energy is resting in a bubble or consciousness at the top of your head at the moment, and we're getting ready to start the journey. The questions you have posed will direct the guides to find you some answers in terms of life experiences and so we're ready to go. First of all we go higher, and higher, to a place where you will be put in touch with your guardian angel or angels, guides, or power animals; some higher energy form which emanates as a Being. They are there to accompany you, not just through this afternoon, but through your lifetime. I'm getting a sense of a presence coming in now, making their way, and I have indication that there is at least one Being with you at the moment. Do you have any sense of that for yourself?

Clare: I have a sense of some kind of male presence. It's Native American, that's the feel.

Heather: There's something else coming in as well. It could well be another Being. Now, what now? (Feeling some other presence definitely there.)

Clare: Well, maybe something a bit softer. Is it Anandamaya Ma?

Anandamaya Ma is the Joy-Permeated Mother, who did a great deal of counselling and teaching during her lifetime, when people in need asked questions. The clarity of her understanding was remarkable. She is an acknowledged ascended master. Clare brought a photograph of her along as one of the keys.

Heather: I'm getting the Truth Line, so you are right about that. I think those are the Spiritual Beings who are accompanying you this afternoon. The next thing we do is to move to a sacred place, which will appear to you. It may be somewhere you already know, or it may be somewhere with which you are not familiar. Again the journeying is happening, and I would say, from what I am being shown, that you are almost there now, so do you get a sense ...

Clare: I get a sense of the Sancreed Holy Well.

Heather: Yes I think that's correct. (Information confirmed through the swing of the pendulum.) Now, from that place there has to be some sort of portal or doorway, through into another dimension.

Clare: I think it's down the well. Yes!

Heather: Are you happy to make that journey now?

Clare: Yes.

Hannah: (Hannah is my assistant today. Her responsibility is Holder of the Sacred Space and Keeper of the Keys.) I feel the dolphin energy wants to come in here.

Recent studies are confirming what indigenous peoples have known for centuries, that Dolphins possess an innate healing ability. The dolphin totem will swim alongside one who has the soul of a healer and Clare is herself a healer and a trained Regression Therapist, which is interesting.

Heather: Thank you. Now, what can you see ? Is anything appearing to you?

Clare: Well, it's a bit strange, but I'm in my home at Sancreed, and there's a whole lot of water coming in the door, like a river almost. I'm swimming in a great torrent of water. I'm floating in a river and there's just all this junk around. There's old bits of houses and *all* sorts there.

Heather: Have you any sense of who you are?

Clare: It feels as if it's China/Japan area, and as if I'm a woman. Oh goodness! I'm going down a waterfall now! Ugh!

Heather: There's more information coming in.

Clare: There's a ladder there, and I'm trying to reach it to hang on to.

Heather: More information coming, but I think we need a key in order to receive it.

Clare: I'm feeling that my house has gone. There's been some kind of flood or earthquake.

Heather: More information trying to get through.

Clare: It feels like Vietnam.

Heather: I'm getting the Preselli Blue Stone as a key. If we invoke the Precelli Blue Stone, does that make anything clearer for you?

5000 years ago these stones were considered to have such unique properties that a group of Neolithic people are claimed to have manhandled a hundred or more, each weighing three to four tonnes, and moved them two hundred miles from their source in the Precelli Hills in Wales, to Salisbury Plain in Wiltshire. There they were dressed, polished and erected, as part of the monument known as Stonehenge. They form the inner circle there. In ancient times stones were generally considered to be holy and magical objects, homes of spirits and gods.

Clare: There's a change of consciousness somehow.

Heather: Yes, there is.

Clare: I'm in a jungle now. (Long pause,) lost.

Heather: We need the old key.

This is an ancient iron door key, beautifully crafted and about 14 centimetres long. It came from a special little shop on St Mary's Island which lies about 28 miles off the coast of Cornwall. In this little shop, from time to time, Heather has found objects possessing surprising esoteric qualities.

Hannah: Yes.

Heather: We invoke the old key. If we put the Precelli blue stone on top of the old key ... now what do you have?

Clare: Well, I'm getting an owl in a tree, and the owl feels important, but I'm not sure why ... and a door.

Heather: The owl feels like a symbol for wisdom to me. He could very well be the keeper of the door. "I am !" he's just told me emphatically.

Clare: Mmm. Yes.

Heather: Do you think you are supposed to go through this door?

Clare: I think so, yes.

Heather: I think the key is to unlock the door.

Clare: Yes. There is a lot of light coming from behind the door. .. There's a whole new place to live, almost. This woman has lost her house. I've gone through the door and it's very light.

Heather: It feels that you've, "Gone into the light," doesn't it? I would imagine that is just about all you can see at the moment? It seems like the release of the spirit of the woman from that life, where she experienced the onslaught of chaos. Does that feel right?

Clare: Yes, it felt like the woman got lost in the jungle. I'm not sure what happened to her. It felt that she didn't have a place to live. She was looking for something, but I don't know whether she found it.

Heather: Yes. The guides are giving me the same signal that they gave me before, when we put the Preselli stone with the key. It was to take things forward. I think she was trying to find a way forward, and possibly going to the Light was the best way forward for her to make a fresh start?

Clare: It feels like she didn't find any help, particularly, when she moved into the jungle. That would tie up with a lot of what I tended to do in past lives, which was not to find it easy to find anywhere to live or to make connections.

Heather: So you've experienced this before then?

Clare: That kind of theme, yes.

Heather: So, starting with the light, I think we are to go forward, minutes, hours, days, weeks, months, years .. It looks like one year forward.

Clare: (Pauses, then speaks gently) I'm in the Spirit World and I'm talking to the spirit of my mother in this current lifetime.

Heather: Do you want to tell us …

Clare: (Hurriedly cutting across, not wanting to be interrupted) There's something very sad going on. (Sighs deeply) I have a feeling that we're discussing the life that she and I are going into next, and that .. Oh! She's trying to tell me that it's really *necessary,* that she's going to suffer and that she's going to help me to understand .. Oh God, what is it that ..? This is really *intense.* (Another deep sigh)

Heather: I think we bring in the energy of Anandamaya Ma to be with you.

Clare: So she's going to help me.

Heather: She's going to help you, "process" the information.

Clare: Process? Right. What I'm *getting* is some kind of psychic retrieval process, but there's more *to it* than that.

Heather: Yes, but that's good for a start. I get the feeling we can move. Forward, minutes, hours. I think it's one hour forward.

Clare: She's going to be born, and I'm saying, "Good-bye," to her. It's kind of upsetting, because I don't want her to suffer as much as I know she's going to, and there's not much I can do about that. And I kind of know it's her choice. Oh, it's interesting *stuff*, Gosh! Ohh!

Heather: There's more information coming.

Clare: That she's *choosing* to do it, and it will take her to a higher place! It won't take her to a higher place immediately, but she's *also* to be working on the Mysteries of the Feminine, on a very difficult journey. She's wiser than I *think*. *Yes*, she's wiser than I perhaps *know*, and she, .. she *is teaching me in some way*.

Heather: (Feeling an exceptionally strong spiritual energy flowing through her body) This is *very powerful stuff. This is* **very powerful stuff.** (Deep sigh from Clare)

Hannah: I've moved the laser crystal, but only slightly. It's slightly *off* the table, at the moment. (Another deep sigh and shudder from Clare)

Heather: The pendulum is going on the Truth Line like crazy, and I felt, all through that, a very strong presence of your Mother.

Clare: Well, it's clear that she knows what she's doing, and it looks like she's *unsupported* at the moment too. I am able to *know* that she's *not*. It's good to see her in that light, because she looks stronger than I knew her on the earth.

Heather: Yes. The energy's settled down now too. And now I think we can move, forward, minutes, hours, days. This time it's one day forward.

Clare: (Speaking quickly) she's gone, and I'm actually concerned for her. I don't like what she's gone into.

Heather: More information coming.

Clare: Ohh! Something horrible!

Heather: I think we need another key.

Hannah: My hand has gone towards the indigo.

Indigo is the colour associated with the third eye, the eye of the seer. In the ancient Maya civilisation indigo was the one colour that was recognised for its soothing effect on pregnant women and their unborn children. Pregnant women often wore this colour in order to protect themselves and their child from danger and to ensure a safe and successful delivery.

Clare: Well, it's my Grandmother. Ohh, it's very strange because I had some information from her recently. There was a message which came via a friend of mine, about her wanting to apologise for the way she was .. and she wasn't evil, it was just that she gave my mother a hard time. And it really *upset*. It seemed to be upsetting for everyone. What my mother has gone into is the psychic stuff around my grandmother. It actually feels very claustrophobic. I know there were six miscarriages before my mum was born, but there's more than that. My Grandmother was brought up in the Raj in India, and was very stuffy, ... stuffy, stuffy. Like .. cobwebs, ... It's horrible when I look at it from the Spirit World, ... It's kind of 'sticky,' and I wish I could clear it away. It makes me feel a bit .. disgusted, I suppose. Ugh!

Heather: Still more information coming.

Clare: I can see my grandfather. Gosh, I wouldn't have thought I would have got this involved. It's incredible isn't it? I can see my grandfather and how 'plodding' he is. I have a lot of warmth towards him. He's very naive in a funny kind of way. I can see that he cares a lot about my mother, and he *will* do.

Heather: That's a very important point.

Clare: True. I see him as warmer than I experienced. He was so incredibly intelligent that it was hard to get to see beyond that.

Heather: And now I think we can move, .. forward again, a very short space of time. It's barely a minute. But there's a change. There's a *shift*. I've got a very strong energy again. I don't know whether that's linked to your mother. The pendulum is really *whipping* through the air again.

Clare: I've gone to a place that I sometimes go to, and it's hard to describe. It's outside my grandparents' place. It's quite a lot further forward in linear time actually, when I was four or five years old and I went to stay with my grandmother. In my mind I go often to the house that my grandparents lived in, because it was such an extraordinary house, and garden. It no longer exists, but it's an incredible place, and, because I found my grandparents awkward to get on with at times, I used to wander around the house and garden a lot. And now I'm outside the house, a little bit down the road. I never know whether I actually went there, but, in my mind I'm often there, just watching my grandparents, thinking about them. They were such peculiar people. They had such strong characters. I'm watching my grandmother at the moment and just seeing what a fascinating woman she was, this very tall, dark eyed woman, who was very psychic and very .. *naughty*, a real *storyteller - a naughty and wild energy*, who gave my mother such a hard time. She was a real force to be reckoned with!

Heather: There's more information that wants to come through, but I think we may need a key to get it.

Hannah: There's a rabbit. I invoke the rabbit energy.

Rabbit teaches us that we create our world through our thoughts and feelings. For us humans this is an important lesson. The idea behind repeating affirmations, focusing on positive images, and programming one's crystals to help realise dreams is that thoughts have energy, and that focused attention on a thought creates a vibration which will help that thought to become reality. This is just as true when you think about what you don't want to happen. Rabbit also has the ability to be alert and aware of its surroundings at all times.

Clare: (Sighing) I'm feeling that I'm wanting to stand up to my grandmother. I feel like I'm floating around the house, but, when I really clue into it, I feel quite angry with her.

Heather: It seems to me that you're showing her some of your power now.

Clare: Yes, *yes!*

Heather: More information coming.

Clare: (Pause) Well I feel now that I could sit in those chairs and be who I am. At the time, I was only four or five, and it was too difficult. But I feel now that I've surrounded that house with so many stories, that I have all sorts of characters of my own in that house, from Cullis Castaneda to Mrs Tweedie to ..

Cullis Castaneda wrote several books about shamanism, including shamanistic methods taught him by the Mexican shaman Don Juan.

Mrs Tweedie is a highly respected Sufi teacher, who lived in North London.

All these people, I have them all lined up, and even, (laughs,) even the plays of T.S. Elliot, I have staged in that house, but they're all there for me now. She's shrinking now, down to size a bit more I feel, and she told me through my friend's channelling the other day, that she apologised for the way things had been. .. I think she wants to tell me that the life in India was quite scary for a little girl, and, there were lots of creepy crawlies. I'm getting lots of strange animals, scorpions even, and, .. well I knew her father used to go on tiger hunts, but, .. there's something about scorpions ...

The Scorpion is a very interesting and solitary creature. They are fierce and lethal and have been known to live for as long as twenty-five years. They are nocturnal and do not hunt their prey, but rather wait until a suitable prospect crosses their path. They will then ambush their victim by giving them a lethal injection of poison which either kills or adequately stuns the unsuspecting creature. The Scorpion's stinger sits at the top of their many segmented tail. The Scorpion is able to control how much venom will be released from their stinger when attacking their prey. They will, if very threatened, sting their victim several times. There are fifteen-hundred species of Scorpion throughout the world, of those, only twenty-five are lethal. These creatures moult frequently in their lifetimes, sometimes as many as five or six times. Scorpions can survive a year without food or water, making them one of the most enduring creatures on the planet. For centuries shamans, priestesses, spiritualists and practitioners of the occult have used Scorpion pearls, found inside the creature, to transfer the powerful magical energy of the Scorpion to themselves and to others in need of this commanding magic.

Heather: A bit more information is still wanting to come, though it's slightly resistant in coming through.

Clare: I'm suddenly seeing elephants. Maybe it's the energy of her father, my great grandfather, who made trips into Tibet on elephants, and treated the natives not very kindly. I know that because I've got his diaries. And his wife, .. he was very down on his wife. .. Now I'm getting pictures of the elephants going into Tibet.

Hannah: I have moved Ganesha.

Ganesh/Ganesha, the Indian Elephant God, sees no obstacles. God and love always prevail.

Clare: And the majesty of it all actually, and I realise what a different time period that was. My grandmother was brought up in a time period when the English really thought they were kind of gods, in a way. When they were going into Tibet they felt that they *owned the place* almost, that they really held a presence of some kind. It feels very *real*, him being there on that Elephant Trip. I suppose being on an elephant can make you feel really *important*, yet there's a certain *wonder* of being on this elephant as well.

Heather: There's still more information.

Clare: There's something more about Tibet coming in now.

Heather: I get drawn to Lao Tzu, the author of, " The Tao Te Ching," as the next key.

Joshua David Stone, in his marvellously helpful book, "The Ascended Masters Light the Way," says:

Everything has a Tao. When you are dating, for example, there is a certain Tao of Divine Timing for moving the relationship along. There is a Tao of working, and even a Tao of sleeping for a given day. There are infinite polarities and and balances, all of which have a Tao. That does not mean you have to think about them necessarily, it is just a matter of staying in harmony with them. To my way of thinking, if you always listen to your higher self, soul, or God, rather than your negative ego and lower self, then you stay in the Tao.

Clare: I can see a lot of the prayer flags and the Golden Emblems of Tibet. And the people walking on these journeys into Tibet.

Hannah: I've moved the picture of Tibet that Clare brought with her this afternoon. It has moved down the table, so to speak, into view.

Clare: Ohh! I'm suddenly on one of these journeys in Tibet myself, and it's very cold, and there's the sense of the yak skins that they wear .. and stopping in a tent, and the fire and the tea, the yak butter tea.

Heather: A little bit more information.

Clare: There are some monks. There's a monk kneeling down. It feels like some kind of ceremony.

Heather: Before you spoke then, I could feel the presence of one monk in particular.

Clare: Yes!

Heather: Has he got a message for you I wonder.?

Clare: Well, it feels like some sort of initiation. They're kissing a ring, or something like that, but it doesn't feel like it's me being initiated. I'm watching it going on. But it does feel like a message and I'm not quite getting it!

Heather: Are you the centre of attention there?

Clare: I'm not sure that I'm a monk, but it feels that I'm part of the scene.

Heather: Are you possibly a Lama?

Truth Line on the pendulum.

Clare: I'm not sure.

Heather: There's more information coming. I get drawn to gold.

Clare: Yes, there's a lot of gold around, .

Heather: It's the gold energy.

Gold has been said to attract honours, wealth and happiness, to provide composure, to stabilise the emotional system, to alleviate tension and stress, and to amplify positive feelings. It also assists one in attuning to nature and its healing forces.

Clare: It's as if I know this Tibetan life *so well,* because they love to *laugh.* Sometimes I want that scenery around me *so much* that I get almost hysterical, laughing! .. I'm in a monastery now. It feels like I am part of a monastic life there somehow. (Pauses) There's something about the Tibetan understanding. There's a lot of whispering going on, and there's an understanding that the Tibetans are going to find it really hard in the future. OOOhh!!

A rush of confirmational energy goes through Clare's body.

The Tibetan understanding has got to be taken on *secretly.* OOOhh! PHEW!

Heather: Are you alright?

Clare: So much electricity around, through my back! I don't know whether I'm a Lama. If I'm not, I'm a wise monk there. I know it very well, it's very close to my heart, the understanding of it.

Heather: And now I think we can move. Forward again, minutes, hours, days, months, years, decades, one, so it's ten years forward.

Clare: (Pause) Ohh! Well, gosh, I feel like I *am a Lama of some kind* .. and there's another lama beside me, and I'm feeling very sad. I don't know why I'm getting this as, when I think about the Chinese invasion of Tibet and my birth date in this lifetime, I don't think .. the dates would tally.

Heather: Just speak your truth. Whatever you get, just speak it. Don't try to analyse and censure at this stage.

Clare: *Right.*

In fact when we looked up the Chinese invasion of Tibet, we found that it took place from 1949 to 1951, in which case it is possible that this could have been a a former life of Clare's.

Clare: It feels like there are prayers being said, for the future of Tibet, and it's quite tense. There aren't Chinese around, but there's the fear of the end of the Tibetan Culture. There's something really difficult, and there's a lot of prayers being said, and they're kind of being said in a slightly secret way. Again a lot of gold, and it feels like there are grave discussions going on.

Hannah: I'm just going to move the star amethyst beside the gold.

Star amethyst stands for the energy of ultra violet star. The ultra violet star is one of a class of invisible stars giving out intense ultraviolet radiation. I associate this with a very high energy vibration which is only just slightly less than angelic.

Gold provides energy of a Divine nature.

Clare: (Pause.) Ugh! Actually it's taken me to a really weird place in this lifetime, when I was a child, and I was sometimes a bit haunted by going to the toilet, because people would climb over the toilet, when I was about eight actually, strangely enough.

Clare had previously been asked by Hannah to bring a photograph of herself at the age of eight to the regression.

A boy would often climb up over the toilet wall, and I used to get a bit freaked out by it. And then one day he put a worm down my back .. But at the moment I've brought all those monks into the Gym at junior school! (Laughs heartily) As a way of lightening that experience, I think.

Hannah: Mm.

Heather: Do you want to say anything at that point Hannah?

Hannah: Well, that's absolutely correct. And the feeling I've got is that with the understanding, there will be the forgiveness of that act, and the taking away of fear.

Clare: Right. Well, thank you for that. It feels that some release has gone up the back of my neck actually, because I was quite frightened by that boy climbing up over the top of the wall. At the time he was a bit of a bully. But I can let go of him now.

Heather: Then I think we move, forward again, minutes, ten, twenty, thirty minutes, forward. Half an hour forward or possibly a little bit more.

Clare: I'm standing alone in the school playground in my mind. When my mother was very ill I was very shaky at school, and when that boy put that worm down my back it really shook me, and I went out in the school playground on my own. I'm just *there* at the moment, and feeling very alone. I can't really ... I don't *feel* I can tell anyone that sort of thing, because my mother wouldn't hear, is not available, for that sort of thing to be told to. My father's not interested, so .. it's, I suppose it's where I make a decision that I'm quite alone in life. Ugh! (Shivers)

Heather: More information trying to get through. Possibly another shift Hannah, or another key.

Hannah: Yes. The sodalite crystal needs to be moved.

Sodalite facilitates the manifestation of the qualities of companionship, and mutual dependence, encouraging self esteem, self trust and trust in others.

Heather: Yes. I think also the chrysocolla, so it's Third Eye and Goddess energy now.

Chrysocolla purifies the home and the environment, and can work to eliminate negativity from within a person. It imparts an energy conducive to stabilising the home and rebuilding relationships.

Clare: I'm suddenly feeling very frightened and a lot of, well, tears I suppose, and upset, that I wasn't really in touch with at the time, because at that time I felt *frozen*. Oohhh!

Heather: There's something about an explanation, to the little girl.

Clare: (Slight pause,) I'm suddenly seeing a lot of pink energy come in. Yes, I'm kind of floating above her at the moment, and ..

Pink energy is representative of Love at a very high level.

Heather: (Gently) What's the message?

Clare: Well, I'm feeling that the Tibetan monks are really there for her actually. I've kind of brought them along. And they don't seem like an *obvious* help, but I think they *could* be. She's not really aware of them at the moment. And they seem a bit, um, *formal*, I suppose, to contact her, but I think there could be a go-between.

Heather: And who might the go-between be?

Clare: I feel that there is a monk, in amongst them, who is very .. gentle, who could go out and talk to her.

Heather: Is this connected to Anandamaya Ma? It feels like the energy of her again.

Clare: That could *well* be, yes.

Heather: Is the monk the masculine energy and Anandamaya Ma the feminine energy of that?

Hannah: Mmm. That's correct.

Clare: I think, yes.

Heather: So is this, in a sense, now being established as an Energy that you could call on?

That is to say Anandamaya Ma and the Tibetan monk, because, in some way, they are one and the same?

Clare: It's quite possible. It's interesting. I always seem to .. pull in a masculine energy, if I'm given the chance, because my mind seems to work in that way, in this lifetime anyway, (chuckles.) I can't see how Anandamaya Ma would be very close the the earth at this point, but, I think, through the monk, she could be. My feeling is, anyway, that somebody is reaching, or is trying to reach, this girl.

Heather: Yes. And now we are going to move, backwards this time, minutes, hours, days, weeks, months. Now, this time the pendulum has gone around the anticlockwise way to reach the Truth Line, which is the guides' way of warning us that something a little bit difficult might be coming up. We're on months, one, two, three, four, five, five months back.

Clare: Well, what I'm getting is so unlikely, but, I'm seeing a crocodile come along.

Heather: Remember, the five months doesn't necessarily relate to this lifetime. 'In the past,' and 'five months,' are co-ordinates, and they are bringing us to a particular location on the Akashic Field.

Clare: OK. I'm just watching this crocodile come along a trench, and it feels a bit menacing.

Heather: More information coming ... or *trying* to come. I feel that we need to invoke the old key again, to unlock the door, and also to bring in Owl, the doorkeeper. (Pause) Now, what can you experience now?

Clare: I feel that I'm an Indian, and I'm trying to fend off a crocodile. I'm waving something at it, flapping something, like a coat or something, trying to make it go away. And then I'm getting out, running away .. I'm a man with quite thin legs, and I'm just wondering how fast I can run ...

Heather: More information coming.

Clare: Now I'm running, and this crocodile is walking after me. I'm running through swamps, and lily pads, and water.

Heather: And now we can move, forward, one minute.

Clare: I can just see this *beautiful* water, and these leaves in the water. And I don't know whether that's the last thing I see before I die, or whether I'm hiding in the water.

Heather: There's more information trying to get through. (Sensing a crisis,) Pegasus!

Pegasus, the mystical, magical flying horse is invoked. Pegasus was a winged horse of mythology. He is invoked here for his enormous capacity for power, his ability to fly fast and come to the rescue.

Heather: And?

Clare: I feel like I'm in the water. And, there's this struggle going on at the moment as to whether I am going *into* the water or whether I am being lifted out of the water. The water's really *beautiful*, and ..

Heather: I get the Archangel Gabriel.

Clare: Yes. something very light. I feel like I'm being lifted up by a dragon fly!

Dragonfly embodies a stripping away of all the beliefs that say we cannot do this or that, It is to remind us that anything is possible when we really get the understanding that we are part of Spirit and, as such, have the power to manifest anything that we desire. Dragonfly is the keeper of dreams, the knower within, that sees all of our true potential and ability. Its energy is the essence of the winds of change. Dragonflies are very ancient, with estimates of having been around for 180 million years. They have a beautiful, jewel-like colouring. The colours take time to develop, reflecting the idea that, with maturity, our own true colours come forth.

Heather: More information coming ... but *not* getting through. I think it's St Francis that we need. St Francis' energy.

St Francis is the patron saint of animals

Clare: (Long pause) I don't know whether the crocodile caught me, but ... I think St Francis is saying that .. I didn't have to be running from that crocodile, that I could have stood, stood my ground. If you have so much fear of an animal, then you create *more* fear.

Heather: There's also a sense of compassion for the crocodile, isn't there?

Clare: Yes.

Heather: Now, we appear to have a pattern of Working /Thinking energy around the Spiritual, or Balance Line.

Clare: Because in that lifetime there was a lot of running around and not really respecting animals as well as I *could* do, it's as if there's an opportunity here to turn that around. There's something karmic, about turning it around and working with animals in a more enlightened way. It seems *that* is the teaching here for this Indian man.

Heather: I'm watching the energy of the pendulum swing out now, into a full Working/Thinking pattern, swinging full circle, taking in the Material World Line of earthly manifestation as well as the more narrow, elliptical pattern of spiritual idealism. In other words putting the thought into action.

Hannah: My feeling is also, that the Indian had a gift which he was very reluctant to use, in connection with the animals.

Clare: He looks a bit *ashamed*, after his life, that he didn't do what he could have *done*. That's *strange*. He looks as though he has gone into *fear* too much.

Heather: And now I think we can move, forward, a *very* short space of time. It's certainly not more than a minute.

Clare: (Long pause) Well, first of all I get a dragonfly, and then I'm standing at the front of the school, the same school that I was at before. It's the perennial thing of waiting for my mother to turn up, to come and pick me up after school. There was always that feeling about, would she be there or not. She usually was, but then, there was just the odd occasion when she overslept or something.

Heather: The dragonfly, does that stand for transformation?

Hannah: Yes.

Heather: So would that be linked with the transformative power of the experience with the crocodile? In a sense, I'm making the link between the ancient form of the crocodile, which could be seen as a dragon, and then the dragon-*fly*, ... the fact that you see the dragonfly symbol, in this particular place.

Clare: It's as if the Indian died in that beautiful water, with the waterlillies, just watching all that.

Heather: But then the transformational quality of that highly significant incident has stayed with him, with his energy, do you think?

Clare: There's something about .. maybe the Indians are quite meditative, they're into being rather than *doing*. That water was very clear and bright, and the dragonfly symbolised something *of* that. And waiting for my mother was a little bit meditative as well, in a funny kind of way. Rather than *worrying*, One can just be, yes? It's just to *wait* and *see* if she comes. But the Indians, when they're not running around being afraid, there's quite a peaceful quality. That's what that man was sometimes *missing* in his life, that sense of beingness, that he could hold that space of beingness, which the Indians can do so well, rather than having to *do* all the time. In which case, waiting for my mother to come was not really an *issue*. *She was bound to come at some point.* Maybe *that's* it. Yes.

Heather: And now we can move, forward again. Again it's a very short space of time, like another minute.

Clare: There's Mum arriving. I've just seen her a couple of times in the car, and us all wearing our boater hats, and I'm watching where she's at. You could slightly see she's on drugs, by just that look in her eye, .. but she's OK.

Heather: And now we're going to move, forward again, another minute. It's very slow, frame by frame.

Clare: And now we're in the car, and she's chatting about the cakes that she's bought for tea.

(Chuckles,) a wild journey this!

Heather: More information trying to get through. We might need a key.

Hannah: Well, I've got the Moldavite out.

Heather: Yes, that's right. We invoke the moldavite. So, one minute forward from the cakes.

The presence of moldavite can indicate a sudden and unexpected turn of events that can be the beginning of a great opportunity, if change is allowed to happen. It can be the wakener and accelerator of spiritual evolution.

Clare: There's something concerning her, and, um, I'm suddenly in a slightly different dimension.

Heather: Yes, I think so. That's right.

Clare: I can tell she's not quite right. Ohh, she's going to take us somewhere. Shopping or something. But what's *really* going on is .. I'm watching this energy that's up in the air somewhere. It's like a caterpillar.

The caterpillar's DNA is totally different from the butterfly's. Thus, it is the symbol of total transformation. Butterfly represents a need for change and greater freedom, and at the same time it represents courage: one requires courage to carry out the changes necessary in the process of growth.

It feels like she's going to go off to Mental Hospital quite soon.

Heather: Is the caterpillar to do with a metamorphosis again? Is it to do with transformation, I wonder.

Clare: It's like I want to talk to her, and I don't know what to say. It's as though I know, because we talked about it before I was born ..

Heather: Mmm. I could feel the energy of this coming in.

Clare: And she's told me, before I was born, that this was going to happen, and she was going to be OK, and I couldn't quite remember it at that time, but I'm remembering it now.

Heather: Somehow Paramansa Yogananda is connected with this. I don't quite know in what way, but that's the energy I'm drawn to at the moment.

Paramansa Yogananda revered Sri Anandamaya Ma, and spoke of her in his famous book

Clare: Ah, that was his story line wasn't it, that he had this shock.

Paramahansa Yogananda, who wrote the book, "The autobiography of a Yogi," which really brought yoga to the West, had a very severe brush with death, and miraculously survived. It was his wake-up call! The suggestion is that the electric shock treatment that Clare's mother received in mental hospital, was in some way a , "Wake up call" for her soul's spiritual development. Likewise the shock of the crocodile's attack on Clare, in her life as an Indian. This is somehow mixed in with the psychic scorpion-like energy around the grandmother which, seemed at the time to be bad for Clare's mother, but never-the-less brought her to the place of Metanoia, or change of direction, the shock of a 'wake up' call. Happenings are neither good nor bad they simply are. It is the Tao – The Way.

Heather: So it was a wake-up call, was it?

Clare: Yes. It feels like my mother went to Mental Hospital several times in her life, and this was going to be one of them. She's driving her grey Morris car and that always feels a bit of a dowdy car. She drives it as if she knew exactly who she was and where she's going, but, quite often I wonder. I feel like, when I get in the car with her, she could take us *anywhere*, but this time I think she's taking us shopping, and it's all very kind of OK on some level, but, (sighs) there's always that unknowing, somehow.

Hannah: What I understand is that she was trying to tell you something. She was trying to get the information *to* you, but found it ..

Clare: Difficult?

Hannah: Yes. There was no language, really, to explain ..

Clare: To explain what was happening, to us children, or at least to me?

Hannah: Yes.

Clare: Well I can accept that now.

Clare is the eldest of four daughters.

Heather: It seems to me that the communication was between Clare's mother and *Clare*, though. That was where the dialogue was attempting to happen wasn't it?

Hannah and Clare together: Yes.

Heather: There's a bit more information coming. We can cut through with the laser crystal I think.

Clare: (With a stifled cry) It feels like she's frightened. .. but at the same time, I'm getting the lily pond from the Indian life. I can understand that she's frightened, and I can, on some level, be the lily pond. I can be calm for her. I think that's it. And

I'm going to try and just ask her how she is, and see what's going on for her, if I can, .. which is kind of what I used to try and do. At times she's inaccessible. She's like .. gone off somewhere, and there's times when there's, "no one at home," at the moment, and other times when I know she's, "travelling," somewhere. It's like she's fast forwarded.

Heather: She's gone to a place where you can't quite reach her.

Clare: Yes, and I'm trying to catch up.

Heather: I get the feeling that that's because she's actually quite an *advanced* soul.

Clare: Really?

Heather: Yes.

Clare: Good heavens! Oh.

Heather: Do you agree with that Hannah?

Hannah: Yes.

Clare: Really? Well! Bless! I always used to treat her like a child, poor thing. (Laughs at the irony of the situation) Oh Bless. She'll probably come and pat me on the head one day, and say, "There, there, you did quite well!"

Heather: There's a bit more trying to come.

Clare: Well there's Dad come into the picture. We must be at home. He's always kind and reassuring. He's not really where it's *at*, but I can tell he's worried about Mum. I get the feeling that I *am* trying to reach her, and, on some level, she *knows* I'm trying to reach her .. (deep sigh.)

Heather: Is there any kind of link between your mother and you and the old North American Indian with the eagle? There does *seem* to be a parallel there.

This is a beautiful picture Clare brought with her to the regression.

Clare: Yes. If we're out of context, it's easier. It's more difficult as a mother and daughter.

Heather: If you take on those different ..

Clare: Yes, different roles. Somehow, we know each other *better* like that than we do at the moment. Being mother and daughter, we don't know each other so well, but, I can't quite see whether she's my teacher, or whether, .. I get that feeling, that on *some* level she's *teaching* me something, but I don't know .. I don't feel like she's a *high* teacher.

Heather: There seems to be an energy interchange. Possibly you're teaching *her* things and she's correspondingly teaching *you* things.

Hannah: I get the word, "insight," and I call in the energy of the Himalayan crystal. This crystal is like a herkimer diamond, but comes from the Himalayas, rather than the oil field of Herkimer, USA. Its message, in this context is attunement. It can be used to attune oneself with another person environment or activity.

Clare: It's as if she's holding a mirror up to me, and, on some level, we're both souls that can .. move around a lot, if you like. We can move in and out of dimensions a bit, which is why I can sometimes reach her, and she *knows* that.

Heather: Yes. I get, "rite of passage."

Clare: My rite of passage?

Heather: I think you've *both* got rites of passage.

Clare: OK. She knows I can reach her, and yet there are times when she doesn't want to be reached, and she's going to "shut the door." She doesn't want me always to interfere in her path, of what she's doing, and she did that before she died. She shut my sister and I out completely. She didn't want us psychologically moving her around, because she knew we could.

Heather: She's a very strong energy. Every time she's called into this regression I get a really strong swing with the pendulum.

Clare: Oh yes! That's what the Sufi Teacher who *met* her told me, .. that if she hadn't been so frightened, she could have moved mountains, but she *was* frightened at times, and a bit hysterical.

Heather: Yes. I've got the Angelic Energy again now. It's calming down.

Hannah: I see two hands linked, and the Angel Energy holding them, so that the passage of energy becomes lighter, not a heavy burden for either one of the humans.

Clare: Actually I can feel that going on in my Base Chakra, where I can sometimes get a lot of fear or panic, because I feel that's what I picked up from my mother. She wasn't really very much on the planet, sometimes. There's something else that I need to understand, and that's that .. there's some way in which we were matching each other, my mum and I, but .. there's some way in which I wasn't on the planet enough, and, by her being so much *off* the planet at times, she was kind of drawing attention to that, for me. (Long pause) but I can't see exactly what we were teaching each other. It's more difficult to get hold of that.

Heather: The pendulum has just come to a standstill, so I'm just wondering if we've actually finished, or if there's still more to do. I think we've finished, unless you feel there's more to come.

Clare: (Amused) I haven't a clue! It's not a journey that I expected at all, so it's really hard to say.

Heather: What do you think Hannah?

Hannah: I feel that there is possibly something that can be said. Whether this is the appropriate time or not, I don't know, but what my understanding is, .. that this is a balancing of energy fields. It's a whole family situation, and somehow these energies have been .. balanced, in some way. .. It's about Balance and it's about the balancing of the energy fields, of the different participants, and once they're in Balance, in union, the cycle can flow. Somehow the cycle was blocked, and I think there has been a freeing of the cycle of energy, so that the spiral of your soul can now move in conjunction with the whole family, rather than trying to spiral on it's own. It wasn't functioning very well. Now it can actually function. That is my understanding. That concerns your energy Clare, your mother's energy, even your father's energy, .. and your grandmother's energy. You have done some family work here, which has been crucial for your family, but equally for you of course, because we are the **one** *and* the **many** in our family. The spiral of your family can now fit in with more unison. It fits together better, with your clarity. It's slotted in.

Clare: Yes, I can hear what you're saying, because I blamed my grandmother and her father a lot, but I didn't see my own connection with India and Tibet clearly. And it was interesting that my grandmother told me endless stories about her childhood in India, but I didn't really think that my own karma with India was involved in all that. So it wasn't just *her* part of the family that was irritating us all. It was so interesting to see my *own* Indian lifetime. My grandmother used to tell us about her father going off shooting crocodiles, and there I was, being *eaten* by a crocodile! Weird.

Hannah: Well the crocodile energy is a very significant one. It's truly significant.

Heather: As a power animal?

Hannah: Yes. And it's one of the *oldest*. You look at a crocodile's skin! It's like an ancient minotaur or something, isn't it?

Crocodile energy: The Crocodile totem contains the unbridled creative forces of the world, the fury and ferocity of Primal Energies. It is the symbol of creation and destruction. The Crocodile is the keeper and protector of all knowledge. She is the primal mother in whom all knowledge rests and waits to be born. People with a Crocodile totem have the opportunity to develop new wisdom but they must be careful not to be consumed by this wisdom. Study each bit of knowledge carefully before going on to the next. When a Crocodile shows up look for an opportunity to touch very primal energies. There will be an opportunity for new knowledge and wisdom.

Heather: And so I think we can bring the regression to a close now. I'd like to thank all the guides, helpers and participants of this afternoon, and we speed them on their journey back from whence they came, to a place of peace and love.

Hannah: Blessed be.

Clare: Blessed be.

As soon as the tape was finished, Clare said, "The crocodile took my foot. Of course! The crocodile had my foot." Clare had been complaining, before the regression, of a long term problem with her foot and part of her original question was about what had happened to it.

Clare's afterthoughts

It was interesting to consider that the relationship I had with my mother had been pre planned to quite an intricate degree, even to ways of keeping in touch and keying in important events. When things looked very rocky, as in the situation when she was about to go into hospital, my precognition of this held and supported me, and enabled me to hold and support her also. Indeed the whole regression appeared more of a teaching experience than I had considered possible or at all likely.

I am not sure how my mother and I related in terms of being teachers for each other. It begs certain questions, such as why was she so childlike, humble, and lacking in self esteem at times? I still can't see her as being a very evolved or a high teacher, but we certainly taught each other some interesting things. She taught me to express myself freely, in terms of both feelings and creativity. One of the lessons I pull from this regression is the need in me to spend more time in being creative. She has influenced my life's work strongly, in that when I grew up I became interested in 'what heals' and she also influenced me, in various ways, not to take ordinary reality for granted.

I liked that Anandamaya Ma came in as a figure to transmute the lonely experience I had at primary school and brought in a Tibetan life as a memory to thread through the experience.

It was curious that the history of my grandmother, told in stories, triggered and wove around images of my own personal karmic history. The crocodile, which always loomed large in the stories she told to me as a child, appeared important both in terms of a totem animal and my having been eaten by one! The crocodile is the symbol of creation and destruction. It is the keeper and protector of all knowledge, the primal mother in whom all knowledge rests and waits to be born, When crocodile shows up there will be an opportunity for new knowledge and wisdom, but each bit must be studied carefully before going on to next.

Somehow the fluidity of the various levels of experience in this regression seem to help me go beyond the linear time frame of events and lives, and allow more of an overlay of experience.

Chapter Eight

Richard – A Second Story

The journey begins with three chimes struck on a small Tibetan bowl which has been cast, and has been embellished around the outside with the Eight Auspicious Symbols, the significant one of which, in this instance, is the Eight Spoked Golden Wheel. The three components of the wheel - hub, spokes and rim - symbolise the three aspects of the Buddhist teachings upon ethics, wisdom and concentration.

Heather: Your spirit is now resting in a bubble of consciousness at the top of your head Richard and I am just waiting for a signal from the pendulum to show us that all is ready for us to make a start on our journey. (Short pause) We have reached that point now, so first of all it's the usual descriptive imagery of rising up, of going higher and higher in order to be put in touch with your Guardian Angel or Angels or Guides. .. I'm told that there is at least one present with you at the moment, but there's more than one I think .. one, two, there appears to be three. Can you feel some presence with you?

Richard: I can't *feel* something, but what I got was an image of a picture which I have on the wall in the bathroom at home, which is of the Three Graces, or three angels, sitting at a table. And so when you said there were three, that was the image that came to my mind.

Heather: So now could you put your question to the three?

Richard: (Pause) It feels like the question is about, "What do I need to lay to rest? What do I need to leave behind in order to move on right now, in order to let go of what is holding me back in my life and my life work?

Heather: Thank you. Next you will be taken to a sacred space in which you can be put in touch with your Akashic Record, or Book of Life. I'm being told that the information is available. Is anything presenting itself to you?

Richard: What I got was the mouth to a cave, and somehow what came into my mind was it being Merlin's cave, which I've never been to, but I know is near to Saint Nectan's Glen, Tintagel, here in Cornwall, and it somehow feels that it connects with that.

Heather: That also connects with the Preseli Blue stone, which is one of the keys. There is a Merlin connection there. Do you feel disposed to go *into* the cave?

Heather: This is an important point to bear in mind, in relation to what happens later on in this journey. Neither of us knew at the time, but legend claims that Merlin used his magical powers to transfer the Preseli stones to Stonehenge before disappearing into one of them, taking with him the Thirteen Treasures of the Isles of Prydain, as Britain was known in ancient times.

Richard: I feel like it's very dark, but it also feels like something is drawing me to enter and find out more, to explore.

Heather: Yes, that *feels* right.

Richard: I *do* feel myself *entering* and moving away from the entrance and it feels like the darkness is *enveloping* me but, somehow it doesn't feel frightening. It feels like there is a way that I need to go forward into the darkness. I don't have a fear of banging *into* something. It feels like there's a big space. I suppose the other thought that I *have* is that I might walk off the edge of something, almost as if there's a cliff edge within the darkness.

Heather: Well I think I'm being given an indication to ask you to *move*, and I think at this point you've to move forward, minutes, days, weeks, months, years, ... *remember* this is *not* linear time; this is just a direction, but it's a year, one year forward, or thereabout.

Richard: (Pause) I feel like I'm waiting somewhere. It feels like I'm sat by a small fire. And I'm waiting. I'm not sure for whom or what I'm waiting, but there's a sense of preparing myself for a meeting.

Heather: There's energy that wants to get *through*. I think that maybe we need a key.

Hannah: I'm drawn to the small mouse, who is a guide. He will come, and if you can follow the path, which is certainly wide enough and broad enough for you to follow, he will guide you.

Richard: It feels like mouse is there and I've seen it and acknowledged it, and, although initially I thought I was waiting for something or someone *grander*, my impulse is to follow, and I'm starting off into some woods, and, .. It seems it's just his role to put me on the right track, and, having done so, then he scurries off into the undergrowth, and I am now carrying on walking. It doesn't feel like it's a dark wood. It's a wood with a lot of light shining through and a lot of green growth on the woodland floor. It feels a pleasing place to be, but again I have the sense that I don't know where the path is leading.

Heather: And now I think we can move. It's forward again, minutes, hours. It seems like one hour forward.

Richard: What I've done is walk out into a clearing, and the clearing is a place of meeting, a place of, ... maybe also a sacred place, ... and there's a big stone in the middle, obelisk-like. It has that *sense*. I'm not sure whether there are other people there. It's almost as if there were other paths that were like the spokes of a wheel, leading through the woods, leading to this point, and it's as if I've come out of one path and there are other people coming out of the woods into the clearing from other directions as well. I'm walking into the centre of the clearing, to where this big rounded stone is, and the other people are around the edge and forming a circle, and I'm walking around the stone, walking clockwise around it. I'm walking slowly, but several times around, as if I'm not sure what to do, or what's required of me. There is a sense of expectation, of people waiting. They're certainly watching, and is there a need for me to act? Somehow I feel a sense of "difference." I'm not sure what that difference is, between me and the other people there, but I feel that they're observing me and waiting for me to do something that will move things on, or change the situation. I don't know quite what that is.

Heather: I think the guides were feeding you information in small pieces, and now that seems to have settled down. They have enabled you to describe the situation clearly so far, and now I think we can move. Again we move forward in time. It's just minutes now. It's one, two, three, four, five minutes, forward.

Richard: I feel that I have turned in, towards the stone. I'm down on my knees, and I'm holding it, almost embracing it, and it feels like there's, ... I don't know whether it's prayer, .. it's almost like beseeching, a wanting, of the wisdom, which is within the stone, to come. It also feels that, maybe there's a sense of grief as well. There's a sense of, "Help *me. Help me, guide me.*" I feel, I'm not sure, "at the end of my tether", but certainly of a kind of desperation, of needing.

Heather: I think we need a key.

Hannah: I'm moving the Preseli Stone into the centre.

Heather: That seems to settle the energy right down now, and on to the right wavelength. It was going slightly off signal before that happened.

Hannah: Right.

Richard: It's almost as if there's a certain point, on this big stone, that I'm reaching for, which feels like, "Touch it." And it connects me into a source of wisdom .. that is .. profound. And it feels like that comes through the palm of my right hand.

Richard came to the session with his own special moonstone and was instructed by my guides, acting through the pendulum, to travel with it held in the palm of his right hand. Just as the moon itself has a relationship with water, moods cycles and intuition, so does moonstone encourage a fluidity and flexibility in all body systems. It's almost like in making the connection with that spot, suddenly is a feeling of .. empowerment, or transmission.

Heather: More information trying to get through

Richard: Um ..

Heather: We need another key.

Hannah: The um ..

Heather: I'm searching as well Hannah.

Hannah: The moldavite.

Moldavite is needed to make us realise that we have been living in a self constructed dream of reality rather than reality itself. Moldavite may indicate an awakening experience of any kind. It brings about a sudden broadening of experience and perception, that changes our relationship to everything which is familiar.

Heather: We are right back on a very strong signal now.

Richard: I was kneeling and now I am standing. I'm still holding the rock but it feels that I have one hand either side of it at about chest height. It feels that that is somehow creating a circuit of connection, through from my right palm, through my arm and I think maybe through my chest, maybe through my heart, and the around through my left arm and back. ... I sense almost that I somehow become a sacred stone as well. It feels that there is a shape shifting and I am a mirror image of this Other, this Great Stone.

Heather: Now I'm getting a working pattern. This is psychic surgery. There is an adaptation being made to your psyche, through the power vested in the guides, by the Divine Power. Now there's a certain amount of negativity there, so I'll just pull that out, and we go on to a second level. Then we've got the Healing Line, very strongly swinging.

Richard: Somehow there's a sense of me ... resisting something.

Heather: Well, there's a working pattern now.

Richard: (Softly) Yeah.

Heather: The energy has gone forward. It's gone forward into the positive, from the negative quarter. I'm pulling out again. Maybe you are trying to resist, but I don't think it's working. It's gone on to the Healing Line again. Now we've got the circle again. And it's gone on to the Healing Line once more.

Richard: It's as if I can feel myself coming back out from rock form, right back into human form. And now it feels like I'm *bigger, I'm different*. It's almost like I have, in that transformation, grown, become huge, and so I'm still holding the stone, but the stone has become smaller. It's as if I'm still growing and growing and growing.

Heather: There's work being done on a very specific part of your psyche now. .... And that appears to be complete.

Richard: It's like I've grown big and it's almost like the big rock is now no more than a little pebble in my hand. It's as if I've, yes, I've taken on a kind of giant proportion, compared to what I was.

Heather: And now we can move. It's forward again, just a very short space of time, a minute, one minute forward.

Richard: I'm not sure whether it's ...

Heather: There's information trying to get through, but it's a bit far out at the moment. I think we need the Ansuz rune.

The Ansuz rune means both god and mouth, and therefore means the mouth of a god. It is the first of the thirteen runes, which make up the Cycle of Initiation, runes that focus directly on the mechanism of self change. Therefore connection with the Divine is at hand. It is a reminder that one must first draw from the well to nourish and give to oneself. Then there will be more than enough to nourish others.

Richard: Feels like, from that feeling of giant stature, I've shrunk right back down to my usual size. So I'm back there in the clearing, but it's almost as if I have taken in something and accessed something, which is about having that capacity, that bigness which was there, and within the giant, now contained within me. It feels like that fills me with a sense of confidence, with a sense of , um, ... It's almost as if I am, not immortal, but something close to that, so there's a fearlessness, I think, which is there, and so I stand there, in the centre of that circle, and now I feel that I'm able to turn around and face all the people who are on the outside of the circle on the edge of the trees, and I'm walking around and I'm looking at them, feeling very powerful in myself, very confident and there's a sense that they are there and somehow in awe and not quite knowing how to respond to what they have witnessed, to what they see.

Heather: More information trying to get through.

Richard: There's the sense that I want to reach out. I want to calm them, to soothe their fears, assure them that I have no malicious intent, that my intention is good, and that what I offer them is care and respect and gentleness. ...They are now tentatively stepping forward, so that gradually the group is closing in and I am greeting them, welcoming them, shaking hands and embracing different people and there is a general sense of relief and goodwill and humour and it feels like we are a tribe, we are a community which I am leading somehow, have been restored to leading. Maybe there was doubt before.

Heather: And now I feel we can move, forward again.

Hannah: The pink coral has been moved.

Richard: Um ..

Heather: (Pause,) and Kuan Yin is invoked.

Pink coral helps one to act in a caring manner, supported by the fact that everyone and everything is connected by the bonds of love.

The message from Kuan Yin is that wisdom comes from sitting still, watching and listening, not from rushing to get ahead.

Richard: Feels like there is something about a woman, as I move around the gathering. There is a woman there who is my Queen ...

Heather: OOOhh! (A huge bolt of energy passes through her body)

Richard: Or my ...

Heather: Powerful energy! Very powerful!

Richard: (Very quietly,) Yes. .. And maybe 'til now I felt that I couldn't meet her, couldn't honour her, in the way that she needed, and deserved to be honoured, and now I feel that I've come to her, and ... I kneel in front of her and am paying my homage, my .. my honouring, of her. It feels that she possesses within herself the

95

archetype of .. Queen of the Feminine ... Power. She's dressed in blue, a long blue dress. She's very still. And I rise, so that we are

facing each other, and I see her eyes bright, her smile warm, and sense that she is in her being, embracing me. (Long pause ensues)

Heather: And now I feel we move, forward again, another minute.

Richard: Everyone else has taken a step back, made space around us, and we still stand facing each other, and I take her hands and it feels there is something that I speak, and it feels the words are important and profound, and they need to be to be the right ones. (Long pause) I don't know whether it's my hesitancy, but it feels that it's so .. crucial, this speaking.

Heather: Yes, it's trying to come through. The feeling is that we need either a shift of energy or another key. (To Hannah) It's a shift of energy isn't it?

Hannah: I'm moving the moonstone.

The moonstone carries the feminine goddess energy.

Heather: That sounds good. That has put the energy back on the waveband.

Richard: Mm, I feel less tentative, and am stronger in myself again. (Long pause) I feel I'm preparing to speak, that every*one* and every*thing* is listening, waiting. (Another long pause follows)

Heather: The pietersite is helping you.

Pietersite assists one in remaining open to experience, enabling the effect of an illuminated glory when one proceeds to "walk the stage of life."

Richard: Somehow it's just about me starting, rather than needing to know the exact words pre planned. Maybe the first word just leads to the second word and the third, so ...

"Beloved woman, I honour you. May I always make space for your wisdom. May I be open to learning from your compassionate heart. May I be worthy to stand beside you as an equal. May I be willing, in humility, to defer to your understanding. May I respect the deep knowledge that you bring forth. Together, may we go forward as guardians of the truth, in the spirit of love and compassion and beauty. I honour you as I honour my own true being. May we live in harmony and peace. I thank you for your patience, for waiting, for waiting for the ignorance to be removed from my eyes so that now I see you truly for who you are, wife, lover, mother of my children, I give thanks to you."

I feel myself smiling now, and I see her looking, as if she's been waiting for a long time. (Long pause) It feels that there's a silence around. There are people all around, but there's a profound silence, as if, somehow, we're all *changed*, and we're all united in some renewal, some understanding that's opened us to a quality of our humanity that we weren't in touch with before. (Long pause) Now she's reached out, reached out her right hand and is stroking my face. It's almost as if that is like the benediction, like the sign of her forgiveness, that reaching out, that blessing. We're looking at each other and it feels that the look has the depth to look without barriers, without bales, deep into each other's hearts, and feeling the sense of connection, of unity, of healing in love. I know she knows me. There's nothing to hide, nothing to disguise. We are well met. And there's a timelessness in that. It is the infinite. A place of beauty and serenity.

Heather, Hannah and Richard: Amen, so be it, blessed be.

Richard's comments

I approached this regression with a familiar mix of nervousness and anticipation, nervous in spite of my previous experience of 3 regressions with Heather, that actually nothing of significance would happen, and that I would not attain the slightly altered state of consciousness in which the regression journeys seem to unfold. This nervousness sat side by side with the sense of anticipation about what might be revealed through the session.

As it was, the regression seemed to proceed with an ease and momentum which made it physically and emotionally less challenging for me than some of my previous experiences. The images and content, which had the quality of a lucid dream, or a dream state while conscious, with my own witnessing observer, remain clear and accessible to me now, and left me, after the regression, feeling a sense of peace and expanded awareness, as if a veil had been lifted from a part of my unconscious and some gift brought forth from the shadows into the light.

It was as if a part of myself, from which I was previously disconnected, and which carries within it some of the archetypal qualities of Merlin the magician, is now available for me to access, in a way that was not previously possible.

I have since felt that energy at various times in the weeks and months following the regression, as a process continued, which feels like it is about integrating the experiences of the regression altered state into everyday reality. Some of this integration I have been doing consciously, through visualising and revisiting parts of the regression story as it unfolded, and by getting for myself a small piece of the Precelli Blue stone, which feels like it now has a talismanic quality for me and connects me back to the menir stone in the regression, through which an energetic and psychic transmission seemed to occur.

Other things have happened at a more unconscious level. A dream, in which the Merlin figure appeared, and experiences in my own work, with clients, in which moments of confusion, as to how to proceed, have vanished, to be replaced by surprising intuitive insight, which feels as if it has emerged from this newly accessible part of myself.

This channel, to a source of intuitive wisdom, which I was not in contact with before the regression, feels like an empowering possibility, something to be acknowledged and given attention, in order to more clearly and consciously make use of it as a resource for use in my work and my life. As I write this, I recognise the *significance* of that gift and the need to honour it and give it attention, perhaps more than I am doing, in order to ensure that, through neglect, it doesn't atrophy and become veiled and hidden again, but instead becomes more and more grounded in the everyday reality as a channel through which guidance and wisdom can manifest.

Chapter Nine

Eva's story

We welcome all the Guides and Spirit Energies who have gathered.
Eva's Question: Please can you help me and show me my way forward?

Heather: Your energy is resting in a bubble of consciousness at the top of your head, and we're just waiting for a signal to begin. (Short pause) Now we can go. First of all we are going to a high place, and it seems that we're making our way there now. This is in order for you to be put in touch with your Guardian Angel, or angels or guides. They may be male, they may be female, they may be androgynous, they could be very young, they may even be an animal. And I feel they are coming and are moving in closer now. If you get a sense of their presence, maybe you could let me know.

Eva: Yes, there are *two* things. One, I don't know *what* it is. It's not a person or an animal, it's something very, very primal, like .. the stuff that everything is made of. I don't know what that would be, .. some sort of basic stuff.

Heather: DNA, or something like that?

Eva: Even before that. Something not even really living in the sense that we know it. It's *really* the stuff that the cosmos is made of. That's *one* thing. And the deer is there as well.

A deer totem animal is about the power of gentleness. A new innocence and freshness is about to be awakened and there is a gentle lure of new adventures.

Heather: And now we can move. We are going to a sacred place, in which or through which you can be put in touch with your Akashic Record, or Book of Life. And that is starting to happen now. The imagery is making its way towards you. .. Do you have some sort of sense of place?

Eva: It feels like .. there's a series of rooms, almost like a tunnel, and at the end of that is a large room, or maybe a cavern, and there's a very, very big statue of the Buddha, all covered in gold, not the fat laughing Buddha, the serene Buddha. It's a *very* ancient place.

Heather: Maybe you can tell me something more about it, and then, from there, we can probably move to another time slot.

Eva: It's a place that's been, .. there's some kind of *energy* there, which *cuts* through things, which is outside time, which can go between times, and that's why they chose that place to be sacred to the Buddha. *Originally* it was a sacred *place*, even *before* the Buddha.

Heather: Could I ask you if this is anything to do with laser, as we know it on earth. Is it a more advanced form of laser, that you're talking about?

Eva: I don't think it has anything to do with lasers. (Pause) I don't understand it.

Heather: OK, thank you. And now we can move, forward, minutes, hours, days, weeks, one week forward.

Eva: Long pause.

Heather: There's information trying to get through now. The yin-yang energy is invoked. There's a slight swing on the pendulum, which might mean that you're not quite sure how to explain what you are seeing.

The Symbol Yin-Yang represents the ancient Chinese understanding of how things work. The outer circle represents "everything", while the black and white shapes within the circle represent the interaction of two energies, called "yin" (black) and "yang" (white), which cause everything to happen. They are not completely black or white, just as things in life are not completely black or white, and they cannot exist without each other. The yin – yang invoked is made of Jade, and so, in this instance, the property brought forward from the sacred jade is that of assisting one in access to the spiritual worlds.

Eva: Nothing is really clicking into place. It's something to do with a tree I think, but I can't see the tree.

Heather: The energy is not steady enough is it?

Eva: I can't quite get it.

Heather: So we're bringing in the elephant, and that does seem to stabilise the energy. .. Let me check the time slot, because I said a week, and if I'm just slightly out, that will affect how you get the image. 1,2,3,4,5,6, .. I think seven days is a bit too far, .. try 6 days and 15 hours. (A long pause follows.)

Eva: I *still* can't quite get it.

Heather: I get a feeling for the cross, because the cross, the tree, ...

Eva: Yes. It's *wood* . I think maybe it's an olive tree, and it's *something* to do with a cross, but I don't know what.

The plant totem for Experience is the olive tree. There is a very ancient olive tree in the garden of Gethsemane, mentioned in the New Testament of the Bible. Some believe it has stood there since the time of Jesus. Whether that is true or not, the extreme antiquity of this famous tree is certainly a fact. Olive trees generally are amongst the oldest known on the earth and thus have experienced millennia of history. Working with Olive Tree energy opens one to beneficial experiences on the spiritual plane.

Heather: There's more information coming. We're bringing in the energy of the ruby, the special ruby record keeper, marked by containing an equal angled triangle within itself. Now there's something trying to get through, but it's coming from a long way out. *My* feeling is to try to go back to the Buddha. Let's try to go back to the Buddha, and work from there again.

Eva: (Sounding shaky,) OK.

Heather: Are you back with the Buddha?

Eva: No, I'm kind of muddled now. I don't know *where* I am. There's something about a, what are those things called, I think Catholics have them, where there's like a world, a sphere, with a cross on top of it. What's that?

The Catholic cross of triumph is usually pictured as a globe with a cross on top, symbolic of the triumph of the Saviour over the sin of the world and the conquest of the world through grace.

Heather; Are you getting an image of that?

Eva: Yes, just an image of that. That's something to do with the tree and the cross.

Heather: Well there were ancient drawings of Christ, as being crucified on a tree, rather than on the cross.

Eva: Yes. It's *something* like that, but nothing's quite clicking into place. I'm feeling quite impatient with myself. I'm normally quite *good at this!*

Heather: You're doing really well. There's really very *difficult* stuff here. *That's* what it is.

Let's try moving again, and see where they'll move us to *this* time. Forward, ..

Eva: From where?

Heather: From wherever it is you are now. (Starts counting) Minutes, hours, days, now it seems like a day is too much, so, 10, 11, 12, 13, 14, 15 ... This business of 15 hours is occurring again. It's important somehow.

Eva: Well, I just get an image of a church. It looks like a sort of oriental church, maybe a Greek Orthodox or something like that, and the priest is walking down the aisle, and they're swinging the incense burner.

Heather: There's more information coming.

Eva: And I'm part of the congregation.

Heather: More information coming.

Eva: It's *very complex.* There's a feeling that this is all, .. superstition, mumbo jumbo .. and that the real energy is kind of being trapped, instead of let go. Again I get that sense of the really primitive energy that everything is made of. (Tearfully) I feel quite upset about it, .. the way that it's being made small, instead of being allowed to be *big and flowing.* And yet it's so *powerful.* You really can't *fight* the Church.

Heather: You're doing really well. .. Is there a bit more you want to say, just a bit more?

Eva: (Hesitantly) Yes. I can't quite get it. Something about groups of people, formulating dogma, when it's different for everybody, because we're all .. like facets of the crystal, and we're all different, although we're all part of the same thing. We're all different, and they're trying to make us all the same. They're trying to take away *our* energy, our connection, our personal, unique connection. I feel really *angry* about them. I don't want anything to do with dogma, and rules.

Heather: Is there a little bit more still that you want to say?

Eva: There's a kind of a helplessness there, because I feel that I need help, but I don't need rules. I need support, but I don't need rules, to connect with the Energy.

Heather: And now we can move.

Eva: (Gives a really deep sigh)

Heather: Back in time, minutes, hours,

Eva: (Cuts in) Oh, *I really want to go right back* to the very beginning. I'm not very keen on this place.

Heather: Alright

Eva: I want to go right back to that very *primitive* energy, where everything is just clean and clear and right.

Heather: Well, I've got to wait a minute for the energy to settle now, before I can actually count the time off, and there is an anxiety, which the guides are expressing, around it. ... so the time slot is *back in time,* minutes, hours, days, week, months, (The energy is proceeding, and is better now.) decades, centuries, millennia, 1,2, .. So we've gone back to around the time of the birth of Christ actually. It's two thousand years back.

Eva: Well, it looks like a sort of desert place. I don't know where it is. It could be the Middle East. Could be Africa. Quite dry. Some spiky thorn bushes.

Heather: More information gathering. The High Priest key has just stepped forward.

Eva: Someone coming, but it doesn't look like a High Priest. It looks like a sort of Arab desert person. May be a High Priest, don't know.

Heather: Closer.

Eva: Yes, just striding forward, very powerful.

Heather: More information coming. .... Now!

Eva: There *is, there is,* ... there's a tradition, or a secret passing on of knowledge, of people who .. *can contact the Primal Energy,* without having to .. gang up with each other for protection, without having to be .. in groups or gangs or ..

The breastplate of the High Priest was actually made of two pieces, which formed a sort of purse, or bag, in which also was kept the two sacred stones, named the Urim (representing light and excellence) and the Thummim (representing perfection and completion). These stones were some divinely appointed instruments by which the High Priest inquired of God about matters concerning the welfare of the Children of Israel. The Bible makes several references to these miraculous stones, but not anything physical, like the shape or size. They were probably two jewels. When someone had to make an important decision, the request was made known to the high priest. He would stand before the lamp stand near the altar, holding the Urim in one hand and the Thummin in the other. As the light from the candle reflected from the Urim and the Thummin onto the twelve stones of the Breastplate, each one of which represented one of the tribes of Israel, this flash of light provided up to 24 combinations (2 x 12). Since there are 22 letters in the Hebrew alphabet, the flashes of light could produce strings of letters. It was said that God breathed through the wind, which in turn causes the veil to move, permitting a breeze to flicker the flames in the Lamp stand to momentarily alter the angle of direction of the light onto the Urim and Thummin, and thence to the Breastplate. Thus God was able to communicate directly, but not audibly, to the High Priest and answer the enquiry.

Heather: More information coming.

Eva: I don't feel *worthy* .. to join them. I'm scared. I'm scared I'm going to .. mess it up, or not be able to do it, or hurt somebody, or ..

Heather: There's more information coming.

Eva: (Deep sigh) It's the same kind of feeling. I'm kind of scared to step into power, scared to step into power.

Heather: Bit more information coming, ... or *trying* to get through. Now the aquamarine has brought the energy further forward.

Aquamarine provides for access to stored information, concerning the perfection of the body, and enhances one's insight into the art and practice of actualising the perfection; it provides for inspiration and for an inculcation of the truths of the universe and the universal perfection.

Author's note: To inculcate – to instil by frequent admonitions or repetitions.

Eva: This feels very familiar, the not quite being able to step into power. I'm needing something. Some support ...

Heather: There's a bit more information coming in, but it's got to come from quite far out, and it's coming in quite slowly.

Eva: It's too much for me, which is why part of me wants to go back, back, where it was all clear and simple. I don't feel big enough or strong enough to carry this through or carry it off.

Heather: The Isis energy steps forward.

Isis is the primary feminine archetype, or energy representative of nature's divine fertility. She is mysterious because she never completely reveals herself to anyone. She is the focus of divine motherhood found in the Ancient Egyptian mystery schools. In this circumstance, the goddess Isis is here to help with self esteem, that is to say, Eva's ability to accurately assess, and act out her potential.

Eva: I'm not fulfilling my potential and it's not just me I'm letting down, it's the whole system which requires that the energies flow forward, and I'm not up to it. (Deep sigh)

Heather: There's more information coming.

Eva: I feel dreadfully ashamed.

Heather: (Gently) And now we can move, forward, minutes. It's just one minute forward. It's very, very close. The phase comes into my mind, "It's only a breath away." ...What sense do you have at the moment?

Eva: Just don't know what to do. Confusion.

Heather: There's information trying to get through here. ..What about the egg?

A blown glass egg, containing an acupuncture needle, a gift to Heather from an artist friend who had done an installation piece using a large number of such eggs. Acupuncture is about freeing up the Chi energy system in the body, and so initiating healing. On the evocation of the egg, there was a very deep in and out breath from Eva.

Eva: There's a kind of sense, a muddled sense, of somewhere in the past, I've tried to go forward too quickly, and stepped into consciousness that I wasn't ready for, or something like that. The image of Icarus flying too close to the sun. The image of Lucifer.

Heather: The eye of Horus is invoked.

The all seeing eye.

Eva: Overreached, too confident, and crashed, and now, no confidence, really scared, really frightened myself. Really don't want to move forward any more. (Enormous sigh.) So now I'm .. in a kind of a limbo. I know enough to know that the rules and the dogma are not going to work, so that's not there for me. I can't even join in with that. Lost the confidence to just step into the light. That's the problem, I'm stuck.

Heather: I think this is why we were told it was only one minute away, as close to you as your next breath. It's going from the Now into, in a sense, the next Now, so that enlightenment can come. It's that close, and can come as quickly. It seems that this links in with a theme that we've been dealing with recently. It's the Forgiveness theme; about being able to forgive yourself, and move forward, and accept. Accepting the "isness" of things, not wishing for a different or better past, and seeing that *that* was a path which brought you to this present moment, the Now, where there *is* an opportunity to put all that behind you.

Eva: And yet I still feel scared, traumatised.

Heather: Paramahansa Yogananda, and the Buddha.

Paramahansa Yogananda's message here is, "Be as a child at play. I am watching over you, with the tender affection and dedication of many, many mothers." The Buddha has joined him in order to aid spiritual growth and understanding.

The energy is on the line of receiving. ...And now enters the bridge key

This represents the passage from there to here.

...The gift is gold ... and the outcome, knowledge.

Throughout this section Eva is breathing in and out very deeply, as if there is an exchange of Healing energy.

The pendulum is continuing to swing on the Healing Line, confirming healing is taking place.

Eva: That's what it *feels* like.

Heather: It's still continuing to swing on the same line. I feel I'm in a situation here, very similar to that of distance healing. ...The energy is just changing. It's gone into a working pattern now. ... Now it's settling on the Fear/Pain Line, and that's symptomatic of negative energy that needs to be pulled out. I'm just doing that now, pulling up and out. The pendulum has gone on to the Healing Line again, ... and then into a working pattern. There are tiny circle swings this time, as if it's working on some specific area, and the energy's gone forward, .. Still a bit negative. Pulling out that negative energy, and so on to the third level of healing. Then we've got the circles of the working/thinking pattern. And now the energy has gone forward into the positive. Still continuing to pull out the negative energy, on to the fourth level of healing. Another working pattern. Now we're right over on to the Healing Line, and I've got a pattern which I recognise as representing a Guardian Angel presence, standing with you, and is continuing to stay. The Guardian Angel is still there. Now we've got a pendulum pattern which means Unity with the Divine. ...That unity is still continuing. Represented by the Balance Line.

Eva: (Deep in and out breath, followed by) There's something which I need to bring forth, and I don't know what it is. Something that only I can do, something that's coming through me, from Heaven and Earth, and, because of my fear, I haven't brought it forth. What is it?

Heather: The pendulum has gone on to the Truth Line. ... Information trying to get through.

Feel accepted. There is a Mother Energy Form stepping forward. ... I'm getting two words. You said that there is something you need to *do*. Do you just need to be.

Eva: Something I need to bring forth. I don't know if it's, "Do." It's, "Bring forth."

Heather: Let me try moving a time slot and see if that will give it to you. Forward, no. It's backwards, backwards in time, minutes, hours, days, 1,2,3,4,5,6, ..between 6 and 7 days. We're probably back to the six days, fifteen hours again. Six days, fifteen hours, fifteen minutes.

 On reflection, I believe this ties in with the allegory of the creation of the world in seven days.

Eva: I keep coming up against this overconfidence, over optimism. *I* can do it, and then I *can't. Rushing forward, "I can do it!"* And then I can't! And it's not *trivial*. It's deep, profound, ...

Heather: I wonder if we're actually going to be allowed to see this today. It's just out of reach. It's out of *your* reach and it's a little bit beyond *me also*. It's as if we need to do this in two parts. We need to carry on with it again another time. We have come as far as we can get today somehow, because it's about clearing away a lot of very old stuff and it's very *tiring* for you I think.

Eva: This is going right back to the very *Beginning*, right back to the very beginning of *Time* almost.

Heather: Does that mean that you recognise yourself as being part of the One?

Eva: Yes, .. and the decision, to create and separate, in order to return. I've kind of overdone it, got lost, or frightened myself, or forgotten who I really am. It's right back at the creation of the ....

Heather: Universe?

Eva: Yes.

Heather: Well perhaps we should leave it for today, but you're so close, just a breath away. If we could only burst through this.

Eva: It's that really basic thing, and it's primal, and it's fear. It's OK to be afraid. Well, it's not OK on one level, but on another level it is. And that seems to link everything. The fear is on one level, but on another level .. I *can't explain it*. It *does link everything*, but you're not in it, you can just see it. It's kind of like a *painting of fear*. So it *does* exist, and it *is real*, but it's not enveloping, it's just something that IS.

Heather: So you can step outside of it?

Eva: Yes. Just acknowledge it. And it has to be. It *has to be*. There has to be negative, and there has to be positive, but they're just on one level. And then there's another level, where there is no negative or positive. I can *see* it. I just can't *explain* it. The feelings go *right back to the very beginning, right back to the very beginning*, when that was the decision. The decision was made, to separate, to be SE-PAR-ATE, in order to experience joining, and that goes way way back to the beginning of creation, and it's like I've been playing this out, in different forms, in different ways for ever. Sometimes I go into the separation bit and forget that I know how to join, and there's something about this lifetime, which is – There's an opportunity here, for it all to just coalesce somehow, for it all just to click in place, and yes, it feels that it's *just on the tip of my tongue*. (Deep sigh)

Latin, separare, – se, aside parare, to put.

Heather: I'm getting a pattern here which is about energy. It would normally be about energy inclined towards a very specific place in the body. I think it's being inclined to a very specific place in the mind at the moment, and by mind I mean Universal Mind. I think there is an energy put to everything it possibly can, to enable you to know this and accept it, but maybe not to put an end to it.

Eva: There is a feeling of letting go of even that, because it's not important. If not this lifetime then the next, and if not the next, then the one after, what's the hurry? It's *only* energy and it's *only* a game.

Heather: And with that the pendulum has actually stopped moving, and I think we've done our work, completed the task. So I'd like to thank all the guides, and helpers, who have been *so supportive*, so diligent and so helpful, and who have allowed us to bring to a conclusion and very difficult piece of work. Our heartfelt thanks to you all.

Eva: Yes indeed. Amen. What a relief!

PART TWO

This piece took place some months later, when the time felt right.

Heather: We are here today to try and find a piece of wisdom, which will somehow, maybe, complete the jigsaw. We have all turned up for work with good intention and we will see what comes of that. There's a good vibration running and my information is that the Guides and the Helpers are assembled and are willing to help us, in our Earthly state, to try to find a sense of Heavenly wisdom.

Heather: I'm just waiting now for a signal from the pendulum to show us that we are ready to go forward. It is making its way forward to the all important connection line, (Truth Line,) which it has now reached. First of all we go higher, the imagery is to go higher, in order to put you in touch with your Guardians, Angels, and Light Beings, who will help you on your journey this morning. They are gathering now, and if you have a sense of their presence with you, please let me know.

Eva: Yes. Well the image is that I am up high, high above the clouds, the sort of feeling you get when you look out of an aeroplane, but I'm not in an aeroplane, I'm just *up there*. And, (chuckles) it's a bit like I'm going to step out on to the high wire now! I've got that long pole in my hand to balance me, so .. I feel quite confident about it, but it is very high.

Heather: Are you ready to go forward?

Eva: Yes, OK, yes.

Heather: So if you could just keep us informed about what is happening with you, I may not need to intercede at all.

Eva: OK, so it feels like a deep breath and Go! It's like jumping off the high diving board, so I'm stepping out onto the wire now, .. and balancing. .. It's OK, I can *do* it.

Heather: Can you see where this high wire ends?

Eva: No. It goes into the clouds, so I'm stepping into .. mystery, or the unknown. (Hesitantly,) I probably don't need the long pole any more, but it *does feel* that I'm kind of picking my way through, finding a path that I can't actually *see*.

Heather: There may be something among the keys which would help you a bit in that. My first thought is for the name of your angel. (Says the Guardian Angel's secret name) Now, that seems to hold the line very steady.

Eva: Mm, mm, well OK. (As if talking to someone) What the angel is saying is, " Well, that was very brave of you to tip out like that, but you're more of a creature of *Earth*, than of Air really. And it's the *same problem*, but I'm now on the Earth and it's kind of a boggy place, picking my way through, trying to find dry bits to stand on. At least I can see where I'm going now. It's kind of the same business, but I feel I'm probably going to make a better job of it on the earth than I was up in the skies. So I'm picking my way through this quagmire, this bog ..

Heather: There's more information coming.

Eva: Tufty little hillocks of grass, that are showing the dry bits ..

Heather: Little bit more?

Eva: Mm, there's a blue area ahead. I think I'm heading towards a beach, or a ..

Heather: Maybe it's simply a beach. The pendulum is swinging quite steadily on the Truth Line.

Eva: Yes, it's a beach, .. and the tussocks of grass have turned into dunes, .. and there's the sea. *That* feels a bit more relaxing, a bit more, .. Ah .. (Relaxed sigh.) OK, right, what now?

Heather: I've got a pattern of .. working energy? No, it's something to do with *thinking* rather than working. I believe there are thoughts which are beginning to .. *gather?* (Long pause) information coming in now. (Further pause.)

Eva: There's a ship coming. It looks like one of those ancient Phoenician ships, like the old tin traders, I mean *really ancient,* around 1500 BC, with orangey red sails ..

Heather: Coming your way?

Eva: Coming closer. Coming towards the beach, yes.

Heather: (Pause,) and now?

Eva: Yes, it's, it's *kind* of arrived. It can't come right up to the beach, but it's shallow enough for people to get out. They're kind of half swimming and half wading, .. coming down ladders off the side and then coming to shore.

Heather: Any feeling of knowing anyone?

Eva: It's *strange! I'm* wearing what I'm wearing now, and *they're* wearing ancient Phoenician dress, not unlike simple Egyptian dress. There is clearly a mingling of times here.

Phoenicia was the area of those land masses bordering the shores of the Eastern Mediterranean. More often it refers to the heart of the territory where the great cities, notably Tyre and Sidon, stood, corresponding roughly to the coast of present-day Lebanon.

Heather: More information coming.

Eva: Everybody looks quite happy and relaxed. .. Everybody seems to know what they're doing .. except me. So I'm just going along with it!

Heather: I've got a feeling that it's time to move now. It's forward, minutes, hours, days .. one day forward.

Eva: Mm, some sort of carnival or trade fair, .. something like that. That's what it is, they've come to do some trading. It must be some annual event. Yes, there's an area, where everybody is setting out their wares and they're ready to do trading. Lots of people, and again everyone knows exactly what's going on. .. I feel a bit like, I don't know, like the invisible man, there and not there. They kind of know I'm there but, but I'm not really part of it, in a way. It's more like I'm an observer, so I'm just hanging around really, just watching and trying to fit in, trying to do whatever seems the right thing to do, so I'm just hanging around in the market place, kind of looking at things, and .. I haven't got any money anyway, so I can't buy anything.

Heather: There's something that wants to come forward now. I think it might need a bit of help to come forward.

Eva: Oh, my dog's come with me, that's nice, Smiler's there. He's just come along for the ride I think.

Heather: Oh, lovely!

Dogs stand for devotion and protection.

Eva: Yeah, he just wants to know what's going on as usual!

Heather: I don't think we move yet. There's something *more*, and something makes me say there's something about to happen. ...... Now?

Eva: Yes. It's something quite unpleasant actually. ... There's going to be something like a stoning, or an execution, or a crucifixion, some sort of public punishment. I don't want to *watch* this! I don't want to *be* there at all!

Heather: (Sympathetically) No, OK. Now can we *move*? (This remark addressed to the guides) No, we *can't move*.

Eva: (Resignedly) OK.

Heather: Now, the energy has gone over to Lethargy, so, whether that's just to move you over, out of harm's way somehow? I think it has!

Eva: Yeah, I've kind of switched off to it a bit.

Heather: Yes, that's *right*. Whatever happens, happens, but you're not party to it. And now I think we can pick up the story again.

Eva: (A bit tearfully) Maybe I *should* be party to it. Maybe I should be doing something! I'm feeling very tearful, feeling it's *my way,* when things get too painful to bear, I don't know what to do, and I just turn away! (Deep sigh)

Heather: Well, "We can only learn by our mistakes," is what comes into my mind. If that's a mistake, then make it a constructive mistake and, next time, maybe, stay with it. And now I think we can move, forward ..

Eva: (Interrupting) I'm feeling prepared to step in and do something about it.

Heather: Alright, (Deep sigh from Eva) well, we're going to move forward anyway, but it's a very short time, about a minute.

Eva: (Obviously struggling with her emotions, and trying desperately to control them) It's a woman, who's going to be stoned to death, for something, some ridiculous thing, like, I don't know, she's had a lover, or she's done something that's not evil, it's just against society. I'm feeling really very tearful about *this*.

Heather: (Gently) Take your time.

Eva: And I'm arguing with the crowd, and saying, "Look, this is just *ridiculous*. Show some compassion. Which of us hasn't made a mistake. Which of us has not done something wrong? Killing people doesn't make it any better. And it's hopeless of course, but it's all I can do .. I can join *with* her. So now we're *both* getting stoned, but it felt like the right thing to do! Ouch! (Still weeping) I think it helped her that somebody was prepared to join her in her pain.

Heather: (Gently) And now the energy is changing. It's gone to, "Unity with the

Divine." And so I would imagine that the Spirit has left *both* bodies.

Eva: I'm worrying about Smiler now. (Still weepy) He only came *along* for the *ride* and now he's looking really *upset*. He doesn't know what to do. He's frightened! (Deep sigh)

Heather: And now there's a *Working Pattern*, (on the pendulum) because, in the position that you're now *in*, you can do something about *this* as well! This is quite a *powerful* thing, your being able to help those you love from the Other Side of Life. I'm going quite *cold* now. My face has gone cold and it's going down my arms as well. Confirmation of a spiritual truth.

Because it would seem to me that you're very *new*, in the space between lives. Do *you* actually have a realisation *yourself*, that you can *do something* to help Smiler?

Eva: It's like all I can do for *anybody* is to join them in their pain, join them in whatever it is they're feeling .. and to "Be It," with them.

Heather: So how does that work?

Eva: It works because it .. makes it .. Conscious.

Heather: That's *it!!*

Eva: Yes, something like that.

Heather: I think that is right, because it takes the energy right on to the Truth Line. *That's* what it is, it makes it *Conscious!* (Deep sigh from Eva)

Heather: Can you take that a little further? Can you expand a bit from that?

Eva: It's like that's the whole mystery of life, duality, the material world, is to make it Conscious. It's like the words aren't enough though. I'm not saying it right. To be aware of it, to make it known, and so to somehow transmute it from lead to gold, from Material to Divine, from Heavy to Conscious. It's hard work, and takes a lot of courage.

Heather: Is this about bringing the form into formless, or the formless into form, the two way flow?

Eva: Yes, it's that place, between form and formlessness, between Material and Spirit which is awareness, which can hold the both.

Heather: So, I think what you are saying is that awareness is the bridge?

Eva: Yes, the bridge, or the electrical contact almost. Some current flows, like the space between the finger of God and the finger of Man, in the famous painting of the Creation of Adam, which is on the ceiling of the Sistine Chapel, the spark between them.

Heather: Now there's more information trying to come through, something to do with The Emerald Tablet of Hermes.

Eva: I think it's something about .. There's no Rush. These things unfold in their own time and at their own pace.

The Emerald Tablet of Hermes was a "key" of paramount importance to this Soul Journey. This we knew a few days before the journey took place.

Heather: And so this search for the missing piece of the jigsaw comes to a

TRIUMPHANT end.

The word TRIUMPHANT was furnished by the guides at this point, meaning celebrating or having achieved triumph.

The Emerald Tablet

The Emerald Tablet, also known as Smaragdine Table, Tabula Smaragdina, or The Secret of Hermes, is an ancient text purporting to reveal the secret of the **primordial substance** and its transmutations. Its claims to be the work of Hermes Trismegistus ("Hermes the Thrice-Great"), a legendary Egyptian sage or god, variously identified with the Egyptian god Thoth and/or the Greek god Hermes. This short and cryptic text was highly regarded by European alchemists as the foundation of their art, in particular of its Hermetic tradition. (Their art being that of that of the transformation of base metal into gold, a metaphor for Human enlightenment.)

Translation, allegedly from the Phoenician.
(Very interesting, since the boat which Eva saw arrive at the beach was one she described as Phoenician.)
1) I speak truly, not falsely, certainly and most truly
2) These things below with those above and those with these join forces again so that they produce a single thing the most wonderful of all.
3) And as the whole universe was brought forth from one by the word of one GOD, so also all things are regenerated perpetually from this one according to the disposition of Nature.
4) It has the Sun for father and the Moon for mother:
5) it is carried by the air as if in a womb, it is nursed by the earth.
6) It is the cause, this, of all perfection of all things throughout the universe.
6a) This will attain the highest perfection of powers
7) If it shall be reduced into earth
7a) Distribute here the earth and there the fire, thin out the density of this the suavest (suavissima - sweetest or most fragrant) thing of all.
8) Ascend with the greatest sagacity of genius from the earth into the sky, and thence descend again to the earth, and recognise that the forces of things above and of things below are one,
9) so as to posses the glory of the whole world- and beyond this man of abject fate may have nothing further.
10) This thing itself presently comes forth stronger by reasons of this fortitude: it subdues all bodies surely, whether tenuous or solid, by penetrating them.
11a) And so everything whatsoever that the world contains was created.
12) Hence admirable works are accomplished which are instituted (carried out- instituuntur) according to the same mode.

13) To me therefore the name of Hermes Trismegistus has been awarded because I am discovered as the Teacher of the three parts of the wisdom of the world.

14) These then are the considerations which I have concluded ought to be written down concerning the readiest operations of the Chymic art.

[Davis 1926: 875 slightly modified.]

One translation of The emerald Tablet, by Isaac Newton, was found among his alchemical papers:

1. Tis true without lying, certain & most true.
2. That which is below is like that which is above & that which is above is like that which is below to do the miracles of one only thing.
3. And as all things have been & arose from one by the meditation of one: so all things have their birth from this one thing by adaptation.
4. The Sun is its father, the moon its mother,
5. The wind hath carried it in its belly, the earth its nurse.
6. The father of all perfection in the whole world is here.
7. Its force or power is entire if it be converted into earth.
7a. Separate thou the earth from the fire, the subtle from the gross sweetly with great industry.
8. It ascends from the earth to the heaven and again it descends to the earth and receives the force of things superior and inferior.
9. By this means you shall have the glory of the whole world and thereby all obscurity shall fly from you.
10. Its force is above all force, for it vanquishes every subtle thing and penetrates every solid thing.
11a. So was the world created.
12. From this are and do come admirable adaptations whereof the means (or process) is here in this.
13. Hence I am called Hermes Trismegist, having the three parts of the philosophy of the whole world.
14. That which I have said of the operation of the Sun is accomplished and ended.

Chapter Ten

Richard's Third Story

Heather: We are all met here this afternoon to help Richard find his way forward. All our preparations are complete, so if you feel ready to state your question Richard, perhaps you would do that now.

Richard: My question is to do with fear and what I need to uncover and understand for myself in order to be able to let go of the habit of fear, which I feel pervades my life, in order to move forward with a sense of greater freedom, flexibility and joy.

Heather: Thank you. Now I'm just waiting for the energy to get to the Truth Line. This tells me that we are ready to start our journey. Your energy is resting in a bubble of consciousness at the top of your head, ready to make its way up to the higher levels, from which point we make our way up higher and higher to a place in which you can be put in touch with your Guardian Angel, or angels or guides. It feels to me as if they are making their way to meet you now, and, in fact, that they are actually with you, so, if you have a sense of that, perhaps you would let me know.

Richard: I have a sense of sitting around a fire. It's a circle gathered around a fire. I'm not sure where we are. It feels that maybe it's outside, under the shelter of trees, perhaps in a wooded glade. My sense is that it's a group of men who are gathered.

Heather: The next thing we need to do is to go to a sacred place, although my sense is that this may already be the sacred place, in which or through which you can be put in touch with your Akashic Record, or Book of Life. I get the signal which means, "More information coming," so maybe there will be more images or words that occur to you at this point.

Richard: I have some kind of image, but I'm struggling with my rational mind over it. It feels as if that whole circle within the trees is somehow sunk down into the ground. It's almost as if we're in this cavern or cave. I think there's an underground lake there and perhaps there's a little boat or canoe, a little narrow skiff that I need to use to go across the lake.

Heather: That's on the Truth Line. I think that's what you do.

Richard: It looks as if there is an old man there waiting for me. I'm not sure whether he's a Holy Man. He's holding a long staff.

Heather: That's *powerful!*

Heather experiences the familiar rush of energy through her body, indicative of a high level spiritual truth.

Richard: And he's there with glinting eyes, showing, somehow, both a mischievous and joyful quality, which I see he has. I see him more clearly than I see me, but my sense is that he turns and I follow him. No words are spoken; he's leading me, and we're going up some stone steps, quite a number, which feels like hard work somehow. For me it's almost as if he glides up, but the steps feel very steep for me, as if they're a test in themselves. At the top there's a big stone slab, like a table, and there are maybe two or three chairs there.

Heather: And now it seems we can move, forward, minutes, hours, one hour forward.

Richard: My sense is that we've stood there waiting. I'm not sure whether it's a period of meditation, but certainly it feels like it's been quiet, and it leaves in me a nervousness, or impatience, but the old man seems cool and calm and unfazed.

Heather: More information coming.

Richard: There's something about light shining. We have been waiting for the sun to come around and there's, perhaps, a chink in the roof of the cave, which allows the sun to shine down on to the table, that big slab of rock, so that there is something on the rock which is illuminated, some kind of carving, or symbols. I was thinking that it is almost like a circle with segments, with different symbols, almost like the signs of the Zodiac, all around it. The sunlight is shining in a shaft of light, illuminating certain of the characters on this stone face. And I feel I don't know what is meant by this, but certainly, the old man is seeing significance in what is being illuminated through the particular characters. It feels like he's observing and nodding, as if it's confirming things to him of which he was already aware in some way. And there's a sense in me of, "Well, I still feel in the dark myself. What does this mean? What is the meaning?" and yet I feel reluctant to ask. I'm not sure whether it's out of respect. Maybe I'm saying to myself, "Perhaps the time is not right. Perhaps I just need to be patient."

Heather: Still more information coming.

Richard: (Short pause) The light is shifting. It's almost as if it's going anticlockwise, and I suppose I have the feeling, if it was to do with the movement of the sun, that it was going to move gradually in a clockwise direction, so there's a sense of a kind of confusion about how that is happening. Where is the light coming from?

At the time, and certainly at this point in the transcription, in the light of what happens later in the story, Heather gets the insight that the anticlockwise movement may be indicative of a warning of difficulties that lie ahead. Always, the guides warn her when things could become difficult, when there are difficult and highly charged emotional issues to be faced ahead, by spinning the pendulum in an anticlockwise circle, as a warning, before the details of a time shift are given. Also there is an axiom, "As above, so below." In a mirroring kind of way, as mirrors reverse things, could this therefore be the light of Heaven rather than of Earth?

Richard: Perhaps there is an alternative source of light that is illuminating .. a light of wisdom, maybe.

Heather: I was getting a pattern of Boxed In Energy for a while, but it's cleared again. and now I think we can move, minutes, one minute forward.

Richard: I think the light's gone off now, as if a switch went and the light is gone!

Heather: There's more information trying to get through, but this is a point at which we may well need a key.

Hannah: I'm moving the Inukshuk.

An Inukshuk is an Inuit beacon. For travellers in Canada's North, an Inukshuk is a welcome sight. It says, 'I've been here before; you're on the right path'. They stand in the landscape built up of local stone into the shape of a human figure which marks the way. A little replica, formed in glass, arrived a few days before this journey was to be undertaken, as a present from a Canadian friend of Hannah's. Neither Heather nor Hannah knew of them before, and so Inuit was researched on the internet.

Heather: That is making a difference. That's better! That's the Way Shower.

Richard: The old man is talking to me now, and he's indicating something about the journey I must take. He's pointing directions with his staff , and it feels like I was expecting him to tell me some truth that was revealed by the light shining on the rock face, but instead, what seems to be happening is that he's indicating to me that I must make this journey, and, perhaps, in me, there is an irritation. There is a sense in me that he knows more about me, more about my life, than he's revealing, and that, why can't he just *tell* me. But he is insistent and clear, and I have respect for his wisdom, and yes, he's indicating this journey that I have to undertake. I'm not sure what it is that I'm meant to be seeking or searching for, but something will be made clear, perhaps, through the journey. And he's saying that he *will* be guiding me, will be alongside, not necessarily in physical form, but his presence will be there. That's all I need and to trust that.

Heather: Now I think we can move, forward, minutes, hours, days, weeks, one, two, three, four, five, between five and six weeks, forward.

Richard: I'm up in the mountains where there's snow and it's very cold. I have a horse and there's a cave which is there for shelter. Although the journey's to somewhere I don't know, it feels that every need is catered for, like this cave being there when I need shelter. The journey has been supported in that way. So I'm there in the cave, and it's dark, but I'm OK. I feel confident that this is the right way that I'm going. .. There's a sense of waiting, but I don't know what I'm waiting for. I don't feel particularly hungry or needful of sleep. I think perhaps it's that we're waiting *for* the weather to clear.

Heather: More information coming.

Richard: The snow stops, and I go on, with my horse, climbing through the snow, a pathway through the mountains, and there's a sense of expectancy or excitement. I feel that I'm coming towards the high point of the mountains, and that, somehow, something will be revealed. ... Perhaps when I crest the top of the pass, something will be seen. It feels like something important is there, down in the bowl which is created by the mountains. Down in the valley, there's this miraculous, I'm not sure whether it's a city, but certainly there's a settlement of great splendour, and it's shining in the sun, almost as if it's made of gold! Certainly there's a very reflective quality.

Heather: And now we can move, forward, minutes, hours, two hours forward.
Richard: I have gone down, down the mountains, down through the valley, into the city. The gates were open and there was no threat of any kind of danger, either *for* me or *from* me. There's a sense of this place being open to whoever arrives here. There's almost a sense of the gates being open to welcome me, and I'm passing through the streets and there are people around, who are just getting along with their own business, their own daily life. There is a sense of wonder in me as I look around, both at the scale of the buildings and also the exquisite nature, the gold and lustre. ... It certainly seems like a magical and mysterious place to be. The feeling is that I'm looking for some*where*, or some*one*. Perhaps the old man, the wise man, is supporting me and guiding me, and it's seems like I'm being drawn towards the centre of the city. The city has a radial quality, rather like the radial quality of what was shown on the stone. In other words the stone had almost a map of the city on it. So I'm heading towards the centre, and, I'm not sure, but it somehow feels as if there's also something laborinth-like in it.
Heather: I'm getting a boxed-in energy pattern now, as if it's somehow got you hemmed in.
Richard: Mm, there's almost a sense of, I can find my way in, and that seems straightforward, but would I be able to find my way *out* again?
Heather: Well, we don't move, but I think we need a key, or something shifted.
Hannah: The Diamond. I'm taking it up to the North, (of the table) and then I'm making a complete circle.
The North is the place of wisdom, so this movement was helping Richard to access his own inner wisdom, to go 'full circle,' and complete the task. The special significance of the diamond in this instance is as a 'stone of innocence,' bringing forth purity, constancy and the loving, open nature with which one came into the physical realm. It can activate the crown chakra and can produce a connected force between the intellect and higher knowledge. It assists in removal of the 'fog' from one's mind, such that one can recognise the obstructions to be avoided on the path towards enlightenment.
Heather: I'm getting that circle reflected by the pendulum as well, so you've gone from one extreme to the other now. You've got the working/ thinking pattern, as energised as it's possible to be, while the Boxed In energy pattern is as hemmed in as it's possible to be. So, does that have an effect on you Richard?
Richard: Well, I feel I've reached somewhere. I'm not sure whether it's a dead end,

and I'm looking around, and it's .. It *is* as if .. the walls have closed in around me. And there's just this small space in the middle that I'm in, like a tiny courtyard. It's like a courtyard without doors now. Somehow, I've come in, but the way *out* seems obscured and I look up and the walls are high. My horse and I are just walking around in the enclosed space.

The Horse Totem here indicates travel of the spirit and a new direction in life. It also represents a guide to overcoming obstacles, the advent of adventure and the spirit of personal, untied freedom.

I don't feel a sense of threat, but there's a feeling of, "I don't know what to do. What now?"

Heather: Well, now we can *move*, it seems. I've got to take you *back* in time, minutes, hours, days, weeks, so one week and one, two, three, four, four days, so it's actually eleven days, back in time.

Richard: It feels like there I am there once again at the edge of the woods and I'm looking out towards the mountains, so I can see the snow-covered mountains, and it feels that there's a very clear delineation. There's the end of the woods, and then a slight incline, and then, very quickly, into the high peaks, and, again there's a very clear delineation of a snow line. .. I think I'm waiting for a sign. I think it's an eagle that I can see and hear, and I'm watching that, wondering if that's my guide, and it's circling around ..

Heather: There's more information *trying* to get through, but it may need a key to get through.

Hannah: The moonstone, is slowly progressed towards me until it's directly under my gaze, (or the eagle's gaze. See the opening scene of Hannah's Journey Six, which took place before this one.) and pointing toward the Goddess stone, (chrysocolla.)

The moonstone is a stone for 'feeling' and understanding via intuition and emotional 'thoughts', rather than intellectual reasoning. It brings flashes of insight, banishing the possibility of neglecting one's profit from that which is experienced. The relevance of the chrysocolla, is that, in healing at any level, it helps one to attune to the perfection of the universe, providing for insight into that which is necessary to the, in this case, emotional body, in order to facilitate realignment towards the perfect state of emotional health.

Heather: Now that's got the energy back on the Healing/Truth Line. Can you go forward, verbally, from there?

Richard: Well, I had the idea that the eagle had to come down, and had landed, and I wondered whether it was carrying something. A fish. That seemed to be what it was. And ..

Heather: This seems to be the salmon.

Just before this journey started, Hannah had asked me if I had any information on the otter. I turned to my pack of Druid Animal Oracle cards. (ISBN 1-84013-440-2) The otter is there portrayed fishing for salmon, and the salmon stands for success through persistence.

Richard: That was my sense, that it was the salmon. And it's brought it and I feel that what I do is .. I cook it and eat it, and absorb the strength that was somehow in that fish, the litheness and suppleness and determination. It's as if those qualities are being fed into me by eating the fish, that, somehow I'm absorbing them as I eat it, and that those qualities are qualities that .. that I will need to take with me.

Heather: That's right!

Richard: And I offer part of it back to the eagle.

Heather: And now we can move, minutes, hours, one, two, three, four, five, six, seven, eight, nine, ten, eleven .. eleven hours forward.

Richard: (Pauses thoughtfully) Yes, I feel there is something transformed within me. I'm not sure whether it's through having eaten what I ate, but I seem to be seeing differently and responding differently to situations .. and .. it's like .. that .. sense of determination that the salmon has in travelling it's huge journey, .. it feels like my determination, when I was back at the edge of the wood, was wavering, and that it feels like now I'm reinvigorated, and I'm feeling that powerfulness of pushing my way on, up through the mountains, with a sense of that .. that instinct of knowing the way to go. It feels strong.

Heather: And now we can move, forward again, minutes, minutes, ten, twenty, thirty, forty, one, two, three .. seems a slightly odd time, but forty three minutes, forward.

Richard: There's someone throwing snowballs at me! (Gentle chuckles from everyone.) I'm on, and sort of behind, rocks .. and two children are waiting to ambush me with snowballs and we enter into what feels like some playful fighting. Initially I act as if I'm *terrified*, but I .. I start playing the game, and throw snowballs back at them and chase them, and they .. they run off .. to a hut, although I think it's not quite that. I think perhaps it's a bit of a mixture of a building, which is built sort of into the rocks, and has some wood and some rock and some .. it's kind of built using what was there in the nature of the landscape. We're there at this dwelling and the children rush in squealing, and I'm there outside and I look a bit hesitant. There's someone behind me, a young woman whose house, maybe, this is, or she may be another daughter. Mm, I think she's not the *mother* of those children.

Heather: She is something to do with the children.

Richard: Yes.

Heather: I don't get that she's another daughter, but I don't get that she's the mother either. However, she's definitely connected with the children.

Richard: Is she .. like a stepmother?

Heather: I *wondered* whether she was somebody from another dimension, so that the children are not really *aware* of her.

Richard: So somehow she's there as their guardian, a sort of spirit guardian who keeps watch .. protective.

Heather: More information coming. That might need a shift.

Hannah: The boulder opal needs to go much nearer to the right hand side of the goddess, the simple Jurassic stone goddess.

The boulder opal, in this context, provides a connection to the stars, facilitating communication between the Earth plane and the 'star people' of this world and other worlds. It provides for a grounding action, while enhancing the transfer of information. The jurassic heart shaped stone was a brought back by a friend from an English jurassic beach. The Jurassic period was 206 -144 million years ago.

Heather: We're on a good vibration line now.

Richard: So she's talking to me, or we're talking, and I think .. she's quite .. elusive about who she is, and she's wanting to know about me and where I'm going .. but my sense is that perhaps she already knows. Perhaps there's been a sense of her .. expecting me. And she's looking at me and, almost, sort of appraising me, as to whether I'm , " Up to it." – Up to the task, up to the journey. And I think she gives me something. It's a little bundle, which she says will be .. yes, there if I need it. It will help me. It will give me the, I'm not sure what the word is .. the way, the solution.

Heather: 'Solution' seems to be a very good word.

Richard: Mm, so I want to know what it is, but she's very .. She say's I know *enough*. Don't press. And she, like the old man, is quite light, and a little mocking about my questioning about my desire to know, and have all the facts, so she's encouraging me to just trust. She puts her finger to my lips, just to quieten me.

Heather: (After a short pause, feeling they need a little quiet time to themselves) More information coming.

Richard: I get the sense of .. her looking deep into me, and me seeing in her something of great beauty and a shining heart .. and there's a feeling of connection and, .. I think , longing .. for her .. but a feeling that I also need to go on, that this isn't the time or the place, and that something in me, or for me, is incomplete.

Heather: And now we can move, forward, minutes, one, two, three, three minutes forward.

Richard: I see myself riding away, and she's there, stood near to the house, watching as I go, very still, and I'm looking back at her also, and feeling a sense of being wrenched away, and looking and looking, until she disappears from my view.

Heather: More information coming, but it's a little far out. I think another shift of the keys is necessary.

Hannah: The heart stone moves slightly nearer to the sacred white elephant.

In Indian culture the white elephant belonging to the god Indra is considered to be both royal and powerful. The name of the elephant is Airavata and it is a flying elephant. Airavata, always successful, was made king of all elephants by Lord Indra. Indra is linked to the European thunder god Thor, and is sometimes known as the "Smasher of the enclosure." It has also been said that when Airavata shakes his head an earthquake occurs.

The heart stone, a symbol of love, is a stone from the ancient jurassic beach, (See above) in the shape of a heart.

Heather: That's better. Now, we don't move Richard, so there must be more imagery

coming towards you.

Richard: Mm.

Heather: We're on the right *line* now.

Richard: Something about a landslide, or a .. a .. rock fall! And I'm not sure whether that's going on in front of me or behind me, but, whether I gallop forward in order to avoid it .. It feels that, somehow, .. that it is .. cutting off the way back. It's like there was part of me that was wanting to go *back*. I've lost sight of her now, but there was part of me that felt that real .. yearning to return, but it's like .. the rock fall .. was not just a literal blocking of the path, but that it was also symbolic to indicate, "Don't turn back!" And so I'm moving on, up through the mountains.

Heather: And now we can move, forward, minutes, hours, days, weeks .. now the pendulum has gone around the anxious way, one week forward.

Richard: So is this where I'm back in the city?

Heather: More information coming. Don't try to work it out literally.

Richard: Feels like I'm there, in that blocked space, and I'm sitting down, and I'm wondering what to do next. I'm not sure whether I just need to wait or whether I need to try to find my way out. And I feel the pouch the bundle, that the woman gave me, and .. I'm holding it. I haven't opened it yet .. I'm wondering whether this is the place. Will the solution be found in there? But there's also an anxiety about, "What if it's not!" It feels like, within that is my last, or my only, hope. And so there's almost a fear of opening it, in case it doesn't .. help .. is not the .. solution that I hope. So I'm still with it and holding it, and .. kind of stroking it, and trying to guess .. what it is .. but, in the end, I feel like I need to undo it. It's tied with a kind of ribbon, that I pull the end of, and it undoes. .. It's a little bag, and within the bag, it feels that there are two things, one of which is a round disc, like a coin, perhaps gold, I'm not sure, and the other is a piece of paper, or parchment. So, there are these two things, and they, they don't quite make sense to me. I hold the coin, the disc, and it feels heavy .. and the paper .. and, somehow I know that they're linked, but I don't quite see how.

Heather: I can't move you, so is it a key we need? It's a key.

Hannah: I'm going to move the poem. ... I've moved the poem. I've moved it at an angle, so that the top of the page points towards where you are Richard.

Here follows the poem.

Ceremony

I have been into the dream
of sorrow pain and weakening fear.
There did I meet with an
orchestrated demon
who told me lies and deceit

to defend itself from the
terrifying Angel of death
and the awesome Angel of truth
which is love eternal.
Now I give my word
you are not alone in this place
for Angels do guide thee.
Hannah 24-11-06

This was written in the early morning,
before the journey took place.

Heather: We've got a very strong swing from the pendulum now .. on the Truth/ Healing Line.

Richard: Something about the sun shining *in* to where *I* am, somehow mirroring the experience of when the light shone down, when I was with the old man in the *cave* and it feels like that's .. connected, and, is it the coin that I put down in the sort of circular courtyard where I am? And it's .. It's got a certain .. shape on it. It's like the coin isn't flat, it's not totally smooth, and so the way the light shines from it reflects patterns on the walls around me, and, somehow, some of the patterns seem to match some of the, the shapes that are there on the paper. (Pause) And I feel like I'm trying really hard to make sense of .. what this all .. means, and then I kind of get the idea that it's something about focussing. There's something about .. moving the coin in the middle, little by little, feeling like it's about creating certain series of patterns, on the wall, that match what's on the paper. And it's almost like opening a safe with one of those knobs that you turn, and I turn it one way, and it creates a certain series of patterns, and I turn it another way, and that creates a different sequence, and it feels like there's a formula, there's an order, within which those patterns. Those reflections of light need to be created, and I'm concentrated on that. I feel a sense of excitement, of euphoria almost, of being so close to something, so close to something that feels so profound, so secret, so deep, so essential.

Heather: (Pause) We've gone slightly 'off line' for energy. We need something. Another key? No, it's another shift.

Hannah: The Inukshuk, the Way Shower, has moved and it's now pointing from the Goddess stone, in the middle, towards Richard. Now there's a link in the energies. I'll move the poem slightly back too.

Heather: Now we're right on the right wavelength of energy.

Richard: So was there something in what I said before that was taking me away or, up 'til then, was it, did it feel clear, in terms of the energy? Was that .. ? .. Maybe I don't need to know.

Heather: I think you were very close to something very refined and very precious, but you haven't quite got it yet. .. Is this a bit like Plato's story of life in the in the cave, which is about the different levels of awareness? My pendulum suggests that it is.

AFTERWARDS

Imagine prisoners who have been chained since childhood deep inside a cave. Not only are their limbs immobilised by the chains; their heads are chained as well so that their gaze is fixed on a wall.

Behind the prisoners is an enormous fire, and between the fire and the prisoners is a raised walkway, along which shapes of various animals, plants, and other things are carried. The shapes cast shadows on the wall, and the prisoners watch these shadows. When one of the shape-carriers speaks, an echo against the wall causes the prisoners to believe that the words come from the shadows.

The prisoners engage in what appears to us to be a game – naming the shapes as they come by. This, however, is the only reality that they know, even though they are seeing merely shadows of images. They are thus conditioned to judge the quality of one another by their skill in quickly naming the shapes and dislike those who begin to play poorly.

Suppose a prisoner is released and compelled to stand up and turn around.

His eyes will be blinded by the firelight, and the shapes passing will appear less real than their shadows.

Similarly, if he is dragged up out of the cave into the sunlight, his eyes will be so blinded that he will not be able to see anything. At first, he will be able to see darker shapes such as shadows and, only later, brighter and brighter objects.

The last object he would be able to see is the sun, which, in time, he would learn to see as that object which provides the seasons and the courses of the year, presides over all things in the visible region, and is in some way the cause of all these things that he has seen.

Once enlightened, so to speak, the freed prisoner would want to return to the cave to free "his fellow bondsmen". Another problem lies in the other prisoners not wanting to be freed: descending back into the cave would require that the freed prisoner's eyes adjust again, and for a time, he would be one of the ones identifying shapes on the wall. His eyes would be swamped by the darkness, and would take time to become acclimatised. Therefore, he would not be able to identify shapes on the wall as well as the other prisoners, making it seem as if his being taken to the surface completely ruined his eyesight. The other prisoners would then not go to the surface, in fear of losing their eyesight. If someone were to try and force a prisoner to come to the surface, the prisoner would become murderous, and kill whoever tried to force him to come to the surface.

Richard: The sense that I got was that, when I turned the coin, the dial, it kind of felt that something was completed. There was a point where the sequence was done. Then it's almost as if there was this crack which appears in the wall, and reaches from the top right down through, a zigzag line of a crack. And, when it reaches the ground, the crack opens and widens and widens, as if it's a doorway, a doorway through which I can pass. It's still quite narrow but it's wide enough for me, and, I think, still with the horse following behind, I pass through, into this narrow canyon, like the canyon which is near the ancient city of Petra in Jordan. That feels the same, .. going through. And there are carvings along the way. This is .. an ancient place that I've come into. It's as if it's opened into another world. It feels that this is a different city to the Golden City, a different place that I've entered into. It feels that it goes right back in time.

Heather: Now it seems we can move, minutes, hours, days, weeks, months, centuries, one, two, three, four, five, six, seven, eight, nine, ... It looks like a thousand years .. forward.

Richard: I'm there in that same canyon and I'm feeling that real sense of the familiar, of having been here, and knowing it, and .. and it feels like .. attending so carefully. It's like every sense, every part of me is .. wanting to .. wanting to .. understand .. what it is that I am feeling .. connected to .. I'm experiencing as familiar. There's that sense of, I'm there, so still, barely breathing, as I try to .. try to remember, try to .. access .. something that feels like it's just out of reach. And this feels that there's a prayer that needs praying, for guidance, for clarity, for .. the key to this .. situation, because it feels so .. fundamental. It feels that it's .. I feel the tension in me, that feels like it's a tension that's been carried lifetime after lifetime .. as I try to find my way back to this understanding, that feels like it's so .. embedded and related to this place. And I sense it around me, I sense it so close, but feel .. kind of powerless really .. to know .. what to do. My sense is that I stop trying so hard, and I sit .. and I think someone else is coming, coming towards me. ..... It's a woman .. And it feels like .. yes, she's the woman from before. I know her eyes, I remember, within me, that look .. that we shared. And I feel we greet each other. We say, "Hello" and we look, and we .. And it feels a bit embarrassing and .. uncomfortable, about how to .. proceed. But I want to tell her how this place feels to me, .. feels known, and that she feels part of that knowing. And I feel I tell her that, and .. there's no surprise. .. I sense her .. serenity.

Heather: The pendulum is very still.

This happens very occasionally when the information I am trying to reach is beyond me, or, at the opposite end of the spectrum, when what is happening is so obvious that I don't need the pendulum's help anyway, because there's no need to ask.

Richard: We're walking together, and I touch her hand, and she seems happy to walk with us holding hands, and we're in this place and it feels so timeless, and I have a real sense of belonging. (Long pause) It feels that there's something about destruction. It feels as if, in that place, suddenly, there's .. I'm not sure whether there's an earthquake

.. or it's .. And, just, seemingly out of nowhere there's this tidal wave of rock and debris, just .. kind of flying through the air towards us.

Heather: I've got the Boxed In pattern being shown to me, .. and now the pendulum is swinging up and down on the Balance Line .. so I don't think we can move.

The up and down swing on the pendulum at this point stands for Unity with the Divine.

Richard: No, *I* don't. I feel it just comes over us and overwhelms .. and I'm not sure whether *it kills. .. Everything in its path is anialated .. It feels anialated .. Then buried. And this .. holding ..* I'm not sure whether we just moved instantaneously, or whether .. we just got there. It feels like my conception of time is just .. I don't, I don't .. I'm not noticing .. I haven't noticed .. how I got there.

Heather: I don't think we've finished, but we can't move for the moment ... and now we can,.. minutes, hours, two hours forward.

Richard: Something about the old man, the priest, or wise man.

Heather: We need a key.

Hannah: I'm going to take .. the Jurassic Heart Stone .. and turn it around .. so that .. the bottom of the heart is towards Richard. (Pause) And the Sacred White Elephant is placed slightly nearer as well.

The jurassic heart shaped stone, from a time frame of 206-144 million years ago, here represents an ancient, deep love, love, in fact, of a Divine Nature, and the Sacred White Elephant represents long memory and purity of intention.

Heather: And is there something about the bloodstone?

Hannah: Yes, that's got to shift slightly too.

There is an inherent strength to the energy of the bloodstone, allowing for the transmission of practical and dispassionate guidance. It can also be used to dispel states of bewilderment

Heather: We've got a good swing on the pendulum now.

Richard: There's something about an Eye, an All-Seeing Eye. I'm not sure about the Third Eye, but there's a quality like a big eye, and it feels that the old man is scanning through the rubble, with this eye, and it's as if it gives him a sort of X-Ray vision.

Heather: More information coming.

Richard: And with that he's located where we are, where we're buried.

Heather: Now I think we can move, forward, a very short space of time, barely a minute. (Pause) We're on the right line. Now .. more information coming.

Richard: The ... breath .. being restored. It's almost as if the old man, in locating us, has then .. re .. reanimated or re .. It's almost like feeling the Breath of Life .. passing through and between and kind of caressing .. us. (Urgently) I'm not sure whether it's both. (Poignant pause, with anxious breathing)

Heather: Well, it seems to be just you.

Richard: And ... I .. feel .. this .. kind of pain, .. which feels .. heart .. felt, .. heart breaking, of being *there*, .. of being entombed and then being .. revived, to find that *it's only me!* .. And the touch of the hand of the woman beside me, is still there, with her holding me, but knowing that she is not restored, is not reborn ...... And there's this ... despair of ... is it worth living if she isn't, .. or, why me? So there's also that despair, and guilt and shame and self blame, that it was my fault.

Heather: More information coming.

Richard: And there's a feeling of ... not wanting to leave her, but ...... not being able to stay; that being *alive*, being reborn, I can't .. I can't just lie there, entombed. It feels like there's a *pull* that I'm getting from the old man, which is .. clearing a pathway, a tunnel, through the rock, to reach me. Energetically it's creating that space, and that, also, is sucking me .. a way through that tunnel, and I feel my resistance, my wanting to hold on tight, and being pushed and pulled away, and I feel that last .. fleeting .. touch, as our hands separate, and it's almost as if I'm on this .. energetic conveyor belt, being *pulled* through the rock and the rubble .. and out.

Heather: (Pause) There's more information trying to get through, but it's not quite .... . We need a shift.

Hannah: I'm taking off my white bracelet, the one that came from the North Cape of Norway, which seems to be important .. and am placing it around the bloodstone. Also I'm moving the bloodstone nearer to the centre of the table.

The North Cape is up in the very north of Norway the traditional home of the ancient Sami people, who travel with their reindeer. The pure white rock, from which the bracelet is made, is indigenous to the area, and was bought for Hannah on the day when Heather visited this farthest, most Northerly point of Europe and met Niels, the Sami shaman, and his wife.

The bloodstone, in this instance, supports the decision making processes, and is used to access the principles of mysticism, providing for insight into the immediate spiritual intuition of truths which transcend ordinary understanding. The reason it was moved closer to the centre, was to tighten up the focus of the energy.

Heather: Can you tell me where you are Richard?

Richard: I feel I'm on the outside of that big pile of rock and rubble that came down the valley. I'm there and the old man is there, and there's this place out of which I've come, and inside of which the woman is still lying, and .. I want to get her out, but I know I don't have that power, and so I feel like I want something tangible that is of her, even just a hair, or it's ..... (Obviously struggling with his emotions) And I feel ... I'm not sure whether it's incensed, raging with the old man, blaming him, why he couldn't have stopped what happened, or why, if he could have saved me and restored me, why he couldn't save her and restore *her*. He's looking at me with .. compassion and .. softness and sadness, but without answering. And I feel I collapse into him, crying and ... just weeping, sobbing, just feeling shattered, feeling broken .. and feeling so ..confused and so .. ashamed, actually, to be alive. And dazed .. and numb. And it feel like he's guiding me away, and .. I feel we're back, somewhere else. We're back in the cave I think. I'm not sure whether we just moved instantaneously, or how we got there. It seems that my perception of time and what's going on is just .. Um .. I'm not noticing .. I hadn't notice how I got there.

Heather: (Long pause) This feels, to me, like the end, which, in some sense, is the beginning, which is the end, which is the beginning. .. Samsara, the wheel of life.

Richard: I suppose there's something for me. It's about .. Is it worth it? Was it worth it? You know, the doubt, and setting out on that journey .. the quest, with the optimism and then that sort of desolation and that ... Feels like I'm left with a deep *emptiness*.

Heather: Grief! Is it grief for the human condition?

Recognises, through experience, something of what he's feeling.

Richard: Yes! Yes. That feels it. Grief for the feeling, "I can't go on, I must go on." .. That sort of unbearable quality, bearing the unbearable ....

Heather: There's really, in a sense, nothing more to say, is there?

Richard: No.

A necessary pause follows.

Heather: So, with that, we'll thank the guides and helpers, and all the different characters, who took their places in the telling of your story, Richard. Thank you so very much for being here. This is a complex piece, which will take time to digest and understand, because there is, surely, a very important lesson contained within it. Amen.

Richard: Amen.

Hannah: Blessed Be. Amen.

This story is very profound and illustrates an initiation into the state of deep awareness brought about by unbearable loss, which, nevertheless must be born. It has the potential to open our Eyes, Ears and Hearts, through the experience of our own plight, to the plight of our fellow creatures. It has the power to broaden our compassion and strengthen our awareness and desire to be of service, both to mankind and to the world.

Sogyal Rinpoche, in his book, "The Tibetan Wisdom of Living and Dying," says that if we really practised we could experience the wisdom of the Bardo state (that is to say the wisdom of the space between lives,) while we are still alive. The one thing that the Bardos teachings are showing us, is choice. They are showing us the wisdom in us, and at the same time they are showing the confusion in us, and saying, "Which do you want to choose, which do you want to follow? And it is what we follow in this life that determines, in some ways, how we follow in death. So, in many ways the Bardos teachings are giving us a choice. Sometimes in the teachings it is called the Wisdom Nature, or Emergent Wisdom. There's also a similar name for ignorance, Core Emergent Ignorance. Core Emergent Wisdom means the wisdom that is already within us. It is not something from outside, but something which is within us already. Things are not just black and white, we have choice.

All major healing systems have Shamanism at their root. Concepts and techniques, such as soul retrieval and time line travel are borrowed from ancient shamanic practices. The word shamanism comes from the Evenki people in Siberia, and means, "The one who sees, or knows." The shaman is a person who travels between the worlds, usually in trance, forming a bridge between the Spirit World and the world of humans. The objective of this is to bring about healing, sacred teachings and guidance.

When the Austrian psychologist Carl Jung was visiting the Tsos Puebls in New Mexico, he talked with the Native American chief there. The chief told Jung that western people were crazy because they, "Think with their heads rather than their hearts." Here lies the fundamental wounding of the human. The heart, desiring surrender and union, knows that we are all one organism. The head is ruled by the ego, which desires control and personal gratification, but the shamanic path is the way of the heart.

Shamanism, although an ancient spiritual system of wholeness and balance, is still highly relevant in our modern world. Many people feel lost and isolated, besides having a sense that a piece of them is missing. From a shamanic viewpoint, separation can cause fragmentation of the soul. In other words, due to the trauma of isolation, part of the soul, or essence, can actually split off. When the soul leaves, it takes with it the worst of the pain, and maybe, all, or at least part, of the memory of the trauma. This allows the person to function on a day to day level, but leaves a sense of incompleteness. By working together with the client we are able to retrieve lost in-formation and they are able to reclaim their lost power and return to vitality and wholeness.

I believe that the stories which emerge in these soul journeys are beautiful teachings, and fascinating ways of learning, both for the journeyers and the readers of the journeys. We have choice. We can choose the wisdom, and learn, or we can choose the ignorance and give the matter no further consideration. If we can really listen to the stories in this book, they possess great teaching power.

Richard's Commentary on his third journey.

Following this journey, there was a period of six to eight weeks which felt bleak and without consolation, almost as if, at some level of consciousness, I went through a mourning process associated with letting go of the ideal of meeting my "dream partner."

Instead of the happy ending, I was then faced with a profound challenge, which has involved acknowledging and facing up to the "Orchestrated Demon," a dark egotistical pattern, which, until now, has had a powerful hold over me. Its dominance in my psyche feels like it is receding, and with it the fear that I alluded to in my question at the beginning of the journey. In its place is dawning a greater sense of self value and connection to heart, which was not possible when I was obsessively feeding, and in the grip of, the dark side of the ego.

The process of breaking the mould of my behaviour, turning away from the entertaining delusions of "shadows on the wall," feels like it is taking tremendous effort, but there is also, at times, the insight that reminds me I am not alone, that newly recognised resources are available to me. As I let go, I am guided, step by step, out from the stuck centre in the labyrinth of my life, and so, along with a sense of ending and loss, is now emerging the aspiration and momentum towards a new beginning.

Chapter Eleven

Hannah's Story

The primary purpose of this journey, like all others up to this point in the book, was healing. We were seeking a reason why the psoriasis on Hannah's ankle was not perfectly cleared up as a result of several normal healing sessions. It was suggested that Hannah, who was new to regression, might try it as a healing method. Certainly Hannah's skin became clear, but also a totally unique and unexpected event took place. At the close of the journey Hannah's voice changed and there was an invitation from a Light Being, speaking through her mouthpiece, to "Entertain your presence at a future occasion." Eventually this gracious invitation became recognised as the seed for this book to be written.

A dog is heard barking in the background, the sound coming through a partially open window.

Hannah: It's funny. I thought about devotion, because that's what dogs are about.

Heather: It feels to me now as if your angels and guides have reached you. Do you have a sense of something being with you?

Hannah: I'm sitting on a stone bench. It's like Greece. It's very similar, and I've been welcomed with these beautiful Beings in white robes and wearing cords of gold around their waists.

Heather: There's more information coming.

Hannah: Beautiful birds ... Oh, they've shown me the bluebird, the one I came back to Cornwall with.

Hannah was living quite happily in Wales, and one night she had a dream of coming back to live in Cornwall again. In the dream she was walking to St Michael's Mount, carrying the Bluebird of Happiness on her hand. She rang me, whom she barely knew, to ask me about the dream and to see if I could discover whether it was her destiny to come back and live in Cornwall once more. It was immediately shown to me that it was. Many of the journeys in this book are the fruits of that insight.

Heather: And now it seems we can move. (Sensing something unusual, in terms of regression) Are you moving?

Hannah: Well, I'm sort of walking around generally and they're showing me this beautiful garden. It's where I was recently. "Yes," they say, at Jacob's Workshop. That was the garden. I saw the entrance to it and it was within me but it was also here, where I am now. Very beautiful. Tall, beautiful plants, and there's some music as well, very beautiful ...

Heather: And now we can move, because I feel you are already within the regression...

Hannah: I seem to be ... It's quite easy to travel, in a sense, between here and there. (sounding bemused) It's very, very *easy*.

Heather: Now we're going to go forward, minutes, hours, days, weeks ... We're going to go one week forward.

Hannah: I'm in a council chamber. I'm sitting there and I'm being asked about ... I'm being asked to remember something in another time ...

Heather: More information coming.

Hannah: Oh, they're showing me pictures, that's better ... They're showing me pictures of *body parts*. The inside of bodies. The human body is like a map. Goodness me!

Heather: (with a certain urgency) More information coming!

Hannah: Yes, there's heaps of it. And the maps are .. Ah, I realise, the picture with the gold dots I did on this one, only the body parts are like .. If you have a body part, it has the dots around it so it's like the living cells .. It's not like it, it *is*, They're gold. They're *light*, so all the inside of the body is *light*. And, and the bloodstream is the river ... It's, it's, (In awe) ... Oh, it's *extraordinary*, extraordinary. It's difficult to describe in words, in human words, it's so beautiful! And everything is beautiful and connected. It's like a turquoise sea! The blood is like a turquoise sea! ... Ah, that was the early poem I wrote, about that ...

Because the body is composed of light, diseased areas of the body, which will have become darkened, need to be visualised and addessed using light energy channelled through the Universal Heart. (Information disclosed on proof reading – See medicine' on following page).

Heather: I've still more information coming.

Hannah: Yes .. Oh my goodness, the hearing is just immense. Hearing is different levels of hearing and it's just beautiful, and you can extend your hearing. If you are in one place, it's like seeing behind and in front and you can hear behind and in front, above and below, you can hear. Oh it's awesome. It's like..... music is everywhere. Oh .. sound is really important .. sound .. and light. Sound and light .. And something else ...

Heather: I think now we can move. Forward. One year.

Hannah: (After a gap of about twenty seconds) I have a very large heart, and the light from the heart can melt anything .. and forgiving .. The light from the heart is like a laser. On earth they've discovered the laser light, but there is a different higher quality than laser light, which comes from the human heart, which is part of the Divine Law.

It can melt hardness of any metal, it can melt and heal bones and any illness. It is .....

Heather: Information coming.

Hannah: Truly from the Creator. This is only a little of the knowledge. This energy is called Love. It is the strongest thing in the known and unknown universes, known by Man, unknown by Man. This energy holds the planets in perfect motion, the stars in their courses and the sun in its path, and all the planets. It guides the birds in their migrations and the geese in their flight. It is the web the spider spins. It is so *beautiful* there are no words to describe it. It is so powerful, that Man, with all his knowledge, has no concept, but **It Is**.

Heather: And now we can move. Forward. Centuries. Five centuries forward.

Hannah: My back is hurting. There's something burning it, but it's not uncomfortable.

Heather: There's information trying to get through here.

Hannah: (Pause, then hesitantly) I feel this is the last connecting point with an Earthly life. I don't feel any pain in my legs, I don't feel any *pain*. I feel as though I'm burning, but my consciousness has gone and ... OH ... Goodness Me ... The struggle to remain conscious is going. (Whispering) I feel two angels coming. They're lifting me up out of this body and they've laid me to rest ...

Heather: (Gently but insistently) And there's more information.

Hannah: I was burnt. I was burnt with my sisters and my brothers .. because we knew too much. They tried to drag the information from us but it was not possible. We were sealed against them having the knowledge and we had to leave, and they took us away and burnt us, many of us, many of us, even the young ones they burnt. They said we were contaminated ... (Clearly upset) contaminated with the thing they called the devil, but as we were leaving we forgave them, we forgave them for they did not know the devil was of their own making. (Two deep sighs)

Heather: There's more information, I think, still trying to get through.

Hannah: We had discovered some kind of ... it was a medicine. We had discovered a medicine that healed the body.

Heather: (Having been shown that more information on the medicine is not reachable at this point) And now I think we can move. Does that feel clear?

Hannah: Yes.

Heather: Forwards. About five or six days forward.

Hannah: I'm in a garden with some children. There's lots of laughter. Always the birds are singing. There's great happiness here. I seem to know these children and they know me.   (Pause) They bring the ones who are sorrowful. They bring them here, to the children's garden, and they show them how it is. You can free your self from this sorrow and the children will show you all these beautiful things. There are lakes and boats, little boats. It's like fairyland. It is Fairyland. It's the fairyland I saw in Wales, when I was on the Earth plain. They *showed* me! They showed me through the tunnel in the hedge. They showed me the beauty of it. The light is beautiful and it is very very light. The energy is light, the whole thing is light, the flowers, the trees and the animals, they're all made of light! This is another plain of existence. They're very beautiful. (Again in awe) They're very beautiful.

(Pause) They say, "Put your fears into the water and they will dissolve in water. Put your fear into a goblet of water which has a crystal in it and stand it in the sun, and that will cure the sorrow. That will cure the sorrow." That is a cure for sorrow. That's very beautiful. Everybody is equal in Fairyland. It is a very powerful place. They move on energy of light, they have their being in it. It is not a fantasy put about by children on the Earth Plain. It is real. It has it's place in the Divine Order. The children met some of the fairies, the ones they made a film about on Earth. That was very near to it, but could not capture the magnificence of that place.

Heather: And now we can move, forward again, one day.

Hannah: Now, this is different. Here I'm a grown person and I'm living in, what do they call it now? Alaska, here in the wilds and great snows and the mountains, the fir trees and the wild animals. Pristine is the word, very pristine. The rivers are beautiful. In the Spring they are beautiful. It is beautiful in that time. ... Something is happening. We are having to build a shelter here. .. Ah, the people are coming out of the woods. There's a host of them. I wonder what they want. They're surrounding us. I'm in this woman's body and ... Oh (with a sense of alarm) they're going to do a ceremony. I'm not sure what it's all about .. I don't know whether I'm supposed to be here. Am I supposed to *be* here?

Heather: Yes, yes you *are* supposed to be there.

Hannah: Right. (Whispers to herself) "supposed to be here." I've got this long hair, and when we were building the shelter I took off my beaver cap because I was getting warm while we were building and cutting the firs, and .. because my hair is this particular colour, I suppose it's like gold to them ... These people are very dark, very dark skin, and I don't think they've seen a person like me before ... I'm white, and they've got honey coloured skin ... They're quite fierce. The men *with* me, they've got rifles, but, you know, they're not aggressive. The rifles are for killing meat. So we have to have this ceremony. We don't *have to*, but we have to, so let's be with this ... It seems to be very sacred for them ... I have the strange feeling that they *will* kill us, but not before they've done the ceremony. ... Oh, I had a funny sort of upbringing about religion, a bit of this and a bit of that, and now ... I'm not sure how to approach this, but, so I'll just be with this, see what happens. Now they've taken us to this clearing, There's a fire built and ... They're really *curious* about me, I suppose because I'm a white female and they sort of poke and prod me ... I don't know what to do. I'll just sit here for a bit. They're not taking any notice, they're very busy. They're looking at the men ... The women have come. They've brought their children. Oh, Look! Oh they're *beautiful*. They're all so warmly wrapped up. *Beautiful*. What a clever way to keep your *children* warm. And look, there's an old one. I think he must be the elder statesman, and he's given me something to drink. Feels good. It's got honey in it ... I'm feeling a bit sleepy. They've given me a blanket. That's nice, they've given me a blanket. I can't see the men anywhere, but I feel *alright* with the women and children and they're chattering away, but they're looking *thin*. Why are they looking so thin? Why? Why can't they can't they find food? I don't know. There are all these questions. I wish I could speak and understand them. I'm going to sleep now, but it's like I'm dreaming. (Pause) Now there's a Wise Woman. I'm in this tent lying down. I think it's a tent. Looks like a tent ... and it feels like a tent, and the Wise Woman .. I'm lying down because I've had this drink. I'm feeling very sleepy. She's holding my hand. I think she wants to get inside my dream. Well, I don't have much option, by the feel of it, so the dream is ... OOOhh, Oh my goodness me! She's shown me this beautiful place! (Deep sigh) We have been friends, she and I. She knew I was coming. (Whispering) She knew I was coming. She said .. She knew I was coming. And she showed me the way, she showed me the way, how to come and how to go. She showed me how to travel amongst the stars. She has showed me how to disappear, how to vanish, and to come back. How to walk amongst the nations, how to be an influence for the Great Power, how to sit with the Elders, without being seen. How to carry the Gift. ... How to be recognised and to recognise others. I have been on the Earth Plain many times ... The suffering was necessary to bring me, each time to the crossroads, to fine me down like an arrow, so that I may be as light as an arrow and as true, for I am a lover of truth, as revealed by the Sacred Ones .. Many words are spoken which go into my deep memory, words of wisdom and words of power, which I guard each life that I live, on this Planet Earth. She gives me, in the dream, a rose quartz stone, and she says the Bear will be one of my guardians.

Heather: And now we can move. Forward again. (Starting at minutes she counts forwards until) Between thirteen and fourteen centuries forward.

Hannah: (Pause)

(It is very difficult to say quite where the transition from the person Hannah to the Light Being occurs. There is a seamless join.)

This is the time of Great Peace. This is the beginning of the time of the Great Peace. This is what mankind has dreamt of in his heart. It is an expansion of awareness, on many, many levels. It is also the time of great responsibility, for Mankind has fallen before, from his own grace. (Pause) This great awareness comes of that responsibility, first towards himself/herself, which encompasses then everything else. Nothing is separate. There is great harmony here, great wisdom. (Pause) (A dog barks outside the window) Yes, and devotion, thank you. The essence of the animals (Pause) is love, and innocence (Pause). They come each with their wisdom, each with their knowledge. They come, with an awareness, to a human, to show them Sacred ways and the Teachings. All life is sacred. I am not a human as humans would know it. I am a member of what humans would call an advanced civilisation, well not so much advanced as different, but I suppose what humans would call advanced. We are developed like, how would you say, finely tuned instruments. Our bodies have been built differently to the human body, in a sense more advanced than the human body. Human bodies go through different stages of physical development as well as development of their awareness. It is not separate. Everything develops and goes through stages. This is the law, the natural law.   Healing is pleasurable, does not have pain attached to it. Here at this time there's a deep, a very deep level of awareness. Children develop this early here, and our hearts beat at a much lower rate. The, um, how would you call, the spaces occupied by the atmospheres between the planets beat at the same rate. We are in harmony with this. Music is beautiful. We can go to this place another time and you can ask me other questions, if you wish to understand something.

Hannah as Hannah: What about, what about, what about food and water, as they have on the earth plain?

Being of Light: We don't need it. We are composed of different energies so that our bodies are not like the human body. It is just flowing, and very restful. It *can* be energetic if wished, but it has a very different, it's difficult to describe to you in words what I mean, but I suppose you would call it the energy of Love. The guardians are made of the energy of Love. (Long pause)

Heather: (Politely) Thank you so much for that. We would love to come back another day and speak some more with you.

Light Being: I would be happy to entertain you, not to amuse you, but rather to entertain your presence. Thank you.

Needless to say, this journey was amazing, both to Hannah and myself. Remember, Hannah had only had experience of regression once before, facilitated by another practitioner many years previously, and in all my years of experience I had never come across so direct an approach from a Light Being. We were astounded. Also, we needed to think long and hard as to whether it was appropriate we take up the extended invitation.

Chapter Twelve

Hannah's Second Journey

Heather: First of all I am going to wait for information from the pendulum telling us it's time to go, so let's just gather and settle for a minute. I feel the guides are coming to you, they're making their way now. As soon as you can feel their presence with you, perhaps you could let me know.

Hannah: Well it's a bit like walking across the causeway leading to St Michael's Mount but it's in a much higher place. It's like a reflection of the Mount. There are people coming here and meeting with each other. First there was a seagull, who just came to tell me that everyone was coming, and the magpie was there as well. Oh, two magpies, that's lovely. A beautiful dog is there as well, the yellow dog with the wavy tail, and he likes being in the water. He's very important.

Dog energy here is about protection. People with a Dog totem are usually helping others or serving humanity in some way. Dog medicine embodies the loving gentleness of best friend and the fierce energy of protector.

Lots of waving tails. I'm seeing quite a few animals today. ... Oh! Here comes the Polar Bear! (Laughing) *That's* nice.

Polar Bear energy represents good spirit connection and breaking through emotional barriers.

And now, here come the Guides. Here come the two girls ...

Heather: Is that Hannah and Vania? (Two young women in Spirit, daughters of Heather and another healer friend, Yvonne.)

Hannah: (Unable to reply at first, choked with emotion, then, in tears) Beautiful, beautiful! They're bringing me to the other guides, and there are .. ah .. the very tall Angels. Gosh, there are so many .. so *many* .. and they're bringing me in now .... I've come into a hall and there's a round table. We sit around a round table and there's a speech of welcome for everybody there, but we're still *waiting* for somebody. We have to wait a while. Everybody is quietly talking. There's some music going on in the background, very uplifting music.

Heather: (Feeling a powerful energy) Somebody important is just about to come in.

Hannah: Yes, there's a red carpet and it's lined with gold.

Heather: Can you see them coming now?

Hannah: Yes there are two of them. They would be ... High Angels. Ah, there's going to be a ceremony, and this ceremony is the link between the Heavenly Realms and the Earth Plain. There's a book in which they are looking ....

Heather: Is this the Akashic Record? (The data base wherein everything is recorded)

Hannah: I think possibly it is. I'm being asked if I passed through the Ring of Fire. "Did you pass through the Ring of Fire?"

Heather: Mmm, they're checking things carefully aren't they?

Hannah: Yes. I look at them and I say, "Yes," because I *have* passed through the Ring of Fire."

See Chapter Eleven, Hannah's story where Hannah's faith and steadfastness was tested in the fire.

Heather: And now I think you can move.

Hannah: Yes

Heather: And we move forward, one year, forward.

Hannah: There's an acrid smell. It's a factory that's caught on fire, and the humans were warned about this. It has been written that one of the most dangerous things they have are the chemical plants.

Heather: Is this atomic energy?

Hannah: It's atomic energy but also it's the chemicals that they use to make things because they pollute the air and it goes into the air and it falls upon the land, and pollutes the land. Great care must be taken by the chemical factories.

Heather: Their emissions?

Hannah: Yes. And certainly the nuclear factories. In some countries it is very good. They do their very best. There is a special Energy Being you can address for the protection of Nuclear Plant and there is another Energy Being you can approach about the protection and guardianship of the chemicals. People need to be informed about this. The information will come. It will be given.

Heather: And now I think we can move, forward again, minutes, hours, days, weeks, months, years, decades, centuries, millennia, I think we're going forward about ten thousand years here! Ten thousand years forward.

Hannah: The planet has moved. The planet earth has moved.

Heather: There's a certain amount of anxiety about this information .. I think because it's very ... Top Secret. There's more information trying to get through. We are now using the oyster shell as a Key.

Oyster energy is precious. It filters out life's static and knows when it is time to close things to save on energy. It is sensitive to the protection of the environment,.

Hannah: Good.

Heather: With the pearl.

The pearl has been known as the "stone of sincerity", bringing truth to situations and loyalty to a cause.

Hannah: Excellent!

Heather: Now that brings you on to a line where you should be able to get more information

Hannah: Yes, because you have given me the key to show me that the way is open. Now I may have a little problem with language, because the vibrations are quite different here.

Heather: We are invoking the little brass owl of Athena, the Greek Goddess of Love and Wisdom to help you.

Hannah: Yes. Thank you. That's better. Now, ... The planet of Earth has moved into a different realm. (Hesitatingly) The Earth Mother has birthed herself into this .. space.

The light is different, sound is different, the people are not like the humans that were left ...   They weren't left behind, but their energies were dispersed, so that the ones on this planet now are of, how do you say, they breath a very rarified atmosphere. It is the type of which you humans would call rarified. I believe that is the word, rarified, very exquisite. This is the *Earth's dream.*★ The beings who live within and on her planet, on her body, are beautiful! They are in line with her. They are in harmony with her and her attendant moons. There are three moons, each circling in their different time scale. There is the mighty Sun, whose volume is not jumping around any more and giving many explosions and, disturbing the atmospheres of the planet, which it has done before. It was trying to help the Mother Planet align, but now its work is in harmony with what has happened to the Mother Planet. There is much work going on on the Mother, with the Father Sun, and the beings here are able to reproduce at great, in a sense, quality.... It's like a thought process, so they are very careful in what humans would call their thought processes. Each word is very careful. It's like designing. They design their words, or the Sound Words which they use, and they don't overdo it. It is within harmony. And then these beautiful beings may visit with other planets and with the Mother Earth system and the different other systems. That is all the information I can give you at this point in time. Thank you for your presence. It is very beautiful, the work that you do. I hope to speak with you again when the time is right. Thank you. ★ See Ch Fourteen – Afterwords I.

Heather: Thank you. And now we move. We don't move forward now, we're going backwards in time, nine centuries earlier.

Hannah: There are great changes going on. There is quite a lot of fear, but there are many here now who understand this thing about fear. It is fear that keeps them in darkness, and they will be relieved. (Murmurs) A lot of fear. There are safe places where people can go and where the Wise Ones will be there to help them.

Heather: There is a little hare just come in to help you.

The hare totem is connected to the goddess energy. It has associations with the Celtic Goddess Cerridwen and the Norse Goddess Freya, while in classical mythology it represents Aphrodite and Venus as a symbol of fertility and sexuality, due to its associations with Spring, renewal and abundance. In China and India it is believed that the Hare can be seen on the face of the Moon - The Indian legend tells that the God Indra placed him there following a supreme act of self-sacrifice so that people would remember and be inspired by his courage.

Hannah: Yes, that's good, that's good. They must remember the animals. The animals remember *them*. They have a duty, the animals have a duty, but also it is the animals who remember. They must remember their Power Animals and work closely and acknowledge them. The animals will show them the way to the places of safety. The Medicine Men and Women have always known this. There are caverns within the earth which will not be disturbed and so there *are* places of safely. Oceans can be turbulent but there will be places.

Heather: The horse has come.

Hannah: Yes, well they know the way you see, they *do know the way*. And they can go there very fast. They can fly. They will fly with the Humans. They will know the magick of that. It is very, very important to remember all the Sacred Contracts we had with all these beautiful creatures. They were all gifted here.

Heather: Yvonne has just brought the dolphin in.

Hannah: Good. Excellent! Our friends and companions. But Dearly Beloved, one of the highest energies of the system, of the whole of the Solar System is the dolphin, and they will take you to the caves under the oceans, they will take you under the waterfalls, where you will be safe. There is a land, beneath the great ocean, the dolphins bring the message of that. They bring it. They say, "We cannot tell you yet, *but believe that there is this beautiful, beautiful land, which is full of lights."*

Dolphin energy represents wisdom, intelligence and harmonious balance in life, communication as a healing voice, and trust in others, via community spirit.

Heather: And now I *think* we can move. Does that feel right?

Hannah: Well just ...

Heather: Or is there more coming?

Hannah: Well just remember that what you see in the Earth Plain, in sometimes the most funny and least expected places, brings the tears, makes you the tears, the emotion. That is true. Hannah knows this, Heather knows this, Yvonne knows this. They can watch, and they will see, and they will hear and they will know. Bless them all. Thank you.

Heather: And now I think we *can* move. We're going to go forward. It's almost an hour, forward.

Hannah: (There is no response from Hannah)

Heather: Fifty five, fifty six, fifty seven ... Fifty seven, it's actually a very crucial space here. Fifty seven, fifty seven ten, fifty seven twenty, fifty seven thirty, fifty seven forty. It's very precise timing this time. Fifty seven minutes, forty seconds, forward.

Hannah: It's an angle. You have to *remember this*. It is an *angle*. This needs to be worked on. There are combinations of numbers within that number and it will reveal something to you.

The angle of 58 degrees is very important in the construction of a funnel. It makes for faster more effective funnelling! We may be able to speed up and make for more efficient communication by using the 'code' of 58 degrees. However the angle of 57 degrees 40 minutes has since been found to be a very important Time Line for Hannah.

The moment you are born your soul imprints and resonates into the planetary energy grid. Because of the etheric quality of the planetary frequencies – etheric energy carries memory, ie the Akashic Records – all past incarnational memory is triggered and resonates into the places and experiences that in this lifetime are important for you to deal with. For example, by going to these places you may get past life memories or retrieve fragments – parts of your soul frequency left behind or fragmented through a powerful energetic or emotional experience. 57 degrees 40 minutes is approximately the degree of latitude of three of the stars of Ursa Major, the seven stars of which distribute the energy coming in from the Pole Star as the seven rays. The three are Mirak, embodying the 8th ray of Devotion, Megrez, the fourth ray of Harmony through Conflict and Alioth, the third ray of Active Intelligence. These are also found in Vedic astrology as the stars that carry knowledge into the earth. An incarnational pattern would seem to be involved with the repetition of alignment and connection with channelling that knowledge.

As the energy of the seven rays streams forth from the Great Bear constellation (Ursa Major) they interact with the seven stars of the Pleiades, the "Seven Sisters" or "Wives of the Rishis, " the seven stars of the Little Bear constellation, Ursa Minor and the star, Sirius. The ray energies then travel through the twelve zodiacal constellations and toward our solar system, where they are **"funnelled"** through the physical sun into the solar system proper. Researched by Astrologer, Jennine Auther.

Heather: Thank you. Now we will move. This time we move forward again, four years forward.

Hannah: Yes .. it's cold. You have a book. Hannah knows of this book, its called, "Entering the Circle." You need to read it, and discuss. A really important book.

Entering the Circle was a book I had not heard of until this point in time. It is written by Olga Kharitidi, a Russian psychiatrist who now lives in America. It is the story of her introduction to shamanism in Siberia, and is an extremely interesting and informative book. Maybe even more important to this current book is her second book, The Master of Lucid Dreams.

Heather: More information coming.

Hannah: There are, in the Ural mountains in Russia, crystals. You will need crystals from there. This will be to do with another angle of alignment, and you can use these.

Heather: Could I ask what crystals?

Hannah: Clear quartz, absolutely clear.

Heather: Clear quartz. Is it diamond?

Hannah: You can, if you have diamond, use it, yes correct. That will come. But if it is in another form, ...

Heather: Like a Herkimer, but not a Herkimer.

Herkimer diamonds are so called because they are found in the oil fields of Herkimer, USA, similar crystals are found elsewhere.

Hannah: Yes! Good energy! Good energy in herkimer also. Pure diamond, not necessary, but herkimer is very important for the three of you. It will help the bonding, and also hold you in safety. That is to do with the triangle, as above, so below. We have the triangle at the high level and you have the triangle at the bottom level, which makes the diamond. I'm not putting it perhaps terribly well, but do you understand? The triangles will make a diamond.

Heather: Yes, thank you. It calls to mind, the record keeper ruby crystals, where there is and equilateral triangle in the record keepers.

Later a stone from Russia, a wonderful example of a crystal like a herkimer was found, and a star link was also found, to a Healing Star twenty eight million light years from the earth.

The diamond is said to have been one of the stones used in the breastplate of the High Priest. It can activate the crown chakra and can produce a connecting force between the intellect and higher knowledge. It assists in the removal of the "fog" from ones mind, such that one can recognise the obstructions to be avoided on the path towards enlightenment.

Hannah: Soon it will be easier for the three of you. You will all work together beautifully. We are not quite familiar with working with the energy of this person Hannah, but we like her energy, with the lovely Yvonne and the very beautiful Heather. We are not obliged, but we are pleasantly happy with you and we enjoy your company. We shall see you again. Thank you.

Heather: And now I think we can move, forward again, I would say ten years forward.

Hannah: People, people on the Earth Plain,

Heather: Here comes a shell, from Australia ....

The shell represents Invulnerability - "The arrows turn, the swords repel, let nothing pierce this mortal **shell!**" Mortdredd.

Hannah: Yes, people on the Earth Plain

Heather: There's information coming.

Hannah: Destruction

Heather: Amazonite.

This mineral helps one to simultaneously attune to both the spiritual dimension and the province of chaos in order to facilitate the complete traversing of all boundaries; this aspect of the energy of amazonite helps one to access the harmonious centre within the kingdom of perfection and to integrate and synthesise the duality. It helps one to both manifest and retain the pure energy of Universal Love.

Hannah: There is an ability here to see energies. There will be problems of sickness and great sadness, but the Light will never go out. It is, how you say, past the point of no return, in as much as the Light will not go out. It cannot go out now. The work has progressed, well enough to hold the Light, but there's still much work to be done.

Heather: More information coming.

Hannah: I see earthquakes ...

Heather: The little pink stone .

Represents the Heart energy of the Earth Goddess.

Hannah: I see Refugees. There is an Exodus of peoples, only this time they have remembered their animals. The last time there was an Exodus they were in such a hurry that they forgot the animals. Fortunately animals are intelligent, and although they wanted to stay with their human companions, they actually left, most of them had left. Now, this time, their human companions are taking them and making sure that all is well. They are like their children. They have made a recognition of the importance of the animals. The little pebble is really a big boulder, it is merely disguised as a little pebble. The quality of this stone will reveal itself in good time, but not today. The movement of people is in progress now, in this time factor, Twenty First Century movement of peoples, Refugees move out of places, into other places, and all is in accord with the plan so all is in Divine Right Order. People already stationary in these places have trouble accepting them, but even that acceptance will come about. There will obviously be *some* trouble about it, but we will try to hold the Energy for these people. They are very necessary for there to be the blending of the nations. It is really important. The alignment with the animals is important. That is in place, and the next phase of the plan is in progress now. All is well. You may recognise me, I am from your recent history and I have come here to study the stars. I have a sense of humour and I do not tell you my name. I am to tell you that the departure of the animals was as arranged by themselves. Some of them will be waiting and some of them come and go in your lives and that's very beautiful. Feeling of loss for any person or animal, not necessary. You miss touch yes, but a leaf may fall and touch your bodies. In the water, when you are bathing your feet, you will feel little ripples. These feelings on your body have come from the immense love of those that have gone before you, the immense love in both animal and human energies. There is only Energy. You are energy bodies. YOU ARE MADE OF STARDUST. The stars make the humans. You are never separated from that. We are always with you. We always have been and we shall continue. That is the plan. Never different.

Heather: May I ask a question?

Hannah: You may.

Heather: Is there any way in which we can improve our service to the Divine

Energy?

Hannah: If I tell you you are already perfect, you cannot improve on perfection. You are in the likeness and image of the Most High. It is only your concept that you need to improve or get nearer. You do not need to be any different from what you are. It is how *you* see it. You perceive beauty in another being, like your beautiful dog. A lot of people they look with Human eye and make judgement. But those who can see with the eye of Ra, with the eye of the Sun, with the Eye of the Most High, with the Eye of the Goddess, will see her beauty. The animals are beautiful exactly as they are. The birds are never ugly. The birds don't need to improve and neither does your Misha,

Misha is Heather's little scrap of a poodle, who never weighed more than 1.5 kilos in her life!

She is perfection, and so, Children of the Most High, you are already perfect, in the Divine Ray. Keep to your path. Keep your faith. Keep all that you have and it will flow from you, constantly renewed. The more you give, like Hannah's bag of crystals, as she gives out, so the bag refills, and as you give out so you are perfected in your image, always. It has long been so. But you have been corrupted, and as the wise and beautiful Shaman, Angel Ruiz says, you were *domesticated*. If you know that you *can* have freedom, you *have* freedom. You have everything you need. All you need is with you. Just stay with your realisations. You are doing perfectly. We love you deeply and abidingly and we bless you and thank you. We may come to this table again with you. There are many energies here, around this beautiful table. The majesties are here. They preside. They will govern it, and what is to be held for each time. We bid you farewell, and the girls, in their beauty, will carry you forward. Abide in the peace of your hearts and know that you are loved and cherished beyond reason. Thank you.

Heather: Thank you.

Chapter Thirteen

Hannah's Third Journey

In this journey Hannah felt she needed to obtain and clear some information and negativity pertaining to her own earthly life, in order to be a pristine channel for the conduction of sacred knowledge of a higher order to the Earth Plain.

Hannah: I'm not sure where we are to go.

Heather: I think you are going to be taken to a place of Spiritual Awareness.

Hannah: Right.

Heather: And I believe you're actually there now.

Hannah: I seem to be in the usual place. It's as if I cross the causeway, go up the pathway to the St Michael's Mount, and about three quarters of the way up there's a stone bench to the left of the path and there I find the two angels.

Hannah here refers to the daughters of Yvonne and Heather, who passed at the ages of young womanhood into Spirit.

I can sit here with them and look out over the water and towards Marazion. It's a lovely day. It's very peaceful. There are only the birds, and it seems to be around midday time, but there are no people around. They've all gone off somewhere else, so it's quite comfortable to be here, and they say I must count, and go back, ... five, four, three, two, ... five, four, three ... Age three is the first pinpoint. I can't remember where I was at age three in this lifetime.

Heather: Well, the information is coming through in a minute.

Hannah: The back of my head is hurting.

This is where the Ancient Brain, known as the Cerebellum is.

This is where all the information is stored. I'm sitting on my own in a field, or is it a big garden? I can't see very far. It feels like a big garden. ....

Heather: More information coming.

Hannah: And I'm *two* people. I'm Hannah, because that's what they call me, but I'm also this other person. Hannah is sitting and playing with the flowers and the grass, but the other person is, how would you say, an aspect. This is to bring information from the Higher Dimensions into the Earth Field. By sitting on the earth it can be transmitted down. So how? There is no how. There is only sitting on the earth.

The back system is like a pathway. You have nerves, and the nerves are transmitting information, also conducting information *from* the earth. If you can imagine a circle, and halfway along this circle I am sitting, and the energy is... some of it is stored in the brain and some of it is coming in. ... If you sit on the earth, the energy goes down into the earth. It goes right into the earth, comes up the nether regions or plains, and then goes down. What *needs* to go down into the earth *does* so, and some of it is .... It is like there is a whole exchange of energies. I can see it, but it's hard to describe what is happening, because this part of the brain is not, is not available for many. This is the beginning part, when a child is young and still fresh and still able to transmit without too much stress. The child is happy and relaxed in the situation. It is able to give and receive information freely. It's as if what is stored in the brain when you come to the Earth Plain is stored in the deep brain, and then that can be transmitted. Then other energies come through, and you hold that for a certain period of time, and then it's transmitted again. And so there is a constant stream of energy going through the body, being stored, programmed, and let down into the earth, while *other* energies coming up in exchange, on different levels, and then coming down again. And that process continues. At certain periods during its life, the child is programmed. That is an uncomfortable and insincere word. It is the gift that some beings bring. The child knows, at some level, that this is happening. At another level it is playing in the grass. It is able to recognise all the different realms of Mother Earth.

As I write this up, I see in Jude Currivan's latest book, The Eighth Chakra, she is talking about the ninth chakra of the human body, which she says is a non-personal root chakra going about a hand's width down into the ground, thereby making good contact, for the human, with Gaia, the goddess of the Earth. Hannah says that what she is talking about is similar in a way but is operating on a much bigger non personal scale.

Do you have understanding of what is being told? If not, you may ask a question, if you wish.

Heather: I understand.

Hannah: (Sounding very weary) Thank you very much. This is very old ... information .. It is rare. (Deep sigh) Now, shall we go back to the stone bench? I need to rest a minute. The head feels very heavy.

★★★★★★★★★★★★★★★★★★

While Hannah has a rest I would like to share with you a delightful extract from another of Hannah's spirit journeys. It concerns the distribution of gifts to children, prior to birth, while they are still in the Spirit world. It is obvious to me, through the work that we have done together, that Hannah was an extraordinarily gifted child, but this gift has largely gone unnoticed in this lifetime, partly because of the obscure nature of the gift, although it does run through her truly remarkable painting and beautiful poetry also. It is really when she and I get together that the brilliance of her gift becomes visible.

Hannah: There's a great gathering here .. and there are all the Elders. The circle is very large and behind this large circle is another circle, with the *other* Elders, who care for the Soul Children, those still in spirit form, before they come into incarnation. The Soul Children step forward between the adults of the inner circle. They go forward to the centre of the circle, and then turn to face the Elders of the inner circle. Here they each are gifted with the knowledge and the companionship of their soul animals, and also their companions in the crystal, mineral, and plant kingdoms. So each one is imprinted before they go to the Earth Plane. Also a particular attribute is given to each Soul Child, and it comes forward to each one at a certain point in their lives, when they have reached the Earth Plain. They could have intimations of these great gifts when they are very small, and their Elders of the Earth will see this, and so these things are nurtured. At other times the gifts will be disregarded, because the Earth Parents will not understand, but each and every one of humanity *comes* with this. It's going into the circle, and then going out again, with the gifts, but only the elders of the inner circle know the gifts, and which are to be given to whom. This is just one of the degrees of learning that each Soul Child has before it comes here to the Earth Plain.

Hannah: What we lack are the elders who see. Well, we don't necessarily lack them but sometimes the elders are not respected and sometimes the children are not respected. When something is not recognised and respected then it begins to lose its own momentum. It can atrophy. The older people need to be encouraged to remember their place as Elders.

★★★★★★★★★★★★★★★★★

Hannah: Three ...We are counting together. Three ... two .. The age of two. Significant for its attachments made to the different realms in the earth plain. (This is delivered very slowly but surely) The child is sometimes confused, because it's not sure where it's home is. It feels lost. It feels sad. It feels, it feels, um, the head hurts, it feels like ... screaming, and then there's lots of anger. These people say, " Be quiet, Shh. Don't make noise and it will be better," and all these sort of comfort noises, but it misses its own, the child misses it's own true mother. It's earth mother is not its true mother. This child has to, what's the word, ad, ada, adapt, and it is sometimes difficult to *do* that. There is the other child. The brother. He is bored with this child. No understanding. So there is a sense of loss. But the small child will endure. That is all for the two years ... and I can go back now, to the bench.

This has been a very difficult passage to download. Its delivery has been ponderous and slow throughout, possibly due to the age of the child and possibly due to the difficulty of translation, because the information is coming in in one language and has to be simultaneously translated into English. Also the information is coming in to Hannah very quickly, and she slows down the speed of the incoming information by slowing down her delivery.

Hannah: What age next? From Two to One Year. Noise! At one year, lots of noise. Lots of feeling of unhappy. Only when talking with the other realms, then at peace. Then peaceful. Do not like dark rooms. Do not like angry voices. Do not like ... *spitting*!

This comes from the angry little brother.

Heather: (With a sense of urgency) More information trying to get through!

Hannah: I don't like, I don't like ... What are they called? Covers. I don't like covers. I don't like, I don't like, I don't like being here, I don't like this place. I have left my home. I have come to this place. I don't like it and I can't get away. I don't feel welcome here. I don't, I don't, I don't! I have been left here and I don't like it. I shout about it but nobody hears me. I call to them to come back for me, but they have left without me, and I can't go *on* like this. I don't know what to do. Deep sigh) I don't know where I can go next. I feel very cross about this. Why could they leave me here? Why did they leave me here? Why didn't they carry me with them? Why didn't they carry me? Why didn't they come for me? They just dropped me down here and left me here. Why did the Star Beings leave me behind? Why? (Deeply upset) I don't know .....

Heather: I think you go back to the safety of the bench Hannah. You'll be fine. (Sigh from Hannah) Are you back on your bench?

Hannah: (Sounding normal again) Yes, I am now.

Heather: (Gently) Take a rest for a minute or two. You are doing really well. Now there's more information trying to get through.

Hannah: I think I carry, I think I carry that grief, it's like a lump in my head, but I haven't known until now what it was. I didn't know, I didn't *know*. Now I *do* have an understanding of it, and that feels alright.

Heather: More information coming.

Hannah: Now I feel that ..... it is beginning to fall into place now, in one way, about this communication, that nothing ever left. It was *I* who left *it*. This enduring person, who stayed and endured what was necessary. Now I'm here on the bench and I'm not sure in which direction ...

Heather: To go?

Hannah: Yes.

Heather: Ten thousand years, fifteen thousand years, sixteen, seventeen thousand years, forward.

Hannah: (Deep sigh) Now there's (much hesitation) Excuse me, there is much problem with language, bear with me. I see a collection of rainbow bridges. There are also the holders of the rainbow bridges. The rainbow bridges are in the Human mind. Actually being, how would you say " Out there", they are also "In there," being inside the human mind. They are also connected with the Larger Mind patterns. So each person now has a unique quality and the humans back in what you would call the Old Days had inklings of that, and now they're actually able to use these bridges for a type of travel in the different dimensions. You travel the colours and each colour has a sound vibration, and if you're not with your being, then you can align with a certain colour. This is very difficult to describe, because the emphasis in the old days was about making manifest in the physical and then, in a sense, the power was taken away, because it was used for ul .. ul .. ulterior motives, and so the information had to be kept, how you say, "Under wraps ." Now we have much progression to living in harmony. Here is where the species on earth, called extinct, fit in. No such word as extinct. There is only evolution. And so all the species which would be appear to be lost are not lost, never lost. Every realm species has value. Nothing created is without value. No high value, no low value, only value. All species live here, in harmony. All space is in harmony. All energies in harmony. Here humans are, how would you say, as a species, evolved. Some fell away. Some species fell away. They were not able to evolve, but what they became was a necessary part also of their own evolutionary pattern. It would appear, in the old days, that they thought all humans were as one. They were as one, but their patterning was, a difficult word, ... different. Made differently. So there are ... other many plains of existence, to which the other ones fell away. But they are also evolving. Everything is a con, con, how you say, a constant. Would you like to ask me anything? I am not sure what you would wish to know.

Heather: Well, I'm curious as to why we are being taken forward to such a long way ahead.

The last time when we went into progression one of the masters took us forward to between thirteen thousand and fourteen thousand years.

We now acknowledge that we are receiving Progressions, and have started calling them that.

This time we have been taken forward even further. Is there any reason why we, in particular, are allowed to access this information?

Hannah: It is wise you ask this. It is not for, how would you say, general information. You share it within a small group, because if everybody was to know this they would become (with great emphasis) UNMINDFUL, and NOT CAREFUL or RESPECTFUL.

We have since received permission to release this script, because of the urgency required, and because only the enlightened ones will, in fact, both find and take seriously the information given.

At the moment, in your time frame, there is a very difficult period at hand. Hannah has indicated, ... we have indicated through her, that this time is CRUCIAL for the contracts, that you came with, to be remembered, to honour your life path, to honour your contracts, with all the planetary realms, even those you don't know about, to acknowledge them by just saying your greeting and your thanks and also to all the animal realms who were here long before you on the Earth Plain. The animals came and they grew from the earth. They were given star knowledge, because the planet earth contains the star knowledge, and man has forgotten his contracts are with the animals, with your loyal and trusted teachers and friends. They honour you with their love and their devotion.

Heather: Thank you.

Hannah: You may ask another question if you want to. I have the energy for one more, if you so wish, and I would like to say *my thank you* to all of you gathered here.

Heather: Could I ask about .... This is a very *ordinary* question in some ways, but could you tell me something about the choice of things that people eat, for example the eating of animals or the eating of vegetables or fruits or nuts. Can you give me any advice on that?

Hannah: Indeed yes. As long as you acknowledge the gift, of the wheat that makes your flour, of the animals that make your ... Hannah's particular favourite is butter. If you eat the organic that is the best that you can do. You can always ask if this is correct for the body. Your body can respond and say, "Yes, thank you that would be nice." Take for example, Hannah has ice cream, and late last night she was told she could eat ice cream. In the ordinary course of events, we would not recommend eating ice cream at that late time of the solar night, but that information was correct, because if you deny, constantly deny, yourselves the beauteous and bountiful gifts of your Mother Nature, then you set up war within the body. But if you acknowledge that you like these things, then *have them*, a little. Or if you know yourselves to over indulge, then that necessarily teaches you a lesson not to do so. Be governed by your feelings and honour the gifts from this beautiful planet that you are travelling on. By the way, you are all travelling, and time measured in your years has some significance but not as great as you would esteem it to be. It is only a measurement, but there are many measurements. Yours is not the only one. What is a long time? It is only really a short time, for all is coming and going, and it is where you've chosen to be, at separate times, for your growth. We bless and honour you. Your little group is very large. Never underestimate the power of three.

Heather: Thank you.

Yvonne: Thank you.

Hannah: (Deep sigh) I believe I'm back on the bench. I feel much freer now. It is a burden for the physical body to carry some of this information, but to be able to share it among the esteemed company is of great value. Thank you.

Is there another place? There seems to be an indication of a totally different direction, to which we have not been. I don't know where that is.

Heather: (Confidently) Now we can change. We are going backwards in time. It looks like a thousand years back and that may just be a device for finding something.

Hannah: I get a very funny feeling, like laughing. (Chuckles) I think it is the fault of the Buddha you brought. There is a huge teaching going on. In the early days, ... Oh *no!* Oh *yes!* I am a disciple of the Buddha! Oh! (More chuckles) Oh gosh! Oh gosh! How can you live in Heaven on Earth? (Still more chuckles) Oh my *Goodness me!*

Do you know, we walk above the ground, we walk above the ground. Like hovercraft we glide, so that we may not damage *anything* upon the earth. We glide over the ground. Our energy can lift us up mountains or take us beneath the earth. Indeed we are blessed. This is a state of bliss. You can hear the Heavenly choirs, and the grunt of pigs! (Chuckles) All the contradictions of the world are one. They are not separate, they are all linked together. The horrendous and the beautiful, all has meaning. All has no meaning. All is ridiculous and all is Holy. Oh my goodness! I can understand now, people like Mother Teresa. She ministered to those who needed ministering to, and it was difficult, but not difficult, for she was in love with everything. The true attainment is to be in love with everything. That is the state of Bliss. That is what we attain to. We dream it. Live it and change your lives for ever. All is all, and nothing is lacking. Be present as much as possible. In the most everyday is the most Divine. I must leave now. I have places to go and things to do, while I remain present with you, always. (Deep sigh) I've just been told, no you can't, but go back to being a hermit in a wood. (Chuckles) I have to be Hannah. (More chuckles)

Heather: Thank you to everyone and everything.

Hannah: Blessed be all, thank you.

Chapter Fourteen

Hannah's Fourth Journey

Heather: Hannah, we've met here this afternoon for another Spirit Journey, a Regression/Progression as we have learnt to call them. I'm sure you are well prepared and I feel that Energies have been gathering anyway, over the last hour, so we are probably ready to go. I'm just waiting for the final signal from the pendulum. (The pendulum shows the Love, Truth, Gift, Healing Line.) And now we can go.

Hannah: I'm standing at an entrance to a garden, and the garden is like no other you have ever seen. It's very difficult to describe, except that everything is tinged with gold, all the flowers, and it's very light gold. It's like dusting (talcum) powder. I've opened the gate and I'm stepping into the garden and what I'm struck by is the immense peace. ... There's somebody coming towards me.

Heather: They're coming into view. They're taking their time. They're coming from a distance. (From this point on Hannah has two identities, herself and her Higher Self.)

Hannah: Yes .... I'm finding it difficult to speak this because the Hannah part of me realises that the Biblical phrases leap up in front of me, and, although it's *similar* to that, it's not that. It's more than that. It's the Garden of Gethsemane after the Crucifixion, but there's some confusion about the whole thing, because the Crucifixion has been, .. misaligned I think is the word, or misinterpreted.

Heather: Misaligned is better.

The pendulum shows, by means of the Truth Line, that 'misaligned' is the right word.

Hannah: Right. Oh, my Goodness! Someone took the energy of that part of the dream.

It was stolen for power. It was misaligned, for power!

AFTERWARDS

Hannah: Everybody comes to the planet with part of the *dream* of the planet. They also have their own personal dream. All the worlds have dreams, the Animal kingdom, the Plant kingdom, the Mineral kingdom and so on. If I sat with a stone, for example, the stone would begin to tell me *its* dream. If the stone was a very expensive diamond, it could tell me its worth. I could then take that knowledge and use it, because the stone had given me a teaching. I could use it to acquire things like wealth, status and position. It says here that part of the dream was stolen away for power, in this case for religion, (rites of worship and a system of beliefs) as opposed to spirituality. (The state of relating to the world of Spirit) This is most important. Through religion you get power. If that is misaligned or misused, that is when the illusions can be set in place.

Heather: So the dream refers to what? The dream refers to the incident?

Hannah: Yes, because in a sense, even as we sit here, we're in a dream. Of course we can feel our physical bodies, but in actual fact, while we sit here we *could* also be somewhere else. The point is, however, that we're *actually* here and we're *doing* this. We're bringing the dream into *form*.

Heather: Into manifestation? So if there's a *Stealer* of the dream, they can bring it into a different manifestation?

Hannah: Exactly, and that is why you have to be careful with knowledge that you are given, because another person can take it and use it for *their* part of the dream, which they might *think* is correct, while also using it to their own advantage. But there's a bigger thing still going on here, especially with the power of religion, because people are always seeking, and the very thing they seek of course, they have inside them.

Heather: Spirituality, as opposed to religion, may be experienced by the individual through their own six senses of seeing, hearing, touching, tasting, smelling, and of course intuition. We can be in direct link with all that is, with no intermediary, although wise beings who have themselves been in incarnation, are often guides as to how life could best be lived. Good teachers on earth such as Jesus, and the Buddha, to name but two, are important way showers, helping us realise our own divinity, grace and beauty. I have a lovely friend whose belief system is encapsulated in the sentence, "I lift mine eyes unto the hills, from whence cometh my help." Holy Bible, King James Version, psalm 121 verse 1. The psalm is a song of pilgrimage, the pilgrimage of life.

Heather: More information coming.

Hannah: The three days is important. The three days of coming from the Darkness into the Light. The three days of transition.

Like the quotation, from the Apostle's Creed, concerning Jesus of Nazareth, "Jesus Christ, his (God's) only son, our Lord .... was crucified, dead, and buried, He descended into hell ; the third day he rose again from the dead, He ascended into heaven." The Book of Common Prayer.

Heather: More information is very close. If you need help, just let me know.

Hannah: I think I need to be asked some sort of question that will actually propel the answer because working through Hannah is sometimes difficult. She has a certain resistance to the dogma of Christianity, as it is put about, and rightly so, because that has been her defence, but she needs to see beyond that, and she still has difficulty.

There's quite a battle going on, well not a battle, but quite a struggle. Is there a question?

Heather: I've got a key here.

Keys open doors, in regressions and reveal hidden truths.

I wish to invoke the laser quartz wand.

Hannah: Right.

Heather: To cut through this.

Hannah: Now, now we're *properly* in the Garden. I hear the phrase, "Thou art with me always".

This is the power of the Holy Spirit, which is in One, always, and is not divided against anything. It runs through all genuine sincere Spiritual belief systems. In a sense we have not lost that connection, because the Holy Spirit is in the flowers, and you have only to look at the sky at night. The Holy Spirit resides in everything.

The truth is available, and the truth of the matter is in the Energy's possession. An Energy is speaking ... *They're going too fast.* (Speaking to the guides) " Please slow down."

AFTER WORDS

Heather: Could you tell me something of what it feels like for you to be in regression? How do they give you the information?

Hannah: Well, I have to ask them to slow down because the information is a bit like a speeded up tape. There's so *much* information coming, and I have to be really clear about what I'm receiving. The clarity is there, but it's just the speed of it. Also sometimes they'll show me pictures, so there's so much coming and going and I'm thinking, "Hang on a minute, could you just *slow down?*" I'm not saying this out loud but in my other consciousness. This is all so that I don't miss anything. Of course there are things I'm going to miss, but the guides soon come and give it to me a bit later on.

Heather: When they give you the information in some foreign language or suchlike, is there any way that you can explain to us what that might feel like to you?

Hannah: Well, with most of it I feel quite comfortable.

Heather: Do you hear sounds in your head or do you see things written down or what?

Hannah: No, nothing like that. The Energies plug into the energies of my speaking voice, which is connected to my heart and my intellect. The intellect, in order to make a correct choice, needs to be linked with the heart, so that everything works together to bring the information. Because in a sense, human language is still quite dense, they have a problem with the density of the language. In a way their language, when talking to me, is simpler than Human language. They can say something extremely succinctly in just one word, but then they sometimes use many words in order to get the meaning clear to me, and they're very careful, because they have to be impeccable. And we need to be impeccable as well, because in a way the whole process is one of alchemy, of transformation, of the raising of dense, human matter towards Divine Level.

Hannah: (Great difficulty here.) It's as if some, how would you say, walk - ins appeared with some of the early Disciples, who were in a heightened state of awareness, through grief. Their consciousness was raised. There was a vulnerability in that, but also there was a reason for it. Because of this, the disciples acquiesced to the powerful Walk-ins, letting them into their psyches.

Acquiesce - to rest satisfied, without making opposition, Latin, ad , to, quies, rest.

The Walk - ins used the vulnerable energy of the disciples and the fact that they were not strongly rooted in their physical bodies at this time, for political power, because the walk-ins had a more world view. Now, at the time this seemed to be appropriate, but it wasn't for humanity, and that's where the great mistake has been made, a mistake as in missing the mark: some disciples missed the mark. They were not intentionally evil, but evil intention came of it. The thing is that this can be rectified, extracted.

Walk -ins are Energies who are able to take over the consciousness of a person at a weak moment, maybe when that person is feeling vulnerable after a shock, illness, or suchlike. This is, however, done by agreement at some level between the Walk - in and the host person's consciousness. The word is sometimes bandied about, but genuine walk -ins are very rare.

Hannah: The vision of the Garden with dusting of gold, that was a metaphor. And so the garments, robes, bodies of the disciples, they got touched by the gold. The misalignment was not intentional, but the things that were written were not truthful. They were garnered in something other than truth. How would you say? Polluted, the River of Truth was polluted. And so the energy of the river could not flow as freely. As a result your concepts, ideas and even your realisation of beauty, that so many struggle for, has been polluted. That is the greatest sadness.

AFTERWARDS

Hannah: The garden is the Garden of the Heart. When this event happened the gold dust was touching everybody in that situation, except one, except the one whose energy was not quite in line (with Love, Truth, Gift, Healing). This creates a weakness, so the walk - ins were able to search out the energy of the weaker one, the weak link, and obtain that energy. They stole it. They stole the knowledge, not all of it, but enough to make power. You will not be able to see the beauty of the world as it truly is until you recognise your own beauty. Remember Beauty is Truth, Truth is Beauty. The body of another, for example, may be misaligned through genetic structures and so on, but when you see them through the truth of your own beauty, then you will see something which is truly amazing. Beauty also has a feel of course, or a sound, and so beauty is something which is inherent in everything, experienced through the power of the human senses.

Hannah: We are now come to a point where this can be altered. This is the task. For you are not just on earth as you see it, walking around in your physical bodies and your other bodies, but you are also are in …You call it Heaven. It has another name, but because you have been tainted, touched, by this other, then you cannot see it. That is why the sight is not clear.

Now through a glass darkly. Then face to face. (1 Corinthians 13:12)

Heather: I keep hearing in my head, "Elysian Fields."

Among the Greeks, "The abode of the Blessed Dead." - Chambers 20th Century Dictionary.

Hannah: (Brightening) That's right, that's right. Absolutely, that's where you really live! That is the beauty of it! There is nowhere to go, you are already here! There is no need to struggle Here on earth we are going to Heaven, or as you might say, you would be going to the realm of little light if you were a really bad person.

AFTER WORDS

Hannah: It all depends which way you are looking. You can look towards the light or you can look towards the darkness. Don't get too heavy about it. You are here, and if you are doing the work, whatever form that takes, then you will get the realisations that are right for you at this time, as part of the work. The higher self is already perfect, but there is the mundane matter self which needs to be slowly but surely perfected. This is Alchemy. The perfection needs to be RE -MEMBERED, put back together again. Choice is about responsibility and responsibility is about how you **respond** to any given person or situation.

Heather: So often over the years of working in healing I have had to remind people that they *do have choices*, but we need to take responsibility for the choices that we make.

Hannah: With that realisation, and with the opening of the sound waves and the colour waves, this is the medicine. This is the medicine that will open Heaven's door. The Higher Intelligence which recognises the beauty of these energies resides in all the organs of the body. We humans know what sound belongs to us, in terms of music and the sounds of Nature. We know what colour we need and so on, if we learn to listen to our intuition. You are already here. Hannah's resistance was due to her fight with her own Demons of Negativity. For a time she was dis - abled. Sometimes she would get glimpses, but if there were no others who appeared to know, then she was not willing to face the fear of the Great Aloneness. That was her concept, because she has been what she *felt* was alone, and she has not been so. Now she has had glimpses, certainly in the recent past, well all her life really in this lifetime, of what Heaven is, but *still* she resisted, because she was frightened, frightened that too much joy would kill her, too much happiness she felt she did not deserve, too much bliss would take her away from her Family of Nations, but that was the pollution of her river. That was the burden, but the burden was hers, unshared by others …

Heather: And now I think we can move. We're going to go forward, minutes, hours, days, weeks, months, years, decades, centuries, millennia, more than millennia! We'll go forward in increments of five thousand years, five, ten, fifteen, not fifteen. Eleven , twelve, thirteen, fourteen, fourteen thousand years forward.

Hannah: You will have to bear with the language problem, maybe. The Earth has ascended into Heaven. This is a human concept, is that understood? And there is great clarity here. There is this thing. It's not a black hole, but it's more contained, more like a square. If you had a map, and black squares on the map, denoting ...

Heather: A grid?

Hannah: Yes. Upon the grid are black spots. They're not voids which you can pass through, they are spaces with doors. These are very necessary to indicate information to the energy beings which we now are. With timing, when the timing is right, you may open these little doors. If you open the door, that would be the equivalent of Humans' past history, It's very difficult to explain

Heather: Archive?

Hannah: Yes, but the dark doors indicate to the energy beings that we are, that, when we have an expansion of the numbers of energy beings happening in our midst, we need to take the new ones along to the doors to indicate to them how it is. When new energies step forward, the new energy children, as they are before they are born, are shown different aspects and possibilities for growth before they go into incarnation.

Heather: (Misunderstanding) Excuse me, when you say growth, do you mean like a growth in the human body, like cancer?

Hannah: That is one of the black spots, or dark doors.

Heather: I'm just thinking about the piece that Heather and Hannah did yesterday about the matrix, about the cellular structure of the body being affected by the will of the Matrix, the Divine Feminine Energy. One definition of the matrix is, 'Intercellular substance, cementing material.

Could this be the net? "Truth" says the pendulum. It is the linking together of all things.

Hannah: So you have a net, and on the net are squares. Some of the squares are how would you say, dark. The squares are like doors, and if you open the door, you can see down through history. Oh, it's so difficult to describe *history* because it's just not like that at all. But for the sake of reason, ... Excuse me, my colleague is saying, "Limited reason".

Heather: Could I ask, who is your colleague?

Hannah: This is a Chinese Mandarin, who is a shaman.

Heather: Is this Being there with you all the time?

Hannah: No, only from time to time, when I need assistance.

Hannah: (Continuing) You open the dark door and then you can see what humans would call Hell. There would be wars, famine, all sorts of destructive blueprints. Now, these are necessary only in relation to where you are looking, so this has to do with sight. If you have the example of a woman with cancer and you open the door on the grid to cancer and you look down through the history ... (Remember the word history is his story, or her story.) ...you could then do a regression to tell her story. A woman, if she feels able, needs to tell her story and if she looks at it from her point of view, then she will *see* and she can understand cancer. Understanding has great curative effects. WISDOM AND UNDERSTANDING PUSHES OUT FEAR AND PAIN. Even children get cancer, sometimes at an extremely young age. These children come, in a sense as an angelic being, bearing angelic energy and so that is what predominates. They come for only a short time to teach other humans what the angelic energy is about, and then they leave. But they always leave their mark. This is a profound sacrifice, and also a profound teaching.

Now when we have a new energy on this ascended planet, we need to bring the energy to look through the doorways so that they may have a choice. They may have a choice to look down through the history of Humanity as it used to be, with the wars and the famine and destruction, but they also have a choice to not go into that, but to look instead towards the light, and the "future". Until you know that you have a choice, you are *floating energy in this ascended planet and the magnificent aura of this ascended planet.* The new spark of consciousness would be able to choose which way it would settle. I feel that this is probably quite a definite, significant shift, because at this time, which is also the present, there are more and more beings than previously, choosing to bring an enlightened viewpoint into incarnation, while still keeping a recognition of the dark energies.

When we talk about the Matrix. This IS, just as some of you on the Earth Plane at the moment would say God IS. The Matrix, just now, on humans' earth, is merely a concept, but let me explain. It is certainly round. Round, like the Earth is round, round like the spirals are round, round as the Space/time continuum is round, as a womb or an egg is round. Women carry this in their physical bodies, and when they get a sense, a realisation of who they really are, it is then that Peace can return to the Earth. Men can begin to realise this also, if they work on the development of their intuitive feminine side.

The Matrix is a creation. The Matrix IS.

Heather: I get "Perfection", in my mind.

Hannah: Yes, I have to be really...

Heather: Impeccable?

Hannah: Yes, What I'm being told is that, at this point in humans' history ...You see in times gone by ... It's very difficult for me, as a Being, to be able to speak in terms of time, in humans' terms, but in times gone by, and this is to do with the moldavite, when this knowledge was given to humans previously, it was misused.

The moldavite tektite is a seed carrier from the Matrix, a deep green, glasslike jem, known as the star born stone of transformation, which is said to have fallen to earth 14.8 million years ago. There is a book, Moldavite, by Simmons and Warner, Heaven and Earth Publishing, Vermont USA, ISBN 0-9621910-0-0

Hannah: You will hear this knowledge. You may keep this one tape and that's all, and at any given time you might be told to destroy it. Do you understand that? Hannah doesn't need it, she carries the energy of what is happening.

The guides have since given permission for this information being released, because there is a sense of urgency to save the planet.

So, the information, about the Matrix –

This is the Seat (Long pause) of Knowledge and Wisdom beyond Time itself. It is carried like a seed, in the womb of the unnameable, so your bodies, in human form, have that seed. You carry that seed within you and it can be in the bones, in the blood and in any of the organs.

Doctors have recently discovered something called cellular memory. It occurs sometimes in organ transplant patients, who develop traits which seem to be part of the personality make-up of the person by whom the organ was donated, as if our individual uniqueness goes through every cell in our bodies but is capable of 'crossing over' into another host body.

There are also cells called stem cells which are developed in the bones, which can be separated out and then reintroduced into the body by being directly injected into damaged organs, such as the liver. When this happens the stem cells appear to be capable of searching out the damaged area of the organ and bringing about rejuvenation.

Hannah: The organs on the inside of the human body are a Sacred Garden. You have clever people and not so clever people acting on the human body, but unless they're aligned completely with the Sacred in that moment of performing surgery, or whatever is being done, then their experiment will have to go on and on through Humanity, but you are reaching a point in your time scale when you can only do this, achieve this, with an open heart, because if the heart is not aligned then failure and tragedies happen.

On the other hand, in the matter of the small boy you were working with today, you were working with the seed that was placed many aeons ago in the Compassionate Heart. You must realise you are not really in control. Your own compassionate heart will bring the things that are needed exactly to you. There is no struggle, there is flow. It flows towards you, it flows through you and that which you do *not* need will flow *from* you. That will then be taken up by the people who need it, so you are like a storehouse of energy, and the energies, like magnets are drawn to you, there are great healings and great compassionate moves. With the beautiful movements and your beautiful impeccability, *there is the Beauty*. The beauty is in the word, and the beauty is in the movement. Now you have asked me a question. Could you repeat that because I seem to have strayed a little from the going into the squares of what I would call the dark doors.

Heather: Well, we were talking about the dark door phenominon, and I asked whether that could be a representation of a cancer or other problem in the body. I was saying that yesterday Hannah and I were talking about the Matrix. I was given the word Matrix, and the information that the Matrix actually bore the ultimate responsibility for the well being for each and every cell in our body. Thus without the Divine will of the Matrix, wishing it so, there could be no Healing.

Hannah: Correct. correct. Then the human must go through the dark door, and what they perceive as their darkness is shown. You hit the dark door and you go in, and then nothing can help you except the light of your beloved soul, and it may only be a matchstick, a small light in the dark.

Heather: The Divine Sparklet as spoken of by Meister Erkhart?

This is the sparklet, existent in us *all*, which we inherit from the Divine Source, and carry throughout our lives. Meister Erkhart is a 14th century German mystic.

Hannah: Correct, and with that you can then feel your way. You see, humans have been so blinded. There is no blame attached to this. We are trying to do work similar to rescue work, but, with you humans, be assured we have passed the point of no return. We cannot go back to complete darkness, ever again. The way now is to assist.

Heather: I was writing a book this morning. (Heather Bray's first book, "Keys to Wisdom.")

Hannah: We *admire that*. We are so enjoying what you are doing, and we sometimes have movement with the energy, and that is for amusement.

AFTER WORDS

Heather: What do you mean when you speak about movement of the energy for amusement? Hannah: Well when they see you thinking, "I'm tearing my hair out here, trying to do this *difficult job!" they say* , *"Oh, look she's at it again."* And the paper gets thrown through the printer in great handfuls, so that you can only laugh, and so the tension is broken!

Heather: Well, there have been strange and funny moments at times, when I can't get things to come right, and suddenly the printer starts throwing out loads of paper all on its own. So they're playing me up a bit then, for amusement? Just to see how much I'll take!

Hannah: They don't mean to be harmful, but they'll push you to the very edge.

Heather: Just to see if I'll pass muster really.

Hannah: Oh yes. To see if you've got stickability!

Hannah: Do not struggle Dear One. You are wonderfully well equipped with your inner knowledge. That is all coming forward. Excuse me, I interrupt. You were saying, with your book?

Heather: Well I had the insight this morning, because I was going through the different energies that I read from a person who came to see me. I worked through Body Energy and Everyday Mind Energy and got to Spiritual Energy. I realise it was an insight that came to me because I was trying to explain, to whoever is going to read this book, what the real energy of spirit (spiritual energy) was like.

The four energies, which all need to be aligned for perfect well being are Body energy, Everyday Mind Energy, Spiritual Energy and Deep mind Energy, Therefore the spiritual aspect of the human is fundamental for well being in its broadest and truest sense.

I was given an example from my guides, through a movement of the pendulum, that would translate as "Just keep going, it will be alright" and I was trying to explain what I would say to a client when I saw that pattern. I then came to the realisation that, unless we have this direct, almost laser - like beam to the open heart, with our Spiritual Energy we're not perfectly aligned, and therefore we cannot have perfect well being. This is true if we have just one energy which is slightly off alignment.

Hannah: Yes.

Heather: So the spiritual aspect of the personality is fundamental to well-being.

AFTER WORDS

Hannah: You can get to the point when you know you're off, but if you have fear you will pursue whatever you are pursuing, despite knowing that things could be another way. The fear will stop you. I know that one.

Heather: Fear will stop you doing what's right?

Hannah: Yes, exactly. It's fear of the unknown, so again, it's, "What is your darkness? What do you fear in the dark?" There's no blame attached to this. It's only discovering what your fear is and then you can go into it and go past it.

Heather: You joust with your demons as it were?

Hannah: Absolutely.

Hannah: Absolutely. They *must be aligned*. When your planet earth was giving birth to herself, her SELF was *more* than she was. Now we reside here in MORE THAN SHE WAS, and we can reach you through the different intermediaries.

Each one of us, in the course of our Earthly incarnation, has the task to rebirth ourselves, in order to become more than we were.

The alignment *had to be*. Humans liked the planet earth. They are in no way separated from her, and as she labours, so the labours are coming to an end because of each and every energy (person) on the planet. Don't be too sad that the animals are going because they have done their task, and their energy has evolved. Even your prehistoric animals did their task, and then they left. But nothing ever went away, nothing, because you are continually evolving.

Heather: We're part of a process.

Hannah: The planet is. The *whole Universe*, as you can even conceive it, is. This is really a bit big for the human brain, but the heart understands. So there is a continual process of evolving, and then folding, and then coming up, because death is not real as seen by humans. Death is a process of evolving. The human body is dense matter. Its considered concept is dense matter. Think of how your doctoring has evolved from knives cutting up things, now to your lasers. That is, you would say, an advancement, but it was always there. It's just that the humans, because they were so polluted, could not see.

AFTER WORDS

Hannah: Those who knew probably had a fear you see, so there was a darkness which came down. It's about timing as well. We know there's always a perfect time for everything, and it can't be too forward or too backward. It's got to be absolutely 'spot on.' In a sense, although there's no time, we need time to evolve. It's an eternal paradox isn't it, because time IS and time ISN'T, and when you're in the ISN'T there' no time at all. So when people are evolving, they're already evolved, but they've got to do it in their own TIMING.

Heather: Yes, and of course the laser was always there. It was just that people hadn't found it yet, they weren't looking in the right place I suppose?

Hannah: No. They hadn't asked the right questions. They weren't evolved enough to ask the right questions.

Hannah: There was power and all sorts of negative things. Now that is being cleared away. That is evolving. It is so difficult to explain. I hope I haven't made too much difficulty.

Heather: No, I feel it's fine. I understand perfectly.

Hannah: (Cheerfully) Hannah's negativity is quite strong sometimes, but the energy is good to work with.

Heather: We need to be as perfectly aligned to the energy of our true (and perfect,) self, as possible.

Hannah: Excellent. (Claps her hands) Excellent, thank you. Yes we do.

Heather: I get that you should take a few minutes rest.

Hannah: Bottom back is hurting of the Hannah. There's something happening.

Heather: Now we're ready to go somewhere. and we're going to go forward.

Hannah: Yes

Heather: Minutes, hours, days, weeks, months.

Hannah: Birth.

Heather: Yes, nine months, I think. Nine months forward.

Hannah: Yes, difficult birth. Difficult birth.

Heather: More information trying to get through. I invoke the polar bear.

Hannah: Difficult birth. (Utters a sound of birthing)

Heather: Now you're alright. You're born in the Caspian Sea. (This information was dropped directly into my mind.)

Hannah: Now the dolphins are here, and the Water Lights, and the Sea Beings, and they are bringing me to one of the most Heavenly places. And now I am joining in the Spirals, the dance of the Spirals. (Long pause)

Water lights are Spirit Energies of the water.

Heather: I have a working pattern. Something is being done to your energy here.

Hannah: The energy of the dolphins. Hannah was really supposed to be a dolphin, but was given a choice. She had two ways to go. One was a human, and one was a dolphin child. (Pause and sigh)

Heather: It was as if it wasn't a very equal choice. (Shown by means of the pendulum.)

Hannah: No (sadly.)

Heather: My information is that the choice was much biased towards being a Human child.

Hannah: Yes. (sadly)

Heather: (Pause) More work being done. Now the energy is on the Fear/Pain line. This is psychic surgery.

Hannah: Right.

Heather: Pulling out now. Energy on to the healing line again. Little circles (very specific work being done).

Hannah: (Sigh)

Heather: Opening out into slightly bigger circles, and bigger

Hannah: (Another sigh)

Heather: And bigger.

Hannah: (Another exhaling of air)

Heather: The negativity has gone forward, just forward of the Balance Line now, so I pull out again. It's come on to the Healing Line and there's an impetus to go forward. And I think I need another key. The key is the pyrite.

This is the fire stone, so-called because it is struck against a piece of flint to make a spark and thus fire. Hannah is a keeper of the children's fire.

AFTER WORDS

Heather: This made me think of the Ring of Fire (spoken of in Regressions One and Two). I need to explain the North American tradition of Talking Sticks and the Children's Fire. Three simple rules are often set for council:

Speak honestly, be brief, and listen from the heart. The group chooses one or two leaders or facilitators whose job it is to keep the process on track. To empower each person to speak in turn, a "talking stick" or other object is chosen to be passed around the circle, traditionally clockwise, in the "sun direction." The talking stick can be anything from a flower to a traditional hand-crafted artefact. If possible, a fire is built in the centre of the circle or a candle is lit to set the mood for storytelling. This has come to be called the "children's fire," following the Sundance teaching of Hyemeyohsts Storm. When we say, "Never cross the children's fire," we mean no one is to interrupt the person holding the talking stick except, that is, as in the traditional Native American councils, to express approval of what has been said by saying, "Ho!"

Hannah: Yes. So there's a link there between the dolphins, the child and the Children's Fire. So maybe this is part of the children's fire story.

Heather: The pendulum is saying Truth.

Hannah: Yes, somehow there are many children who come through that way, through being granted that. It is an honour, having that, because it's about existing in a different

161

dimension, as a dolphin cum human child. Then what happens, if you're granted that, is that you become, by dint of passing through that way, a protector of the Children's fire. In other words you protect the childlike innocence of mankind, the innocence of the One and the many.

Heather: And now we've got Balance. I'm just waiting to see whether I've finished. No, I don't think so. We seem to have gone on to Obsession. So I'm going to pull that Obsession out because that's "Love gone too far ." Now we're gone on to the Love Line. (Deep inbreath and outbreath from Hannah) A little bit more negativity, and now we're moving the *right* way. (Clockwise) We've come on to the Healing Line. Now there appears to be some very fine work being done somewhere, on to the Healing Line, and now the pendulum has stopped. I think that's because there's no real appropriate affirmation to make.

Hannah: That's correct.

Heather: Because I can't name the Unnameable.

Hannah: (Whispers) Yes.

Heather: So the affirmation is, "In Praise of the Unnameable." (Long pause)

Hannah: That feels different. What happened was that I tried to stay too long in the water,   Love gone too far. See healing above.

And the conflict was between the Human and the Dolphin energy, but the human had set up that conflict, it was not the dolphin. However the dolphin energy says you cannot stay in the water. You must come out of the water, while acknowledging the gift of the water. And I never knew how to do that.

Because dolphins are higher beings, their knowledge is higher than the knowledge of the human at that point.

Heather: And that's the Truth. (Confirmed by the pendulum)

Hannah: Yes. And my Dolphin Family never left me. It was I who had to, not leave them, but recognise where they were and where I was, and who I was without them. Part of the bending over is what dolphins *do*.

Hannah has a curvature of the back.

They leave and dive down into the water. And I was continually, in these last years, trying to go back there, and I'm not supposed to do that, as yet. (Chuckles, and sighs.) I feel that the body takes on the Mind Set. It acts out the Mind Set, so if you undo that, you allow the healing. It makes it open like a woman giving birth. It breaks the waters so to speak, and then the correct procedure can go forward. (Deep expulsion of air, followed by a sigh.) Busy Brain Hannah is coming back!

Both healing and regression can be a most useful tools for correcting the Mind Set.

Heather: I'm getting an indication that that may well be the end of the journey. We're nearly there now. What's been the custom is to keep the tape rolling so that if there's anything interesting to be expressed it happens now, rather than have a break.

Hannah: Yes, I felt, instead of swimming .. it's really interesting, because, instead of swimming in the water, I must now *walk upon* the water. That feels like a pretty profound statement. (Pause) Born as a fire sign, the fire was nearly put out with all the water. There's so many questions I would ask and they're all sort of jumbled together at the moment. Making this journey has been really the profoundest thing in my life. I'm just so grateful.

(Long pause)

Heather: Well I'm only an intermediary.

Chapter Fifteen

Hannah's Fifth Journey

The Labours of Hercules - Labour 5
The Field of the Labour
"Originally the zodiac consisted only of ten constellations and, at some date practically unknown, the two constellations, Leo and Virgo, were one symbol. Perhaps the mystery of the sphinx is connected with this, for in the sphinx we have the lion with a woman's head, Leo with Virgo, the symbol of the lion or kingly soul, and its relation to the matter or Mother aspect. It may, therefore, signify the two polarities, masculine and feminine, positive and negative"
Alice Bailey.

Heather: We know what job we are intended to do, so, without hesitation, whenever you're ready to start Hannah ...
Hannah: It's alright now? The energy is right?
Heather: Yes, fine.
Hannah: (Deep breath and pause) I see a huge flock of seagulls, huge. I'm not walking across to the Mount, I'm being lifted by the birds. They've taken me up to the top, where the lion is, and the lion carries the sun.
There is an ancient sphinx, that looks like a lion, at the top of Saint Michael's Mount. It is said to have come from the Red Nile in Egypt and to be about 4,500 years old. Now I'm joined by a very tall Being in white. This is the Moon Goddess, so we have the all powerful sun and the all powerful moon, and in between them is a space, and in the space is a gateway. Now, we're ready to go on a journey. I'm finding this a challenge at the moment.
Heather: There is information trying to get through.
Hannah: I am supported by these two energies, of the sun and the moon, and they are in balance, but I am nervous about the gateway ...
Heather: The polar bear, Polar Bear Energy.
Hannah: Oh, right, the polar bear will carry me, that's nice. The polar bear has pressed a latch on the gate, and it has swung open. The Sphinx and the Moon Goddess will support, in a sense, from this side, on each side of the gateway, and so they'll be there

again, when we return. At the moment we're just inside the gateway and I'm making myself comfortable on the back of the polar bear. It's a cobbled path, and it goes downhill, but, surprisingly, the bear is quite confident about this. I'm a bit curious, and nervous, but that's alright. This is to be quite a long journey, on which there will be other gateways. How to open them? But with the polar bear, he can do this. (Pauses)

Heather: More information coming.

Hannah: I'm going down quite a steep path, and now there are some steps, and then a rock. In the rock is a gateway. The polar bear asks me if I need to go through, "Would you like to go through? Do you *choose* to go through this rock?" I say, "Yes," although I don't know what I'm choosing.

Heather: That is the correct answer.

Hannah: Right. He presses his nose against the latch and it sort of flies open. .. It's quite dark in here, but his coat is very .. luminous, and I'm ..   Oh gosh, there are some sort of clingy things. They're clinging to me and they're clinging to *him*, but he says, "Just focus on the light of the heart. You can .."   Oh, I find that curious 'cos I *am* nervous, but he said to, ... " 'Laugh it off,' like the humans do." so I sort of laugh and 'cos it makes you, like, wobble, they come off, these clingy things, but they're just inhabitants of this place and they're drawn toward the polar bear's light. Now we've passed through this one room, and we're going into another, and under an archway. We're coming to somewhere where there's a waterfall. There's a waterfall inside this cave and it's, oh it's such a lovely sound, *lovely* sound of a waterfall, and it's all composed of these hundreds and hundreds and *hundreds of water beings.* They're playing and singing and making this wonderful sound and they fall down and they fall on to the rock surface and then they *bounce* to one side, and some get absorbed into the rocks and the others leap up. They leap up again to join the waterfall and cascade down once more. (In awe) That's *very beautiful,* in this semi-dark cave. There is an angel of the waterfall, and (again in awe) I'm permitted to ask a question, about darkness, and the question is, ... now I have to be careful of this question. (Pause) How? ... not how ... The question is, "Does the light of Heaven reach everywhere, to the darkest corners of the Dark Universe and beyond?" The answer is, (Pause) "So be it, that is so, for without darkness there would be no light." (Long pause) ... I think that is an answer that can be considered in all it's energies and extensions and widths. There is no division. There is only energy.... The polar bear is getting impatient.

Heather: I think it's time to move.

Hannah: Yes, I agree. We now have to step on to a time zone. The polar bear and I will be prepared to go on a Time Journey. If you could give us some direction, I would appreciate that.

Heather: Well, first of all let us decide whether it's forwards or backwards. It's quite definitely forwards. You are going forwards in time, minutes, hours, days, weeks, months, years, decades, centuries, millennia, ... It's one thousand years forward.

Hannah: Well, ...

Heather: What did I say? I beg your pardon, I don't think I got it quite right. If I don't get it quite right you can't get the picture. It is not one thousand, ... It's eleven hundred years forward.

Hannah: And of course eleven is the gateway. Thank you. We have changed our energies now, both of us, and we've become, how you say, " swirling," swirling energies, which is interesting, and the polar bear, he is also swirling energy. We have moved. We are in another dimension of the planetary system and it is possible, in these energy forms, to move in and out of the particles of light and the particles of, how would you say? Dark Energy.

The figure of around 74% of the total universe has recently been given for Dark Energy. This is known to be considerably less dense than ordinary matter, and therefore it is possible to understand how Hannah and the polar bear, in their present energy forms, could weave in and out amongst the particles.

Now Dark energy and ordinary matter are like twin energies, I think you say, and they get born at different times. There is something here about the Creation story, which has been misaligned. Now the creation story which as you humans take it ... From science is Big Bang. From Holy Books is similar type of thing only in Religious way. Both having missed the mark, they put the missed mark about, and then it confuses people. Now I am only permitted to say limited amount, I would like you, if possible, for ease, as I am not sure what you are looking for, to please, if you could, ask a question about Creation? Is that possible for you to do, and please keep it simple. If you could find in your mind a story about Creation. .. It's how you say? They got a screw missing? (Laughs) A loose screw, so it's like a loose screw flying around in space is not good, therefore we would appreciate if you could ask us a question about the Creation Story.

Heather: Well, (Pause) what did Creation start out of? Forgive me if I sound sacrilegious in what I'm asking. I certainly don't mean it that way, but if, if we think about the story in the Bible about how God, that is to say the energy we call God, created the different Forces, the question I would ask about that is, what started the Creative Energy, God? What brought the Creative Energy of God into existence?

Hannah: (Immediately) Dust! (pause) Dust.

Heather: Where did the dust come from?

Hannah: Dust Was, Is, Was. Dust always was. What is it they say, "Dust to dust!" Circling and recycling. You *have it, in your books!* Everything! Dust to dust. Ashes to ashes.

Then shall the dust return to the earth as it was: and the spirit shall return unto God who gave it. Ecclesiastes 12:7

"Ashes to ashes, dust to dust." This phrase is from the English Burial Service

If you blow ash, you think it goes away. It only disappears from your sight. You put dust on your, what's the name of the cloth? Du, du, dusters, and it doesn't go away, it only disappears, but it only *appears* to disappear. It is your perception. Scientists are missing the point, because it is so simple, everything is dust and dust can form into all the shapes that you have in your known universe and in the unknown universes, and when we swirl,

As Hannah and the polar bear did

we swirl into dust.

Heather: Could I ask a question about a substance we've been talking about recently, called myfsk?

Myfsk, a white powder made from pure gold, was traditionally fed to pharaohs at a daily ceremony known as the opening of the mouth, the purpose of which was to sustain eternal life.

Hannah: Yes, dust. Dust. Gold dust, gold dust. That is a bigger form. It's a form you can see, gold dust.

Heather: What *particular significance* does gold dust have above dust, if I might be permitted to ask?

Hannah: The colour. Colours are extraordinary beings of the highest energy, equivalent, as you are correctly thinking, to music. High energy. We even use the same words to describe them. We talk of tones of colour and tones of music.

Gold as a colour energy represents both the sun and the divine. For many ancient peoples the god of the sun was the chief god in their pantheon, and even today pagans worship light, represented by the energy of the sun. The ancient Egyptian name, or sound, for the creator was Amn, from which the 'amen' of Christian prayers is derived. Amn is also linked to the cosmic sound or Word, Aum or Om, as in, "In the beginning was the word." John, Chapter 1 verse 1, and so represents the primal sound of the Cosmos.

Everything is vibration and dust. The dust has a vibration. You cannot see it, however but you *would be able to.* If you take this knowledge to your hearts, your lives will be expanded.

Heather: Well, funnily enough, if you have a strong light source, that's when you can see the specks of dust isn't it?

Hannah: Yes. And rainbows. Rainbows are like dust. They are water dust, droplets, particles. You see humans *love to be complicated,* but we don't mind, we *love* humans. We think, no, we *know,* they are the *most delightful beings! We so cherish them. Dust Humans!* (Chuckles with amusement) Ahh!

Heather: Thank you for that.

Hannah: *Thank you. You give us so much pleasure! Thank you.* I need to go back now.

Heather: Yes, I'm seeing that it's time to move, so now we're going to move again, forward, ... centuries, millennia. It looks like a long way. I'm going to go forward in increments of ten thousand years, (Deep breath from Hannah) eleven, twelve, thirteen, fourteen, looks like fourteen thousand years forward.

Hannah: ONE ... FULL ... CYCLE. (Slowly and carefully enunciated, followed by a long pause) Um, ... Um, ... Um, ... Things are very ... slow here. (Long pause) You would say that the energy, if you were measuring this, is st, st, stationary. It has not reached stationary, but it has reached the place at the end of a cycle, where everything appears to be coming to an end, to stop. (All this is said very slowly, and sounds like an ancient wound down gramophone or a stretched tape.) When it reaches that critical, uh, um, stop, it can m, m, make, a l, leap. Do you under..stand me, because it is quite, im.. portant for this .. to .. be .. said. Phew!

Heather: This is critical mass isn't it?

Heather knew neither where that remark came from, nor its meaning. It was just dropped into her head and then confirmed by the pendulum. However, later research showed that critical mass is the smallest possible fissile particle which can start a chain reaction, a speck of dust so to speak. This is where the connection *could* be lost.

Hannah: Y,y, you a, are correct.

Heather: It's a door, it's a gateway isn't it? It's a portal.

Hannah: Yes, but it's it's, it's, phew, it's on a sp, spiral, and if you are spiralling, if you have come to the end of a journey, ... Oh, gosh it's COLD. If you've come to the end of a journey, ooh! You ... (Much shivering from Hannah. Heather watches her very carefully for signs of over exposure) You can make a, you can make a leap. (Still shivering) You have two choices. You can (Still obviously suffering from cold, although the room where we are working is well heated.) You can be ....

Heather: I think you need the energy of the fire of Love streaming from the Universal Heart, and represented by our lighted candle flame, to warm you. (There has been a candle burning throughout the session.)

Hannah: Yes. (Shivering still) I can, I can see it but I am *not* allowed to touch it. I know I'm not allowed to touch these two energies, because that would be quite, d,d,d,dangerous. So will you just bear with me while I look? I am looking at the dark and I am looking at the light, and that's all I can do. *I MUST step back **from** this!*

Heather: That's alright. That's fine.

Hannah: (Whispers) Oooooh! Ooooooh! That was very frightening! Ohh! Oh, my *hands are cold.*

Heather: (Gently) Just have a rest.

Hannah is still obviously feeling very cold. A minute or two goes by in silence except for shivers from Hannah.

Heather: I invoke the power of Love to warm you.

Hannah appears to be reviving.

A minute or two more goes by.

Heather: I think we ought to finish here.

Hannah: (Now in her normal voice) There's something else though. There **is** *something else. There is something **else**!*

Heather: Well, maybe there is, but you don't have to do it today. We can think about it!

Hannah: No, it's *alright!* There is something else, that *is* all related, everything is all related but there is something else of a, of a, of a, (Whispers) What is the word? What *is* the word? There's something else.

Heather: I think you need *all the moldavite that came to the earth from outer space as a tektite fourteen million years ago.*

Hannah: Thank you.

Heather: You need the whole tektite, *and even more. You need more than that too.* (Goes through the "keys" on the table, one by one.) It's quartz as well. It's the whole of the tektite of moldavite, plus Buddha Quartz, to assist and amplify the energy of the moldavite.

Buddha Quartz has been used to contact and to promote the transfer of information from the elders of the ancient civilisations of India, Tibet and China. It is a stone of Shangri-la, and is said to have been used to bring the harmony and accord of this civilisation to those who share the energy. Shangri-la is Tibet's lost city, an Atlantis in the Himalayas, a paradise where time stood still, the site of the silver palace of the Shang Shung kings.

Hannah: And that is to do with the Ganesh of the, of the pen, pen, pendulum.

Why does Hannah speak of the Ganesh of the pendulum? She doesn't even know the answer to this herself, but, on looking up what is written in Doreen Virtue's book, "Archangels and Ascended Masters," under the heading of Ganesh, the pendulum itself picks out the following: " Ask me to assist and I puncture the balloons of dark illusions."

Hannah: S, So that's Ganesh, the Elephant G, Goddess! God, Goddess, both the same, and we will ride .... No?

Heather: Now, there's either something coming ....

Hannah: Yes, I can just see it.

Heather: We need, we need the whole lot of keys, all together. Everything.

Hannah: Yes, because we're going towards, we're going towards the ROCK. (In awe). We are going towards the stone and I cannot enter without all my, (visibly upset) friends! (Through sobs) All the animals and all the birds, every, every, every one! Every one.

Heather: We will invoke them all to come with you.

Hannah: Yes, yes, they're coming, (Still sobbing) all of the ones, all the ones that were ever born, even the ones that humans can't see any more. (Sobs) And the ones that are being born and the ones that have died and the ones that never went away, they're all coming. (Sobs) And I'm showing them the rock, the green rock, (the moldavite tektite,) which came from the other place, which has no name, but humans have one name for it, they call it Heaven, and now we can go and look at Heaven, for that's truly where we belong.

The energy is VERY strong in this area of writing, even in just reading it through.

We have resided in Hell many, many, many thousands and millions of years. (Sobs) And the rock, we do not need to enter, for in this place we are already here. Everything that was ever born, ever made, ever created, is in the lap of the Mother, the Mother and the Father God Energy, whatever name it is under, it is in the lap. (Pause) Remember this, never go out from it, "Dust is thy Nature, and Gold Dust thou art." Humans are like jewels. (Pause) That is the message. Glory Be to all on High, which is below. Glory and gratitude to all animals, all flying ones, all swimming ones, all creepy crawly ones, those of the Past, the Great Beings of the Past. Time here does not exist. It is Heaven and Bliss. It is everything. Remember your breathing. Every time you breath, you breath Love, which is Light. You breath the Breath of Heaven, with your every breath. You are the dust between the stars. You are the Light of Heaven. Be for ever at Peace, meeting with those that have gone. They have not gone far. They are still here, *holding for you, holding. Everything holds for you.* You are supported eternally. You are blessed and cherished. All your creations are blessed and cherished.

The polar bear is coming back now. I give thanks. I am returning. We have shut one door. We have shut the next door, and now we have shut the other door. Hannah and the polar bear give thanks to the Lion, the Sun Energy, the beautiful Moon Energy, and the Moon birds. We all give thanks.

AFTER WORDS

Heather: When you were in that very difficult, extremely cold place in the journey, what did you actually see?
Hannah: Well, I'd gone through the tunnel in a sense, and creamy white was on the left hand side. It was like an energy only it wasn't swirling. It wasn't a river either, but it was like a liquid. Then there was a divide line. Now it's very difficult to find the divide line, but I suppose you could say it was a bit like a grey pencil mark, only it's *very fine*. But it depends where you are in your consciousness as to how you see it, because although it is like a line it can become wavy and shimmering. The dark energy was on the other side of the line and when you get to the line you have a choice.

In my near death experience I had a choice whether to cross the river or not, because I could see all my ancestors, even my grandfather, whom I never met in this lifetime time, on this planet. He was there, together with various other ancestors. I was told that I could choose to go across the river, and I said "No, no." It was very tempting I must say, and I said, " No, I have to go back. I have three children and I've got work to do." So it was my decision to come back.

But with this experience today, in a sense, it's nothing to do with that. This is about soul level. It's very difficult to put words on it, because it's not higher, but different, there's a different feel to it, and it's to do with "playing another part." It's difficult because the Near Death Experience was a choice, and the choice was the possibility to go towards my ancestors and be involved in all of that, and to grow in a Heaven, .. that was it! And because I'd been so ill with pneumonia the choice was different, because I guess we get the death that we're prepared for, and at one of these choices, a way of being, to choose between the light and the dark, which does point to a fact that if you have that choice, have you made the supreme sacrifice for Humanity, which is to go towards the dark, to reflect for humanity all the *possibilities* of the dark. And that will take you into unspeakable realms. And on the other side of the line, if you choose the light, then that will also take you to unspeakable realms. That is my understanding of what I saw.

      You understand my dilemma, moving in Spirit, that if I would take one *or* the other, Hannah could actually die, because it's not my time. I was in a place of being able to kill my body, make a choice, and that's why, as it rightly says in one of the runes, it can be highly dangerous. (Isa - standstill, withdrawal, ice, " Remain mindful that the seed of the new is present in the shell of the old.") But I knew when I wrote the poem★ and spoke it aloud, my Being doesn't belong to Hannah. I am in my Beloved's keeping, and that is how I was able to do this. In a way, saying the poem was like writing a spell. I don't think I can go any further with that.

Heather: No. Well we do appreciate very much what you do Hannah.

Heather: The keys were amazing, because it took the whole tektite of moldavite, plus the Buddha quartz as well. Goodness knows what actual energy quotient or quantities we were working with. And the keys, the whole lot had to go. There was no question of just choosing one key. It was like, "Well, the keys have been carefully chosen, and they are the right keys, use them *all*. I would like to ask you why you thought you got very cold. We *were on the edge*. It was very dangerous, what we were doing. I *was* very well aware of that. I was watching you like a hawk. I realised that you were getting very, very cold, and of course the danger with that might be that the metabolism of the body would close down. It was like being in a hypothermic situation.

Hannah: That's exactly what it was doing.

Heather: But I knew also that I mustn't do anything which would alarm or upset the energies around that, because I knew you could be brought back, as long as everybody kept calm, and sent you love. Basically, it was the energy of love and light which enabled you to come back, so I suppose I've answered my own question now really, because I was going to ask you why you got so cold, but obviously you got cold because the metabolism of the human body was up to the extreme of its limits.

Hannah: Yes, it was starting to get to me.

Heather: And you were actually shaking, in the physical sense, of cold.

Hannah: There was part of me that was registering this in the physical body.

Heather: You see, we are going further and further each time. Having seen that today, I think we would have to think very seriously about taking you there again. I think it might be very imprudent to expose you to that sort of force again. However I don't see it as an evil force.

Hannah: No it wasn't, no, no. If anything it was quite *precise*.

Heather: Yes, but you are travelling in a space suit, and that space suit can only withstand a certain amount of pressure. I think it was up to its maximum. I think you've done marvellous work, but I wouldn't expose you to that danger again.

Hannah: But it will be different next time, because we've now got foreknowledge of the possibilities, if there is a next time, it's up to them.

Heather: Well, this is the amazing thing. Even after you went through that I was prepared to bring you back, but you still wanted to go on.

Hannah: Yes, because I knew there was more.

Heather: It's almost like, "The mountain's there, so I'll jolly well climb it."

Hannah: I couldn't come back until I had the last thing.

Heather: But that's like laying down your life for your friend, isn't it. That is the supreme sacrifice of being a bridge between the worlds.

I stood on the shores of the morning sun★
Behold I see them come,
My ancestors, my kith and kinfolk.
Surely I would wish to come
across the River of Golden Light.
Strong was the urge towards grateful Peace
but the smallest movement between
head, heart and hand
pulled me back to Earthly cause
and effect
And all those children waiting on Love
and promises made before my birth
So returning renewed in Love Eternal
I resumed my place as the mother of three
knowing that we are all known loved and understood
Wherever we may be.

Hannah, for all the children of the worlds 27-06-2007

Chapter Sixteen

Hannah's Sixth Journey

We were told that another journey was necessary for Hannah and that this was the auspicious time for it.

The Keys for this Journey:
On the day when the keys were put together both Hannah and Heather were asked by the guides to draw a rune. Heather drew the rune number 33 YUD CHET VAV - Revealing the dark side, and Hannah, number 39, RESH HEY AYIN - Diamond in the rough. This set the "Scene," as it were and so we knew that, this time, we were going to be wrestling with the dark side, not so much of ourselves, but with Elemental Darkness. 'Diamond in the rough is symbolic of humanity and the alchemical transformation necessary, just like the turning of base metal into gold, the refining, cutting and polishing processes which go on lifetime after lifetime, until each individual soul shines like the sun itself, reflecting its Creator.
Two Water cards were also drawn, from the "Water Crystal Oracle," based on the work of Masaru Emoto, author of "The Hidden Messengers in Water." One was **"Wisdom and compassion,"** and the other was **"Soul."**

Other keys were a meteoric rock called **Horne Blende**, which helps to insulate one from the abrasiveness of others. It further allows one to 'accept" and release judgemental attitudes, bringing one to the tolerance of the un-programmmed child. The element **Aether** - penetration.
Blue Lace Agate, which displays a blue and white lace pattern, and which can help one reach extremely high spiritual spaces. It contains the qualities of flight, air, movement and grace. **The Buddha**.
The **Yin/Yang symbol**, the yin aspect of which is feminine, one of change, while the yang aspect is masculine, one of harmony.
A special **Brandburg crystal with amethyst inclusions** from South Africa.
Chrysocolla, the Goddess Stone. This is a wand of Chrysocolla which was found broken. The break is significant.

A few of these keys are not mentioned again in the text, but they, nevertheless, display a supportive and protective silent role. They are holders of energy for the unfolding of the story.

Hannah, as you will know by now, is a very seasoned traveller, and, on the day itself very little audible introduction to the regression state is needed. She and I, because of the extent of the work already carried out together, are very much in tune on a psychic level of awareness.

Heather: Hannah, having carefully and mindfully completed all our usual preparations, we are now ready to make another journey. I am watching the pendulum to see what instructions it is giving me, and, at the moment, it is simply telling me that the Akashic Energy is coming in .. and is in place now.

Hannah: It is interesting that, while we were quiet, just before you switched on the recording machine, I saw a valley, but my eyes were not my eyes. They were the eyes of an eagle. The valley entrance was to the right of my sight and I was about half way down the valley, on top of extremely tall cliffs. Then I was taken down and put at the valley entrance. It is very difficult to judge the difference between myself as a being, and the eagle, because they seem to be one and the same, but also when I was taken and put near the entrance to the valley, it was as if the eagle stayed on high in order to keep watch. Then I opened my eyes and was back here with you. This coming and going is something I seem to do a great deal of these days. This can be something of a challenge, because one is not more important than the other. Both are equal in helping us understand who or what people are, as there is not yet enough understanding of the other side of humans and their potential.

It is very easy for Hannah to travel through the dimensions. The veil of separation is very thin for her.

I don't know what time of day this is. It seems to be quite early in the morning. I'll just stand here a moment I think. I'm waiting for something to happen or somebody to appear, in order to bring me forward into the valley.

Heather: More information is coming, or trying to get through. I think we need a key, and the key is aether, penetration.

Isaac Newton wrote, "I do not know what this Aether is," but if it consists of particles, then they must be "exceedingly smaller than those of Air, or even those of Light. The exceeding smallness of its Particles may contribute to the greatness of the force by which those Particles may recede from one another, and thereby make that medium exceedingly more rare and elastick than Air." The word "aether" stems from the Greek, aither, the heavens, and aithein, to light up. The five basic elements were thought of as being Earth, Air, Fire, Water, and the most rarefied of all, Aether, from which the adjective ethereal comes. When carrying out shamanic work it is possible for the shaman to call on one of these five elements to assist.

Hannah: Aether, I can be carried forward on that. The I is not I, Hannah, it is the other I. I can go forward with that.

Heather: (Slightly confused) Do you mean the eye is the third eye?

Hannah: It is, but it is more than that. It's like the eye that the Egyptians painted on the prows of their boats, the all-seeing eye that goes through water.

Keelless seagoing vessels like those during the time of King Sahure (2500 BCE) traded with the Phoenician cities, importing cedar wood, Asiatic slaves and other merchandise. The boat was steered by six oars, the bipedal mast carried a vertical sail and the bow was decorated with an eye.

Heather: More information coming.

Hannah: This is the Eye on which the Consciousness rests, the Eye resting within the aether.

Heather: Is this what the Ancient Egyptians knew as the Eye of Horus?

Hannah: Yes ...

Heather: Although that is not quite enough is it?

Hannah: No. It's like seeing with the eye of God and even that feels, in a sense, too *narrow*, but it will have to do. I do not have the words to explain sufficiently. They probably exist in another language, but I can say that Sight is a dimension.

Hannah hears, "In my house are many mansions, One is sight."

Heather: We're not allowed to know any more about that at this stage. The pendulum has slipped back behind the Balance Line, meaning that the Akashic Energy has retreated and I'm being told that it is time for a move. The move is forward, minutes, hours, days, weeks, with the pendulum travelling anticlockwise, the Anxious way ... months, years, decades, one decade, ten years, ten years forward.

Hannah: ... I feel strife! There's a mass, an invading army, which will impose it's nation's culture and conditioning, torture and pain. ... I am confused, because I don't understand *why*. This .. feels .. like an invading .. force! It is like a sickness, which is Dis - Ease. "From whence comest this?" I ask.

Heather: Now the energy is gone to the Negative side again, out of view. That's followed by positivity with an anxious pattern around it. We need a key, .. the Yin Yang energy.

Hannah: That is better! ..This is felt as an invasion, because the understanding of what this is was not understood at the time. The darkness of the invading force must Be, because you have need of a counteracting energy to the Positive one that is carried. It is because of the shift in the Earth Consciousness, on which you are living, that it went the way, in a sense, it did, but now there is a slow but meaningful adjustment being made to the Consciousness of the Earth. I believe you call it The Pole Shift, and this is the earth now beginning to realign itself with its proper motion. And so it is coming around, despite the efforts of all those who would keep it " Usual," that is to say all those who would hold it back and prevent the change. Those of you who *know,* will find it Usual, now that the *adjustments* are being made, and you just have to be patient and to accept that they, the gods, are patient and long-suffering also, while they too make their adjustments, if they so choose. The energy where I am at the moment is very dragging, but I am pushing forward with it, and I hope this has not been too laboured for an understanding.

Some of the words in this last short section were delivered syllable by syllable.

Hannah: I find the energy on Earth very dense, but it is changing, despite all efforts to not have it so. The Eye that speaks knows the Truth. (Brightly) And be assured, all will be well! Adjustments are being made everywhere.

Heather: And now we can move, forward again, minutes, two minutes forward.

Hannah: Strangely enough, we seem to be in the valley again, and my understanding is that people are coming and going through the valley.

Heather: Hesitatingly, I .. feel I should say that I believe this to be the Valley of the Shadow of Death. Ohh!

A strong blast of energy goes right through Heather's body, signifying a deep spiritual truth.

Hannah: That is correct. That is why it is difficult to be here in this location, but this is the auspicious day for the journey and we are correct in being here.

Heather: And now we can move, forward again, minutes, seven. And I must tell you that the energy has gone around the Anxious way.

Hannah: Yes, we are now following the "map" we were given by Jennine, who traced the time line of 57 degrees, 40 minutes astrologically for us. We are now where the standing stones are at Calenesh in Scotland. This is an ancient tuning place, where the priests tuned the Earth energies. When we came here we could see that the humans were of sincerity and we trusted them, and that was good. Your historians don't know all the story, but here the dreams were placed for antiquity, and the dreams were in the songs, and in the tuning. Now, this place is Sacred. As the poles shift in their graduations, so the energy would shift here, and if you lie down upon the earth within this place and open your hearing, you can hear the tuning taking place. But only a few, who have ancestry connections with the Calenesh stones, will be able to do this, for it is of great responsibility.

The notes are important, and all things will be done in good time here, and spread upon the earth into the hearts of men and women. The goodness is already in the children.

I am much honoured, that we are here today with you, following the ancestral line of this being, Hannah. It remains a very good line, difficult and hazardous, but very good connection and carries great responsibility. The burden will lessen as the shift happens.

Hannah: .... Showing me life as old woman in Forres, on the East coast of Scotland, but still on the same time line of 57 degrees, 40 minutes, a happy life, hard but happiness inside. Great bonding with Earth and other humans.

Heather: Now we've got a Working pattern on the pendulum. I'm not quite sure where we are. We may be getting into psychic surgery. I think perhaps we are. There's negativity registering now, so I'm going to pull out.

Hannah: Yes.

Heather: If you want to stop me at any point, please do, but the energy's gone on to the Healing Line.

Hannah: Yes. There was somebody who was dragging my energy .. in that place.

Heather: It's gone into a circle again, and now the energy is better than it was, but it's still negative, so I'm going to pull out again. It's gone on to the Healing Line again. ... a very tiny circle is on the pendulum .. and now the energy's gone forward, far forward on to the Truth, Love, Healing Line. I think this is helping you to shed that negative entity that got itself attached. Another Working pattern, and we've got a Connection with the Divine Line. Another bit of negativity still, which often happens. The pendulum goes around the anticlockwise, Anxious way, on to the line of Truth again. (Healing Line) Another Working Pattern. Again a connection with Truth, Love and Healing. There is a very strong connection this time. The word "Bonding" comes into my head. Still a very strong swing. A pushing forward of energy, followed by a very strong connection with the Healing Line. A more normal pace of pendulum swing now. We didn't actually move the space, but I think there's a key required. ... The key is the Buddha.

Hannah: Blessed be.

Heather: And now, with the Buddha in place, there's a time shift. Forward again, one minute.

Hannah: I died .. and went to the Buddha. And I didn't know what was happening to me, so I died in extreme distress.

This is difficult for me, Heather, to be told of my friend being in extreme stress. Also there had been audible changes in the depth of Hannah's breathing throughout this piece. Rather than ask questions at such a time, it is vital that I keep watch over the progression of the energies, completing the job I am here to do.

Hannah: And the Buddha, .. Because of the work which had been done previously, I was able to see the Buddha, and rest awhile with him. It was as if somebody had wrapped me in one of those stress blankets that, against all weathers, can keep you warm on a mountain. And this one, instead of being made of silver material, was made of gold.

Heather: There were several Anxious patterns around that psychic surgery, but it's not always practical to mention them. ..And now we move again, to the next minute.

Hannah: As you were speaking then I felt as if the Buddha had removed my heart, breathed on it, and put it back. He breathed on it so that the flame in the heart would still be there. This is the great narrowing of how it is .. just a moment while I find the words, .. how difficult a transition may be, how narrow the way ...

Heather: More information coming.

Hannah: If the thread of connection to Divine Source is not strong it may snap, but, because the thread *is* strong, the work can carry on. It reminds me of spiders' thread, which is *incredibly* strong.

Spider's thread is at least as strong as steel wire of the same size, with the ability to stretch to twice its length without breaking, and having the particular quality of not spinning around, as a suspended rope holding a climber would do. This fine thread is the bit that you inherit from your spiritual ancestors. It is the thing that drags you kicking and screaming back to your emotional centre. It holds you steady. You can weave your web of happiness or you can weave your web of sorrow. You get to choose. The thread is the most precious and exquisite form of love. It supports all the other parts of a Soul's Journey. Each character plays its part, but it's only a part of the whole. The truth lies in the heart, always. Each soul journey is part of your diamond body, and so the diamond body grows in stature and becomes polished. This refers back to the rune, diamond in the rough, which Hannah drew as one of the keys. Remember, she says, we go each way but once.

Heather: That the 'spider thread' is strong is so important.

Hannah: If you lose *everything*, as long as you have truth, then life can continue. The truth is *instant*! It has no debating, no, what is the word, no shilly-shallying. Truth Is! And only the heart knows Truth. Speak Always From Heart, even if it appears to be harsh. You work with whatever is necessary to keep Truth alive, for the other person's heart, if they come *from* Truth, will *know* Truth. You will know those who do not come from Truth. You do correctly when you only give them one chance, or two, three times sometimes, but no more. **You do not waste Truth**. It is available .. to all those with good intention and honourable way of being. Truth is Impeccable. Ahh, (deep sigh.)

Short rest of about 10 seconds.

Heather: And now we can move again. Forward. We seem to be keeping to minutes this afternoon, so just the next moment. This is to do with the Power of the Moment.

Hannah: The power of Now rests everywhere.

Heather: More information trying to get through.

Hannah: It rests wherever you place your .. consciousness. Or, if you are being guided, The Consciousness. You trust that. It's also about trust. Trust brings you well-being. How can you teach Trust? You may tell your story, or someone else's story, as an example. You may ... (Chuckles loudly.) I have Mother here! "...You may talk until you are blue in the face, they'll please themselves anyhow!" But you may still tell your story, because they do listen, and if the heart has asked a question, then the heart will listen. And change may not happen right away, but it will come! You have "struck a note" within the heart of another, from your heart, and so it spreads, and ease, rather than dis-ease prevails. Oh, so many words in English language, all meaning one thing and could mean something else. Umm!

Heather: More information coming.

Hannah: Best way people learn is from example. Be your true selves and unto thyself be true. Others feel presence, feel comfortable, feel trusting, and with that comes more spreading of ease. So much rubbish put out on your boxes. Telly. "Tellee," That's good old Cornish for, "I tell you." Most people watch box, and listen, and believe. Lots of nonsense, lots of untruths. Do not waste too much time on it. Be discerning. If it feels right in your heart, then you may watch, but don't waste time. ...

Heather: Now we are ready to move again, forward, it's not quite years and it has gone around the Anxious way, so it's, seven, eight, nine, ten months.

Hannah: I'm getting the Aleutian Islands of Alaska. Ah, I see. I understand now. On the map that I was given there are three volcanos. The three hearth stones, in the middle of the seven, are connected with the volcanos.

The Hearth Stones is the ancient Mayan name for the tight linear grouping of three prominent white stars, Alnitak, Alnilam and Mintaka, in the 'belt' of the constellation of Orion. Alnilam comes from an Arabic word which means "the string of pearls" The constellation of Orion is associated with Auser (Osiris) in Egypt and its appearance marks the periodic flooding of the Nile and the triumph of life over death in the myths of Auser and Auset (Osiris and Isis.)

Robert Bauval, in the Orion Mysteries argues that the three prominent stars in the belt of Orion may have been used as orientation markers for the three great pyramids at Giza.

Biblical Reference – The New International Version Study Bible. Job 9, 5-9

He moves mountains without their knowing it, and overturns them in his anger. He shakes the earth from its place and makes its pillars tremble. He speaks to the sun and it does not shine; he seals off the light of the stars. He alone stretches out the heavens and treads on the waves of the sea. He is the Maker of the Bear and Orion, the Pleiades and the constellations of the south.

Hannah: These stars bring the energy to earth, so these stars are ..

Heather: Connectors?

Hannah: Yes.

Heather: Transmitters?

Hannah: Yes, because if you put something over the top of something of the same value, it can cancel it. So you've got three hearth stone stars in the Belt of Orion and three firey volcanos. Now, what do they mean? .. Yes, yes, I can do that, put three stars on the map. I need bigger map of Aleutian Islands.

Hannah mutters, "Yes that can be done." She is obviously talking to someone else here. At the point of transcription I question her as to who it is and a mini regression follows:

Hannah: The **Starry Being**, who worked with me through my physical system in a previous life in Ancient Egypt, is standing with me in the temple there. My knowledge of him comes from a spontaneous Past Life recall I once had in a cottage in St Just where I was living at the time. The stairs ran alongside the living room, and as I was going upstairs one day I chanced to look over the banister. To my amazement the view completely changed to the outdoors, and I was standing in Ancient Egypt, within view of the Nile and with the pyramids behind me. I was a priestess in those days. Men and Women were equal in the realm of medicine, metaphysics and the sciences at that time, including the time of the Nebra Disc.

This 3,600 year old Bronze Age artefact is the oldest representation of the stars of the heavens in the world. The 32 cm diameter disc shows a golden ship, Sun, Moon and stars, as well as the constellation of Pleiades just before an eclipse. Astronomers have confirmed that the sky map matches the latitude of the place where it was found. While only a small fraction of the extended site, on a hill near the town of Nebra in Saxony-Anhalt has been investigated so far, it is already being hailed as a "German Stonehenge" in some circles.

The information concerning the cancellation of energies is that cancelled energies go somewhere and in this instance they go to the City of Fatehpur Sikri in Agra, India, and are held there and refined until needed in other energetic forms. The Guides are now saying, "Nothing is lost if you know where it is!"

Researched afterwards:

Fatehpur Sikri, the "City of Victory", sits 35 kilometres from Agra on a low hill of the Vindhya mountain range. Before the reign of Akbar (1556-1605), the Mughal King who built Fatehpur Sikri, the site of the future city had already earned an auspicious reputation. Babar, the founder of the Mughal Dynasty and Akbar's grandfather, had won a battle here over Rana Sanga of Mewar. In gratitude he named the area Shukri, which means "thanks". In Akbar's time the site was occupied by a small village of stonecutters and was the home of Shaikh Salim Chishti, a Muslim astrologer and Sufi Saint, who is directly linked to the aptly named Starry Being. In 1568 Akbar visited the Shaikh to ask for the birth of an heir. The Shaikh replied that an heir would be born soon. Sure enough, Akbar's wife gave birth to a boy on August 30, 1569. In gratitude, Akbar named the boy Salim after the astrologer.

Hannah: This is a **Starry Being**. And we can use these Beings to help us, so you and I, Heather, can use these for quicker access to information. Oh I hope you *understand* that there's a quicker way to work together for healing of people and Earth.

Heather: Do you mean it's a quicker way of cancelling out the dark energy?

Hannah: Yes it is, it is! Because, in a sense it's .. I *do* wish they didn't have such fast moving brains!

Heather: Perhaps we can get somebody to put it more simply for you. Let's ask the Buddha to do that.

Hannah: Oh *that's better*. Gosh! They think like dolphins, do you understand me? Dolphins have extremely quick speech pattern in brain. In a sense, you've got to speed your brain up, the human brain, at the moment. Right, the Buddha ..

Heather: (Interrupting) This is particularly Tania's Buddha. Tania's Buddha, in particular was chosen as a key for this Soul Journey.

Tania is a long time friend of Heather's who is now in the world of Spirit. She is helping us at this stage.

Hannah: Yes. He floats. He floats through the Aether. He never went away.

This is something to do with the energy of Tania and the Buddha together. Each energy needs the other in order to float. Also a mutual friend of Tania's, who was like a daughter to her agrees, "That's *right*, She never went away! I knew she never went away."

Hannah: (Chuckles) He says, "Don't get so excited!

Both Heather and Hannah have a chuckle at this, and it breaks the tension. It is also exactly the sort of comment Tania herself would make.

Hannah: ... O.K. three volcanos, three hearth stones. You know how they cap a well? They place something over it, and seal the well with concrete or something similar, to hold the energy in. This action then directs the energy elsewhere. It would seem impossible, that you can cap a volcano, but all things are possible. The volcano is a metaphor for capping energy that is poisonous. I don't fully understand this. I need some clarity please.

Heather: There is a key. It is the special Brandburg crystal from South Africa. Damaraland, in North West Namibia, where Brandberg Crystals come from, is considered a mystical area. It is famous for its 200 million year old petrified forest, as well as an abundance of ancient rock paintings and engravings. It was regarded as a spiritual site of significance by the ancient Bushmen Tribes. From a metaphysical (and physical) point of view, the attribute of the Brandberg crystal implemented here is its wonderful clarity. This one has amethyst inclusions which, in this instance are providing a clear connection between the Earth plane and other worlds.

Hannah: Yes. They would know about *mines*, you see. My understanding, as a simple human, is that, logically, you cannot cap a volcano, because, even the lava which comes out of it, which is burning, ... Will you bear with me while I explore this a bit?

Heather: Of course.

Hannah: You can't cap it, so it flows out, but it then creates something else, which is not *bad*. What it does, the lava also flows into the water, into the sea.

Lava: Matter discharged in a molten stream from a volcano or fissure. The word comes from the Latin, lavare – to wash.

Heather: I'm getting the word Magma. Does that make sense?

Magma: A doughy mass.

Hannah: That's right. That's what they call it. And underneath the water the magma causes *funnels*. When the volcano explodes it naturally flows down the mountain and often into the sea, but also, having reached the sea, the volcano is still exploding under the ocean, so these funnels are smoking, literally smoking lava. Now, none of this is *bad of itself*, while, of course, people are killed and maimed and frightened very badly in the process, so I think what the Buddha is trying to tell me is that these volcanos are in perfection as they are, that they are teaching us, and are somehow a metaphor for Humans, and that's the part I don't understand.

Amazingly, the extremely close friend of Tania and I whom I mentioned before, and who knows my work well, came to stay for a couple of days, and read this document. She identified with it totally at this point, in relation to her anger at certain treatment by other colleagues, which she had endured. She was trying to help a student handicapped by Aspergers Syndrome and who attended the college where she taught, achieve a place in advanced education. Others had tried to quash her appeal, saying it was not possible, capping her anger at their lack of acceptance and open-mindedness, which made the situation worse, because she believed strongly in the abilities of this student and in what she was trying to do, on behalf of another unable to fight for himself. Fortunately one of her colleagues, operating at a high level, was both able and willing to believe in her and her aims and so hold, rather than cap, the situation. Eventually the handicapped student was helped and a placement was achieved. My friend felt greatly helped by the understanding which reading this section of text provided.

Heather: I am bringing in the Goddess Energy, by means of the goddess stone, the Chrysocolla, does that help? The *broken* goddess stone!

Hannah: Yes.

At this point in the transcription I looked up why the chrysocolla was a key, and I read that it can assist one in communication with the spiritual forces of the Earth, and can help one understand that which is required in order that the Earth may heal herself.

Heather: Something is important about the break, the breaking of ...

Hannah: Yes. For they destroyed the temples. That cost the healing energies of the Temples addressed to the Goddess. They burnt, they plundered and they cast them into the oceans. .. So this energy needs now to be recognised .. The energy is of the Earth, and deeply feminine. When these energies were split there was extreme damage done, not just to the earth, but it reverberated through space, and, obviously to all those living on other planets, and now is the time when adjustments must be made, the realignments *must* be recognised, the energies **held**, not **capped**. You cannot cover these for ever. It is an energetic form. This is not yet in the understanding of Man.

She said, (The Earth Goddess) "You cannot hold me any longer. I must go forth without let or hindrance, and do what I must do. This is a metaphor for all **feminine energy,** that which has been **capped**, not **held**, by **masculine energy**, be it within a male or female body, for many centuries. " She says, "I am Creatress, Mother of All. I will gather all to me, that have been lost. All the children of different kinds will turn, now, to me, for we cannot exist any more in the Earth Energy Field, without that. We shall depart. And when that happens, as you see your moon appearing naked, as if nothing is upon it, I am saying, "Unless you come to an understanding of my Full and Powerful Beingness, so you will see your reflection in the moon, empty. You cannot live without my recognition any longer. I am a force to be reckoned with, and yet I care about you all deeply. You are not se- par- ate from me. (Latin. separare, - se, aside parare, to put) Recognise that in yourself. Honour that, whether you are male or female, of any species. All birds, they know. All fish and swimming ones know. All animals, all the four-footeds, and the little tiny two-footeds, they all know. I rest my knowledge with you. **Work *with*** the volcanos, by all means, in recognition of my power, both under the ocean and on the land, and the smoke that ascends to Heaven. I value you all deeply. I am promised to you as you are promised to me. In the Old Days, which are now, I thank Thee. (Deep sigh)

AFTER WORDS

Hannah: About the Buddha, this one was smaller than the one I have seen before. It is as if there are different sizes of him. But what I got was, because it was a bit of an anxious time, I got this lovely feeling of Peace, and then he said, "Don't get so excited, ... because the information that was coming through was exciting to me, whoever the Me was, and he just smiled gently, saying, "Don't get so excited." It's all very well for him. I hadn't been there before, in the place of Complete Peace. It was just beautiful.

There were so many aspects to this journey. The aspect of Calenesh was absolutely amazing! I think I've got a postcard at home, with the Calenesh stones on it, but that was one of the places that Jennine mentioned, and I did look them up on the map yesterday, so obviously she sent me the e-mail in time, and I had to look at these places. And that was about the sound, as it said on the tape previously. I now believe that this is a place where people can visit, in order to hear the sounds coming from the stones, and get, in a sense, tuned up. I haven't been there in this lifetime and experienced that, although I know what I'm talking about, but I can't tell you the experience of it. However I DO remember it. But people have to go and have their own experience, and some will and some won't.

But then I went back to this place near Forres on the East Coast of Scotland, which is still on the same timeline across the map, whereas Calenesh is on the West coast, and that's where I did have a really happy and fulfilling life, until near the end, where I was able to help people and do healings and I was just a very happy person.

Heather: So you went into a little sort of mini regression there didn't you?

Hannah: Yes, I did, but what happened at the end, because it went into a negative zone, was that somebody, a person or a Being, had tried, in a sense, to steal my power, before I left.

Heather: To hold it and keep it with them, do you think?

Hannah: Yes! You can steal a person's power. You can drain it. A lot of people can drain other people's energy. We know about that, and we know what we can do, and how we can protect ourselves, but the point is, that this was at a different level, and it wasn't very nice at all. In fact it was nearly disastrous, because, while I was alive, and really getting old and nearing the point of dying, which I knew I would do, and was perfectly accepting of that, this other Being, another dimensional Being, and remember we're right up North here, at the power spot of Calenesh, in the North West of Scotland, on the Time Line of 57 degrees 40 minutes ... This Being could have stolen my power, but I went OUT before it could finish what it was doing, and there was the trauma, because, knowing that you're a power person, you carry the responsibility to look after the Line, in a sense. It's like somebody gives you something when you come into this world, so you've got to look after it. You're not sure how, but you're shown how. And this Being nearly Did It for me, and it could have destroyed my whole reincarnational family line.

Heather: You had to find a very narrow gap. You spoke about it, didn't you?

Hannah: Yes, it was SO NARROW!

Heather: Is this the Narrow Way they talk about in Pilgrim's Progress by John Bunion?

Hannah: It is, yes. But they couldn't get through you see. They couldn't. Once I'd gone through it, once I had padded out of this lifetime, then I was not available to them, although they thought that I would be, but there are more powers than even Beings can understand.

Heather: I'm getting a sense that this is in some way connected to the Thin Body. You were travelling in your thin body?

Hannah: Yes, I had left my physical body and gone into my thin body, the body that the shaman uses when journeying so he/she cannot be seen, and so I could get through the gap while that Being couldn't, because their energies were a different shape or colour, or something. There was a difference, and so they couldn't get by. The way that you go is made specially for your energy.

Heather: Like a key in a keyhole.

Hannah: Absolutely! Nobody else can get through that. As we come into Earth we've got our own template. That's part of what makes us who we are. We carry that uniqueness inside of us.

Heather: And then you spoke of the very strong thread.

Hannah: It was like a spider's thread. This is the goddess energy, because it's the energy of Grandmother Spider, on the Native American Medicine Wheel.

Heather: Like Ariadne and the Spider, who used the spider silk to find her way out of the Underworld.

Hannah: And where did I first go? To the Valley of the shadow of Death!

Chapter Seventeen

Hannah's Seventh Journey

Heather: It's the 1st December 2006, and we were told some months ago that today was the auspicious day to be making this journey. The energy is settling down and has now got to the Healing Line .. If you start getting any impressions Hannah, please speak.

Hannah: Well I see .. that was very quick .. I see a scribe writing. I'm in what, to him, is an invisible spirit form, and he's .. He's "cooking the books," so I'm told! Is it about money? No, I don't think it's about money. It is about misappropriation of knowledge.

Misappropriation – To take wrongly for oneself, to put to wrong use.

Heather: I think you can move if you want to.

Hannah: I seem to have stuck there, for some strange reason.

Heather: Yes, but it's time to move really. We're going forward in time, a very short space of time, one minute.

Hannah: He's throwing up his hands, this scribe, and he's saying, "I can't do this! I'll go to the gallows rather than do this." He's a very clever person, but he would rather die that commit an offence against his inner holiness.

Heather: Right. Now we can move again, minutes, hours, days, weeks, months .. The pendulum has gone around the anxious way, one, two, three months forward.

Hannah: People are shouting and yelling in the street.

Heather: More information coming.

Hannah: This feels like .. not a protest, a revolution! Is it France? No. .. It's in Russia. It's very cold. I feel it on my chest .. very cold. The air is very cold. And we're all very hungry.

Heather: More information coming.

Hannah: There's no bread .. No bread. All the people are dying .. of hunger. And yet they are still strong with their revolution. They have to have a *revolution*, so they can change the ways of the governing body, but even the governing body is in a mess. It is in disarray. All is chaos here, and fear, and death. .. They even eat the dogs they're so hungry, but there isn't much on the dogs either, and there's a all sorts of diseases and .. oh, it's horrible. Ugh! Gangrene and ... Ugh! .. I'm in a hospital. I'm a doctor in a hospital, but I can't do anything, .. I've joined the revolution. I know that won't do anything, but what else can you do when all your patients are dying? I'm just so exhausted. There is nothing here any more. I'll probably just lie down with my patients and die!

Heather: We can move, forward, minutes, hours, days weeks, one week forward.

Hannah: (Deep sigh)

Heather: I think we need a key. It's the red jasper from Iceland.

Hannah: That's healing! That's healing all through the body! It also heals the soul!
Red Jasper here provides rescue in a situation of danger, and Jasper of any kind, in this situation, can be used to align the energy of the chakras and to integrate the attributes of the chakras, such that astral journeys can be effected.

Heather: Now we're going back in time, minutes, days, weeks, one, two weeks back. The pendulum has gone around the anxious way.

Hannah: (Pause)

Heather: We need another key, and it's the little temple bell. We need the sound of the little Tibetan temple bell. (Rings the bell.)

Hannah: That has brought me up here on a plateau. This is very old Tibet. It's very cool here, an ideal temperature, ideal in the sense of the human body, not too hot. The view is magnificent.
Below the person Hannah is the valley, but as I am travelling in spirit I am both in the valley and on the plateau. There is no separation in my consciousness, and there are plateaux, which you can climb, and from which you can see the world. You can see the world in illusion, and the world of actual, and it's all coming and going and interchangeable.

Heather: There's more information coming, or rather, trying to come. The little white elephant will help you remember.
The elephant totem gives ancient wisdom and power to draw upon. Those with the elephant totem make excellent researchers and alternative scientists. Elephants are said never to forget.

Hannah: I am a child here, with my dream, and the dream is like a kaleidoscope, the colours of which are amazing .. I have a little dog here. It is really the Temple dog. It likes to trot around with me. It has a tail that curls over its back and it wobbles a lot when when it wags it. It's very funny. He's got big brown eyes. He looks like one of the teachers! (Giggles)

Heather: More information coming.

Hannah: My mother lives here as well. She's one of the teachers. I have other children to play with, which is really nice. We do "Learning by Example," so that you don't have to learn to be kind, because people are kind to you and then you don't know that as a word, you only know it as a doing. Words are not that im-portant. We've got to do the action. .. I'm about 5 years old, and, and (Getting very excited) I like rice! .. Sometimes we have to be very .. serious here. That's like the star .. Sirius! We have another name for it, but I'm speaking in this language now, which I shall know in another time. We don't get to see many travelling people up here, but that doesn't matter, because we can see them anyhow, when we go on the plateaux. Sometimes we go with the teacher and we see the world, or whatever the world is at that time, because it's always changing. I think that if I had a message, from this place, to give the world, I would say, "Stop f,f, .. what's the word?"

Heather: Fighting?

Hannah: We don't do that word! We have dis-cussion, which is lots of words .. and we can do an action after the discussion. Um, um, the world is always a place of learning, so that you can get bigger, inside yourself. Even little things like little beetles and ladybirds, and things like that, they can teach you. They teach us. So, dear world out there, with all of them people doing all of those funny things and not very agreeable things, "Stop it!" is my message .. from me, who's big inside and only little on the outside.

Heather: (Believing herself to have been speaking with a five year old) Thank you! That was lovely, and very energetically given as well. And now we go forward minutes, hours, days, one, two, three, four, five, five days forward.

Hannah: This is another life.

Heather: Information coming.

Hannah: I don't feel terribly comfortable where I am, because I'm not sure where it is. Is it .. Ah, here's somebody coming! That's helpful. There're saying, "Can we help you?" I say, "Yes please, where is this place?" "What am I doing here?" Oh, oh that's very nice. (Starts to chuckle) Oh that's really nice. They say, "You've brought a gift of Happiness!" I didn't know I had it! (Chuckles extensively) There are a lot of monks here. We cannot stop laughing! (Chuckles) (Still chuckling) Oh, somebody's clapped their hands and said, "Can we have Order please!" (Continues to chuckle) Well, that's all very well, but what am I supposed to be doing? They say, "Just be happy." They say, "In the Hannah life, when you wake up, and you start giggling for nothing, just remember all the monks, and the laughing Buddhas. The laughter is all there in the monks." Oh dear, that's wonderful! Thank you so much! My happiness is so great I could be moved to tears. Thank you so much. Apparently everybody has this, only they're so busy they forget! Oh, that's wonderful! They say, "Soon it will be, in your time, (I'm having to look down the time tunnel) Christmas 2006, and they're saying, "Give everybody happiness for Christmas 2006, and don't forget to laugh. And you may start now!"

This causes us both to collapse into peals of helpless laughter, so much so that we have to abandon the journeying for a little while and have a few minutes 'cooling off' period.

Heather: Right Hannah, I'm just waiting for the energy to settle. It's gone forward to the Healing Line now.

Hannah: I'm lying down resting, and they're covering me with an animal skin rug.

We're right up in the mountains where it's quite cold, and they're saying, "Well we were waiting for you." They say ..

Heather: Information trying to get through. We need the record keeper quartz.

In respect of Record Keeper Quartz at this point, the message is that only those with open minds and pure hearts can access the information via attunement of the consciousness with the inner energies of the crystal.

Hannah: Right, OK. (Listening to guides) This is a very ancient city which existed on the borderline of modern day Nepal and Tibet. Why am I feeling anxious about this? .. They say, "When you read something in your books, it's quite difficult for us to convey its meaning to the current mind set. This is much broader than a few sentences can express."

Heather: I've got a working pattern here now.

Hannah: Yes. So what I have to do is trans .. pose the energy into a given form that may enter into another form. Do you understand me? So I am not ... No, let me put it another way. I appear to be first a human and then another sort of human, and then ... there are five stages to this. So there's the human Hannah, living. Then there's another person who's living in the very ancient city between present day Nepal and Tibet. Then there's another personage who is quite a high up person. Then we move again, and all the time we're moving form.

Heather: At this stage, the pendulum is giving me an Angelic pattern, which represents the status of the Being on the fourth shift.

Hannah: That's right. And the fifth one will take you out.

After the journey was over, Hannah spoke about being taken completely out of her body at this point.

Heather: The fifth shift is giving me Balance, Unity, Alignment with the Divine, on the pendulum.

Hannah: So we'll go with the Angelic, number four. So here we are. In Soul shape, it's like your diamond.

Heather's diamond ring was one of the keys. Here it represents "the stone of innocence," bringing forth purity, constancy and the open nature with which one came into the physical realm.

Heather: I've got a Working Pattern on the pendulum.

Hannah: Yes. The Goddess energy is here. It is very high and beautiful.

Heather: That's why we got given the Goddess flame as a key.

Hannah: Absolutely. You are absolutely correct. The flame in your language is the Eternal Flame. Every body, all the bodies, have a part of this flame. Everybody is part of this Angelic Realm. They need to remember this exquisite form which they carry within them. It's like a pattern composed of a flame, like a flat leaf pattern, and the point going up, the fire flame. Everybody carries that within them. And I hear somebody saying, "What about very bad people?" I can't make a judgement here. I find this really difficult, because people make judgements. They say, this is bad this is good and, where we stand, there is only the flame, and the knowledge of learning, carrying your flame from one of your lives, to the next life, to the next life. And the flame is there. Some nearly go away. In fact some do go away, but nothing ever dies. The flame is always held within the heart of the Soul Group Family. The flame is always within that, and so the flame of the individual, through the love and care of the Soul Group Family, can be re-ignited. The heart has a whole meaning, nearly beyond Human comprehension, and humanity ...

(crackle, crackle, crackle as the recording machine suddenly refuses to work.)

Hannah: That was opportune apparently, as I was about to say something which is not appropriate, or rather, it was appropriate, but not yet, not yet. You see, even angels can be slightly off the mark! Now the most important thing is to remember that the heart energy contains far more than people realise, but always, within it, is held the flame.

Heather: I think we move now, but they're giving me a sign of more information coming.

Hannah: I'm high up in the mountains.

Heather: Right. So the time is coming when we can move, and we can move .. now. We move forward, minutes, days, weeks, months, one month forward.

Hannah: (Pause)

Heather: We don't exactly need a key, but we need some sort of prompt. Just bear with me a minute. It's something to do with Pegasus.

Pegasus is the magical winged horse of mythology.

Hannah: That is so. That is appropriate.

Heather: Is Pegasus going to take you somewhere?

Hannah: Yes. Now, when a child, I believed in magic. Now I am no longer a child, I still believe in magic. And Pegasus will take me to the Land of the Snows held within his great wings, .. great wings, for he is an angel .. Pegasus is an Angel and he has brought me here and he is going to wait for me, for I must go and visit ... with the people who have no names. And I'm entering ..

Heather: (Anxiously interrupting) I think you've gone into the fifth state!

This is the point at which Hannah is completely out of her body, and Heather's pendulum was indicating the situation, by it's movement, which was a pattern of "Anxious but absolutely fine." (!!)

Hannah: Here we travel into the mountain, where I have a cat in Spirit, for company.

Cat energy here represents meditation, freedom of thought, and seeing that the physical and spiritual realms are one.

Now we have gone into one of the innermost chambers of this place. And here they are showing me .. that death is a gold robe. Death is not a thing, it is only a state, put about as a thing to be feared. Death moves like the Spirit of Darkness, but darkness is necessary. How else would you see the magic? How else would you see the light? The energies of death are beautiful. You will, no doubt, admire them as you would admire a gold robe. In this place also are stored energies beyond the human mind for understanding. We can access this state, or place, when called upon to do so. It has energies unknown to man.

Heather: More information coming, but I think we need a key. It's the record keeper crystal.

The significance of the record keeper quartz crystal at this point is that the information stored within it could be relevant or non-relevant to physical life on Earth. One must be open and willing to accept all information (even those concepts which one would judge as inconceivable) and must be capable (as we all are) of processing the information and applying it to this physical life.

Hannah: Your akashic records are not the only records. There are others, and they are stored here. These are specific to the Goddess, the Divine Feminine which lies, sometimes latent, within you all, both male and female. They were brought here by the Divine Ones, for the safekeeping of women's knowledge. They have always been here and the wise ones knew that there would be a time when they would be called upon to be read again. These are kept in sound and colour energy forms and they can be accessed through various methods. Although we are able to do this, it is the transcribing of these which will be the challenge, for all over the earth's surface are different notes and colours, and I think you now know that what is above is also below, so, if humanity is looking for the harmonies ... it's like your tower, where everybody was suddenly speaking different languages.

The Tower of Babel

According to the narrative in Genesis Chapter 11 of the Bible, the Tower of Babel was a tower built by a united humanity to reach the heavens. God, observing the unity of humanity in the construction, made possible through a single language, resolves to destroy the tower and confuse the previously uniform language of humanity, thereby preventing such future efforts. The building of the Tower of Babel and the Confusion of Tongues, or languages is mentioned only briefly.

Hannah: Here is a somewhat similar situation, where there are so many notes and colours all meaning different things. We are going to try and give you the evolving language of colour and sound so that they blend together, and, to stop confusion for humanity and others, because others are watching what you do, to bring it into a harmonic of Beauty and Truth, so that you will be able to detect, by people's colour and when a person speaks, that your truth is their truth. That situation will become more prominent. I know that this will be happening more and more on the planet. We shall observe from where we are and give guidance, if you wish to ask.

Heather: Thank you. We have come down into the fourth body now.

Hannah: There's somebody here who would like to speak. It has the form of a holly leaf.

Most of the holly's healing qualities are on the subtle planes, where it helps us transform our "Prickly bits" and improve our reaction to the world. To enable wise decisions to be made before a course of action, holly can be used to meditate with or upon, to calm the mind and body of emotions. 'Of all the trees that are in the wood, the holly bears the crown,' is one of our best known Christmas carols, and this reveals not only the importance of the tree, but also of the solar and lunar cycles and their reflection on earth. It also refers to the guardian qualities of the holly, guiding the precious energies of life. Holly is one of the Bach Flower Remedies. Edward Bach said of it, "Holly protects us from everything that is not Universal Love. Holly opens the heart and unites us with Divine Love."

Hannah: I am inside the holly leaf. My home is my tree. The holly leaf and the tree is the same Being, so if you have holly leaf, you have whole tree. The berries are the fruit of the tree. The holly is a guardian. Do be mindful that guardians can be "prickly." They can be bright and shiny in this beautiful .. green, I think is the colour .. but I am trying to tell you how it feels to be prickly, and why that is necessary. To be prickly is to be on your guard, and although you have nothing at all to fear, others will reflect back something which may not be necessary for your growth, so, "Be on your guard," is my message, because others will try for more! It is fine for me, because I am part of a bigger tree, and I don't out prick anybody, but, if they come too near, I can, because it's about proximity of various bodies. .. But do not fear. There is nothing to fear, except fear itself.

Heather: Can I ask a question?

Hannah: You may.

Heather: Would it be good to do some research on the Holly Tree?

Hannah: Yes. You may look in books if you so wish, and that may give you something, but I am also guardian of place, and the questioner holds a very good place, that is to say, is guardian of a Time Line of big significance, much bigger than you realise, and I am just a Holly leaf, telling you to be, perhaps, watchful. I think you have some concern around little issues, and so I say, "Just be on guard."

I like being a holly leaf. You may admire me, because I have a beautiful (with emphasis,) GREEN.

Heather: I think that ties in with the Moldavite somehow.

Moldavite is a rich, dark green in colour. It is an awakener and accelerator of spiritual evolution. It facilitates a broadening of experience and perception that changes our relationship to everything which is familiar.

Hannah: Yes, we travel together.

Heather: More information coming.

Hannah: However far you go out, you also go in. The moldavite is a travelling stone. It's home is amongst the Stars as you see them. This one is a particular information carrier. It has a message about water, but go away and study. We don't give anything lightly. Heather knows. She came into this life with the knowledge, ask her.

Heather: Water, particularly natural spring water, has a holding quality, a memory. It can hold the energies of plant based remedies, for example the Bach Flower remedies, and of crystals also. Moldavite is the stepping stone to the outer forces of all infinite vibration and drinking water charged with Moldavite energy can be a powerful awakener. The knowledge I now have, and the way it has changed my life are my most important experiences.

I'm back with Pegasus. "Hurry," he says, "It's time to go."

Heather: Yes, it is time to go.

Hannah: And the sky is so blue, it is so blue. You have never seen the sky like it! Imagine the bluest sky you ever saw! You have never seen anything like it, and I can see the sky with stars! Even though it's half light! And the Star Beings, .. and they're waving! Look, they're waving! (Sounding really sad) I don't want to go back! But we've got work to do. I don't want to go back. I want to go again amongst the stars, but I must go back. Thank you Pegasus, thank you!

Heather: The pendulum has come to a standstill. I think we've finished. Thank you to all the Beings who have been here, working with us today.

Hannah: (Sniffing back the tears) Blessed be their Holy Names, and their Holy Beings. We are eternally grateful. Thank you.

Heather: Thank you.

Hannah's comments afterwards

Being in the place of the child in the journey, was not only beautiful, and without fear, but there was no dogma, no should or shouldn't. If the grown-ups are behaving properly around them, the children will know how to be. If you have a family with children, please sit down, make time, and discuss problems, feelings, and experiences of any given situation. Children come with their own truth and beauty and they can be very wise, so that sometimes you may wonder who is teaching whom.

Chapter Eighteen

Coming back down to Earth

"I slept and dreamt that life was joy. I awoke and saw that life was service. I acted and behold, service was joy." - Rabindraneth Bahore.

Do you, dear faithful reader, who have followed our journeys through to the very last, think that we are living in a dream world? Well, it may be that I and my faithful friends who have dedicated so much of our time and energies to the production of this book are the ones who are awake and those for whom this book is an unpalatable diet are asleep!

Throughout this book we have been achieving other plains of consciousness. My clients have been seen to be integral in happenings that are somehow, "out there," removed from normal, everyday experience. Now I want to speak about bringing those experiences back into the physical world and applying the knowledge gained to daily life.

Most of us are very familiar with the physical, psychological, social, sensual, plains of reality. We've built our whole life story around them, and I recognise now, that many of the plains of consciousness that I explore though spiritual practices, were ones that were always available to me, but that, for many years, I didn't notice. It's not as if we are adding something to ourselves that we don't have. It's as if we are tilting the horizon a little bit, so that we can see a bit further and become aware of deeper components of our own being. It's not as if these other plains of consciousness, which are often called the spiritual dimensions of life, are new at all. The only thing is, they are not easily available through the devices we usually use in order to know the world. They are not immediately available through our five senses and through our thinking mind. It's as if all of those are tuned to certain frequencies and they give those plains of reality a solidity, and we say, "That's real." and then the other plains, which don't fit the paradigm we are used to, we either deny altogether or we talk about them as Dream States. Each one of you has had some experiences, in your life, while some of you have had many, in which you have recognised that there are dimensions to your own mind and heart and there are dimensions to your awareness, that you recognise as true, as deep, and as significant, and there is a part of you that seeks to explore these plains of consciousness.

Faith and Spiritual practices over the years have connected me to being part of what Is, being nobody special, being just a part of all that is, someone who has been given a job for a period. It's not MY job, it's simply what I do, or rather, what I'm given to do. It's not about choice either. I don't choose it, it chooses me. Later that part of the job becomes less to the fore and I'm given another area to work in, or at least the opportunity for it, take it or leave it. I feel however that when the job was "offered," as it were, I took it, because I love it, all of it. Someone said to me once, "I know why your healing has gone so far. You have never said, "No," to anything. You have always said, "Yes, I'll try."

At the end, in this final chapter, let's start at the very beginning, with the primary question in life for every single one of us, "Who am I?" Having read thus far, you must surely be feeling the need to at least pose that question for yourself.

Some of us, as Ram Dass says, have, "Seen beyond the billboards at the edge of town." We know something, but we're not quite sure what it is we know, and so it's easier to stick to our long accepted paradigm of reality and discard anything which doesn't fit. Instead, we say things like,"I must have been crazy," or, "I don't know what came over me," or,"I must have imagined it all," things that make what we have seen, or heard or read seem irrelevant, even ridiculous. It feels to me that the other aspects of our being, the other plains of consciousness, often get ignored because of the intensity and seductiveness of earthly desire systems and the ways in which they are fanned and inflamed by our lives.

It's much easier to ignore these esoteric things than to take them on board, because of the implications, for ourselves and our families ... and the radical new thinking we would have to work through ... and there's no time to spare, or so it seems, in our busy daily lives ... and so we throw out and forget the one thing in the world that would save us and the planet!

And then there is a thing called awakening. Some of you never went to sleep, but most of us did. I certainly did, and I didn't even begin to open one eye until I was thirty three! (See Keys to Wisdom, Chapter Two) There is a moment of awakening, in which you see the reality of these other dimensions of your own mind and Being, and then starts a journey to reclaim them, reawaken them, reconnect to them, or quiet down the rest of it enough to be with them. And the qualities of these other dimensions vary immensely, from plain to plain, but what is common to many of them is that there is a different quality of a relationship to energy, a different quality in relation to time, to light, to the nature of phenomena. And so most of the spiritual literature, the religious literature, is concerned with going from the entrapment in certain plains of consciousness and the awakening to what is called the Spiritual dimension of life. And this is only half of the story. It raises your consciousness, but it doesn't get you free. Studying it is not doing it! We have to learn to do it, live it. Knowing it is not enough. It will neither get you nor the world free. Make no mistake, there is HARD WORK involved here, but fun and immense pleasure also.

Knowing it gets you to where you know of these other plains, and you are starting to be comfortable in them, but from then on, the journey seems to me to be quite an extensive job of integrating the plains of consciousness, so that you have them all available at once, being both in the world and out of it at the same time. One of the ways this is spoken of is to say that you, "imbue life with spirit." You imbue the plains of normal waking consciousness with these higher states of awareness. I am not intending to use a purjorative term against lower here, but merely to denote difference.

Modern society is more and more concerned with identity, both from a positive and a negative point of view, with passports, ID cards, and all sorts of proofs of identity. I am a bank manager ..... I live in Wales ..... I have a wife and two children. I live in a four bedroom detached house in its own grounds. My bank balance is ..... Or, ... I have fabricated a false identity. I say I am this and that .... but I have made it all up, because I have my own vicarious reasons for doing so.

And then we have the spiritually aware, who have seen things, who have been shown things and who know things, and they know enough to realise that they are nobody special. Whereas the rest of the world is trying desperately to be, " Somebody special." These people are happy in their, " Nobodyness" in not knowing who they are, and in realising that their experiences have been gathered in many different eras, many different bodies, many different roles and many different locations.

I am not who I thought I was. Of that I am now certain, because I have been shown otherwise. Just in this one lifetime, as an adult, I have played the part of a musician, a teacher, a stay-at-home mother, a commercial art gallery owner, a professional painter, a mystic, a healer, a past life regression therapist, a published author, and a nobody special, and I'm not finished yet. So don't put me in a box! I won't stay there! And if **you** don't realise you are a prisoner then you have no chance of getting free!

To get free, the best way I can express it is, that one stands nowhere. It's not that you stand in your separateness, looking up at the grandeur of God. It's not that you stand as God, looking down at the multiplicity of your manifestation, it's not that it all turns out to be just phenomena in an empty space, it's rather that all of those are true! They're all relatively real, and they're all relatively real simultaneously. And what you will see is that this journey is one that starts out sequentially, and then, over time, comes to be more and more simultaneous, so that there is a period where you just want to sing your way or energetically move your way, or quiet your mind in a way, or understand metaphysics in a way in order to open yourself into these plains of consciousness. If, in the course of doing this, you pushed anything away, then whatever it was you pushed away would have you, because the aversion is the trap. And so ultimately you have to turn the game around and come back into the world so that you imbue your whatever it is each day, cooking, serving, driving, making love, laundry, eating, typing, washing dishes, your all of it, with certain qualities that we associate with spiritual awareness. Qualities like equanimity, qualities like joy, compassion and wisdom. As far as I can understand it you and I are in a training programme to transform ourselves for the benefit of ourselves and everyone else, while serving in environments that are often very chaotic.

We are living in a period of history where very profound changes are going on, in nation states, ecological stability, availability of resources, in all the social forms of family, extended family, morals, economy, polarising and destabilising the world. We are in periods of great instability. Means of communication are changing hugely, and we cannot know all the ramifications and implications of it and yet it is changing all of our lives immensely.

The habits of people are clear. When there is change that gets accelerated there is fear of loss of control, and when there is fear of loss of control, there is contraction and when there is contraction there is increase in prejudice, bigotry and ultimately, violence. And my question to you is ...What is the work you and I have to do as part of the system? What is it that we do that allows us to be in that situation and bring to it the qualities of humour, space, equanimity, wisdom, peacefulness, love, to be those around whom the change may not be as violent as it would otherwise be. And there's certainly plenty of evidence of violence in the world at this moment, .. and pain, .. and fear, so for us to serve in that way, we have to find places within ourselves that are not rooted in fear. We need to explore those plains of consciousness, or those parts of our identity that were rooted in fear, through the systematic clearing of that fear in controlled circumstances, so that the world of fear and disfunction is replaced gradually by the world of space and presence.

In the next 20, 30, 40 years we are facing the strong possibility of Chaos and dark anarchic forces instead of Cosmos and Light. Under those conditions, most people identify with separateness, in which they feel very little and very vulnerable, and they structure an environment to make themselves feel safe, and as those things start to crumble, as the money in their pockets loses its value, as the road has more potholes in it, as they have to lock and double lock their doors and windows, because of theft and violence, there is a contraction in people and that contraction is rooted in fear.

To hear how that situation can become an opportunity for growth and can move from one system into another without violence, requires the kind of consciousness that has a certain inner quality, a certain openness to the unknown, and a certain way in which the chaos of the system doesn't undercut you, because you are not dependent on the external, but rather the eternal, for your equanimity. It feels to me that you and I are in training to be instruments in society for stability in the presence of change. Not holding on to the old system, but being able to move into the unknown and different systems. Making friends with change. Change and uncertainty are part of the curriculum of life. People take birth at different times and at different historical moments to do different work on themselves.

One of the big divides in people is that some are really good at intuiting and others have developed thinking to a fine art. What is required in life, as in all things, is a state of balance, a situation where we all are able to use both sides of the brain, the "masculine" thinking side, and the "feminine" intuition side. Throughout history, people, both male and female, like Einstein and Marie Curie, simply knew how close they were in tracking the blueprint of God.

We have spoken briefly of the mind, but what of the heart? Hsin-hsin is a Chinese term for the heart, not the physical heart, nor the emotional poetic heart, but the heart/mind, the space not of loving but of love, the space not of becoming but of presence, the space of no boundaries, the subjective doorway into the universe, through which manna, substance, is fed to you because you are connected to the Source, the Atman, the Buddha Mind, the Christ Consciousness, The Garden of Allah, God.

The inner part of our being is connected into the universe at all times and it gets to be more and more deeply so, both into the systems and into the One. This is not the false power of ego and it's not the false power of being Somebody. It is the power that the earth has or the sky or the wind or the trees. It is channelled and received power. It has to do with the ability to be with the mystery of the universe, without contracting and without frightened grabbing of the unknown, staying open in a way which makes us able to be with the world, the way it is. It is beautiful and perfect on the one hand, and chaotic and terrible on the other, all at the same time. I have faith in that. I believe it. Faith means something very real to me. The building of the rainbow bridge, the working together of humans on the one side and Divine beings of Light on the other. Co-operation. As above so below.

The awe of it all. It is so profoundly beautiful. People are beautiful. I have been awed, in doing this work, at the beauty of the stories, and the quality of the language and expression, which has arisen unscripted and spontaneous from the lips of these unpreselected , so-called ordinary people, who have come to me for healing, these Nobodys Special that it has been my privilege to know and help. Isn't humanity amazing!

So, deeply connected into the present moment, just look at what is. Just turn up for work, with no preconception of outcome and no attachment to it either. What is, is. But in the words of Don Miguel Ruiz, I will do my best, try to be impeccable with my word, try not take the outcome personally, and try not to make assumptions. That which I know spiritually I know experientially, and those things I have shared with you, both in this book and it's forerunner, Keys to Wisdom.

As Margaret Fell, quoting from her first encounter with George Fox, the founder of the Quaker movement said: "You will say Christ saith this and the apostles say this, but what canst thou say? Art thou a child of the Light and hast thou walked in the Light?
And what thou speakest, is it inwardly from God?"

A final word

Following the Big Bang, if the expanding universe, moving at millions of miles per minute, had been off by a fraction of a second, the formation of stars and galaxies would have been impossible, because the momentum of the explosion would have exceeded the ability of gravity, the weakest force in Nature, to halt it. Only the most delicate balancing act kept the push/pull of two forces so close together that that they can dance together instead of tearing each other apart. Randomness is a feeble explanation for such precision Ervin Lazlo, the Hungarian physicist claims. Something so precisely organised requires the principle to hold it together and a medium to carry information from one end of Creation to the other. (Author's note: I have good reason to believe this medium to be aether.)

In his 2004 book, Science and the Akashic Field, Ervin Lazlo explains that Akasha is necessary, not as a medium for visible light, but as a medium for invisible light and invisible energy in general. Think of a jump rope nailed at one end to a wall, as the jump rope is turning with sounds of vibrating energy, follow the rope to the wall where the rope is nailed. That point isn't moving at all. It is the Zero Point, the beginning and end of energy If you put a supersensitive stethoscope to the wall, the rope's vibration is shaking the whole wall and, and in return the wall is sending some of that vibration back out again. This, according to Lazlo, is also happening at the zero point. Every vibration is sending signals throughout the field, and in return the field is sending signals back. The universe, it turns out, is constantly monitoring itself by somehow co-ordinating every vibration that goes anywhere in the visible or invisible domain. In trying to work out the apparently random activity in the quantum field, we have come to see that there is incredible timing, co-ordination, memory, information exchange and self interaction, but what is the point of it all? the Observer Effect adds the missing link. The Observer Effect is related to one of the cornerstones of quantum Physics called Complimentarity, which holds that it isn't possible to know everything about a quantum event. When an observer looks at or measures an electron whatever is being observed is limited. The total event exists only as a potential. Each and every electron has a probability of appearing anywhere in the universe, It is a non local event with no visible component. This changes when an observer enters the picture. Only under observation does an electron jump from from virtual reality into the visible universe, and as soon as the observer stops looking it falls back into the field again. (Author's note: A Soul Journey subject quickly becomes an observer.)

Ervin Schrodinger the great German physicist devised Schrodinger's equation, one of the foundations of quantum theory, which precisely calculates what these probabilities are and yet the notion that an electron is everywhere until an observer calls it into existence at a specific location defies logic. This is described in the famous paradox of Schodinger's cat The paradox is that, according to quantum physics, an electron has no visible reality until it is observed. It occupies a super position meaning that it can be in more than one place at the same time. The akashic field gives matter a place to go when it vanishes and that place is as meaningful as where a memory goes when we aren't using it.

Taken from Life after Death; The Burden of proof ISBN 978 0 3073457 8 3 by Deepak Chopra

I truly believe that what we have been doing here has a sound scientific basis, and is concerned with making contact with the information stored in the zero point field, in order to heal the soul.

Since Past and Future Lives was completed, ther have been more and more amazing, insightful and healing journeys undertaken by clients. These, it may, sometime in the future, be possible to share with you.

Heather Bray. July 2007

Appendix

The blank mind is the source of all knowledge.
Deepak Chopra

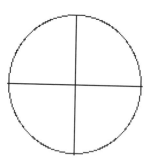

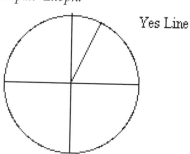

Yes Line

Balance Line
Unity with
the Divine

No Line

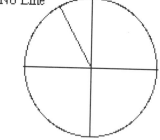

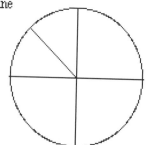

Love/ Truth/
Gift/ Healing
Line. The line
on which both
information and
healing are
received

Fear/ Pain
Line

More information trying to get through

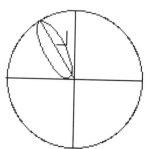

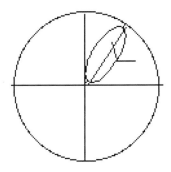

More information
coming

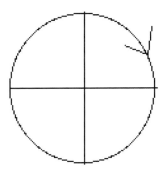

Thinking/ Working
pattern

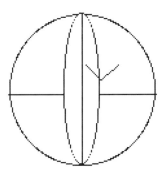

Angelic Presence

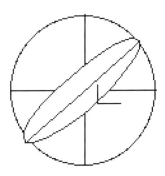

Guardian Angel Presence

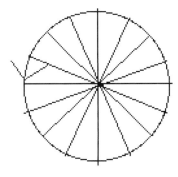

Boxed in, frantic energy

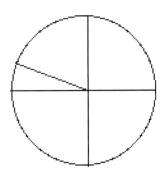

Lethargy Line

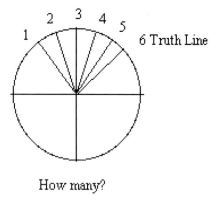

How many?

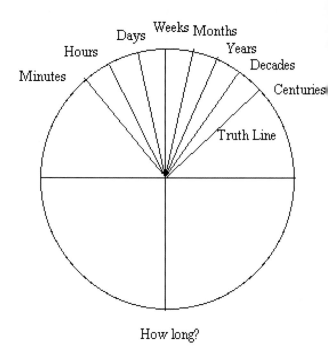

How long?

PLEASE NOTE

These diagrams are only intended
as a reader's guide. If you are a dowser,
then Keys to Wisdom is a Must Have,
as the diagrams are explained much more
fully there.

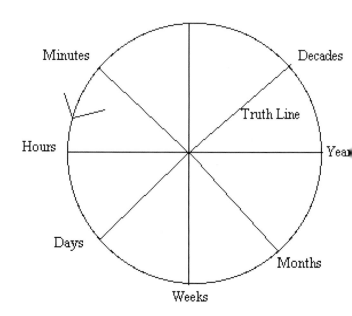

Passing time, with Anxiety warning from guides
Note anticlockwise direction.

KEYS TO WISDOM

The unique working practices of an extremely gifted healer are fully revealed in this fascinating book. Here, for the first time, a fully comprehensive pendulum language is explained clearly and in full detail.

Heather Bray, who is a Quaker, is a member of the British Society of Dowsers. She originally trained as a teacher, and as such has a unique ability to pass on the benefit of eighteen years experience in many aspects of healing, gained in a busy, successful healing practice.

This is a book for those seeking to develop their dowsing skills, those seeking personal spiritual development and those wishing to help both themselves and others by means of Healing Techniques, such as Flower Remedies, crystals and hands on healing.

This remarkable book will interest beginners in Healing and those of considerable experience alike, as well as all those who are prepared to look at dowsing with an attitude of open-mindedness. "Keys to Wisdom" may well be the only book on Healing you will ever need to buy.

BUTTERFLY PRESS

ISBN 0-9550954-0-9

HEATHER BRAY

ISBN 0-9550954-0-9   Website: www.keystowisdom.co.uk

Have you enjoyed reading Past and Future Lives? If so, why not take a look at Heather Bray's highly acclaimed first book, Keys to Wisdom, which describes the unique working practices of this extremely gifted healer, using crystals Flower Essences and Hands On healing methods.

This book, which describes Heather's journey into Healing, will interest beginners and those of considerable experience alike. Keys to Wisdom may well be the only book on healing you will ever need to buy.

This is one of the most important and thought provoking books to be written on dowsing in recent years. There is nothing vague here. Heather has a well worked up methodology, which she shares with her readers. Heather heals people, my words not hers, and these techniques work. She has opened up a whole new way of thinking about dowsing.

Ced Jackson, Reviewer Emeritus, British Society of Dowsers